Luminaries for the Soul

One Year of Daily Inspiration for Muslim Teens and Preteens

Linda "iLham" Barto

Author & Illustrator

Published by

Lit-by-Linda

For reprint permission, contact:
Linda K. Barto
3806 Grady Williams Lane
Maiden, NC 28650-9535
lindabarto13@gmail.com

ISBN 979-8-8689-3511-4

Scriptures are from *A Universal Message Interpreted from the Holy Qur'an* by Linda "iLham" Barto and Dr. Sheikh Ahmed Pandor (Light Switch Press, CO, 2020).

Layout artist: Shakib Imran
Cover illustration and interior graphics: Linda "iLham" Barto

Published by Lit-by-Linda
Printed in the United States of America

BISMALLAH AL RAHMAN AL RAHEEM
Blessed and Exalted is Allah
the Most Gracious, the Most Merciful

MUHAMMED SEAL OF THE PROPHETS
May the PEACE & BLESSINGS of Allah
Be Upon Him

It's okay to be weird.
It's okay to not fit in.
Just don't be creepy.
Be happy being yourself.

Read!

Read in the name of your Lord who created! [He] created humanity from a clinging mass. Read! Your Lord is Most Bountiful. He taught by the pen. [He] taught humanity what he/she did not know.

Alas! People are bound to sin. [Humanity] looks upon itself as independent. Truly, to your Lord is the return.

Have you considered anyone who tries to prevent a servant from praying? Have you seen whether he/she has guidance and directs righteousness? Have you seen if he/she rejects and turns away? Does he/she not know that Allah sees? Let him/her beware! If he/she does not desist, We will drag him/her by the frontal lobes [of the brain]. [They are] lying, sinful frontal lobes. Then let him/her call to his associates. We will call on the angels of punishment. Beware! Do not pay attention to him/her. Prostrate in adoration. Bring yourself closer.

—QUR'AN 96

Daily living tip: All truth is Allah's truth. Never stop trying to acquire more knowledge, understanding, and wisdom no matter where it is found. Your whacko friend may even have a good tip for you.

Today's prayer: O my Lord, grant me a mind that seeks knowledge, a heart that seeks wisdom, and a soul that seeks Your grace.

No God is There Except God.

[Prophet Muhammed,] say, "Truly, I am a warner. No god is there except Allah, the One, the Conqueror. [He is] the Lord of the skies and Earth and all among them, the Victorious, the Redeemer."

Say, "This is the ultimate message from which you turn. I have no knowledge of the chiefs on high when they argue. Only this has been revealed to me: that I am to give precise warning."

Say, "No reward do I ask of you for this, and I am not one of the pretentious. This is no less than a reminder to the worlds. You will certainly learn the truth of it after a while."

The revelation of this Book is from Allah, the Victorious, the Perfectly Wise. Truly, We have revealed the Book to (Prophet Muhammed) in truth, so worship Allah, offering Him sincere faith.

Is it not to Allah that sincere faith is due? Those who take for protectors other than Allah [claim]: "We only serve them in order that they may bring us nearer to Allah." Truly, Allah will judge among them in that wherein they differ. Allah does not guide those who are false and unbelieving.

—Qur'an 38: 65-70, 86-88 and Qur'an 39: 1-3

Daily living tip: There are false gods of today. You may find them as sports heroes, rock stars, movie stars, or anybody else or anything that gains more of your devotion than Allah does. Keep a proper perspective so that you do not idolize anybody or anything. Some of those people are meatheads anyway.

Today's prayer: O my Lord, bring me to a closer walk with You and keep me on the Straight Way.

You Need Allah!

O Humanity, you need Allah! Allah, however, is Independent, the Praised One.

If He wanted, He could eliminate you and bring in a new creation. That would not be difficult for Allah.

A carrier cannot bear the burdens of another. If one heavily laden [with sin] calls on another to help with his/her burden, not even the least mote can be relieved, even if he/she is a close relative. Truly, you can only admonish those who fear their unseen Lord and establish routine prayers.

Whoever purifies him-/herself, does so for the benefit of his/her own soul. The final destination is to Allah.

The unseeing and the seeing are not alike. Neither are the depths of darkness and light. Neither are the cool shade and the blazing heat of the sun. Not alike are the living and the dead. Allah can certainly make anyone [dead or alive] to hear if He wants, but you cannot make those in the graves hear you.

You [Prophet Muhammed] are only a warner. Truly, We have sent you with the truth, as a herald of good news and as a warner. There has never been a people without a warner among them.

—Qur'an 35: 15-24

Daily living tip: Scientists have discovered a "God part" of the brain, so your awareness of God is already wired into your brain. You don't have to flail through life without direction. He is always available to give you guidance. Always be ready for a fill-up on that brain tank.

Today's prayer: O my Lord, my soul thirsts for You as a deer pants for water. Quench my thirst and grant me Your guidance.

He Alone Provides.

Say, "Who provides for you from the sky and the earth? Who possesses [the gifts of] hearing and sight? Who is He who emerges the living from the dead and emerges the dead from the living? Who is He who governs all matters?"

Everyone will answer, "Allah!"

Say, "Will you not then become reverent?"

Such is Allah, your true Lord. After truth, does anything remain but error? Why then are you adverse?

Thus, the Word of your Lord is proven true against those who rebel. They will not believe.

If they charge you with deception, say, "Let me do my work [in ministry], and you do yours. You are not responsible for what I do, and I am not responsible for what you do."

Among them are some who listen to you, but can you force the unhearing to listen when they use no reasoning skills? Among them are some who look to you, but can you guide the unseeing who refuse to see?

—QUR'AN 10: 31-33, 41-43

Daily living tip: Learn to be observant. Look at your surroundings. See beauty in all good things. Listen to nature's sounds. Every part of creation has a message. Even that bird poop on your hijab or kufi is telling you to watch out for the messy parts of life.

Today's prayer: O my Lord, bless my soul with spiritual sight and hearing so I may find You in all Your creation.

Allah is Glorified by All Beings.

Do you not see that Allah is glorified by all beings in the skies and on Earth, including the birds with wings outspread? Each one truly knows its own prayer and praise, and Allah knows well all that they do.

To Allah belongs the dominion of Heaven and Earth, and to Allah is the final goal.

Do you not see that Allah guides the clouds, and then He joins them together and makes them into a mass? Do you see rain issue from their midst? He sends down from the sky mountainous masses wherein is hail. He strikes with it whom He pleases, and He averts it from whom He pleases. The vivid flash of lightning nearly blinds the sight.

Allah alternates the night and the day. Truly, in that is a lesson for those who have vision.

Allah has created every living creature from water. Among them are those that slide on their bellies, those that can each walk on two legs, and those that each walk on all four. Allah creates whatever He will. Truly, Allah has power over everything. Truly, We have imparted clarifying signs, and Allah guides whom He will to the Straight Way.

—QUR'AN 24: 41-46

Daily living tip: Everything in nature is a Muslim because it does whatever Allah created it to do. Only humanity deviates from what is natural. Live the life Allah created you to live in order to be in harmony with all creation. Even the fat, little pig is a better Muslim than many people are.

Today's prayer: O my Lord, restore me to my natural self –the one you created to be in complete submission to Your will.

Allah Protects but Needs No Protection.

It is He who has created for you hearing, sight, and hearts [for feeling and understanding]; yet, little thanks you give. He populated you throughout the earth, and to Him you will reassemble. It is He who gives life and death, and the alternation of night and day is His. Will you not understand?

In contradiction, they say things similar to what the people of old said. They say, "Huh? When we die and become dust and bones, can we expect to be restored? Such things were promised to us and to our parents before us. They are nothing but ancient tales!"

Say, "To whom belong Earth and all beings of this [planet]? [Tell me] if you know."

They will say, "To Allah!"

Then say, "So won't you remember [Him]?"

Say, "Who is the Lord of the seven skies? Who is the Lord of the Supreme Throne [of Heaven]?"

They will say, "God!"

Then say, "Will you not then be filled with awe?"

Say, "In whose hands is the dominion of all things? Who protects, but is not protected? [Tell me] if you know."

They will say, "Allah!"

Then say, "Then why are you so delusional?"

We have sent them the truth, but certainly they prefer deception.

—Qur'an 23: 78-90

Daily living tip: Don't take anything for granted. If your senses and abilities are intact or even if you have some disability, be grateful for whatever you have. If you can eat a pack of cheese crackers and then whistle within thirty seconds, be happy about that.

Today's prayer: O my Lord, make me always grateful. Make me one who submits all my being to You alone.

This Qur'an is Truth.

This [Qur'an] is truly from the Lord of All the Worlds. It has descended with the Spirit of Faith into your heart and mind so that you [Prophet Muhammed] can admonish perfectly in the Arabic language. Actually, it is in the previous Books [of Scriptures].

Is it not significant that [contemporary to Prophet Muhammed] many of the educated Children of Israel recognized this [Qur'an as truth]?

If (the Qur'an) had been revealed to any people besides the Arabs, and had it been recited to (another people), they would have rejected it. Thus We have inserted (disbelief into the hearts of the guilty).

(The disbelievers) will not believe in it until they see the dreadful penalty. But the penalty will come suddenly, without their awareness.

Devils did not bring down this (Qur'an). Not only would it not have suited their purpose, but also they would have been too incompetent.

—QUR'AN 26: 192-200, 210-211

Daily living tip: Learn the meanings of the Qur'an's verses so that you are always prepared to defend the Qur'an when someone accuses the Qur'an of inciting violence or any corrupt lifestyle. Just don't be a jerk about it.

Today's prayer: O my Lord, grant me understanding of Your Word so I may transmit it to others.

Consider the Enlightening Book.

We have indeed bestowed this [revelation] on the Night of Power. What will explain to you the Night of Power? The Night of Power is more wonderful than a thousand months. Therein descend the angels and the Spirit, by Allah's will, on every errand. All is peaceful until the rise of morn.

Consider the enlightening Book. We bestowed it during a blessed night for We wanted to forewarn. Within it, every aspect of wisdom is distinguished. [It is so] by command from Us, for We grant, as a mercy from your Lord. He truly is the All-hearing, the All-knowing. [He is] the Lord of Heavens and Earth and all among them. If only you were certain!

No god is there except Him! He gives life, and He gives death –the Lord of you and your earliest ancestors. Yet, they flit in doubt. Watch for the day when the sky will erupt in thick smoke enveloping the people. This will be a wretched penalty!

—Qur'an 97 and Qur'an 44: 2-11

Daily living tip: When you read the Qur'an, do so with an attitude that Allah is with you and imparting knowledge to you. Don't be a knucklehead. Be conscious of Allah's presence in your life.

Today's prayer: O my Lord, as I read the Qur'an, may my soul hear Your voice, and may my mind see Your light so I may walk with You in perfect guidance.

The Book is From Allah.

Ha Meem. The revelation of the Book is from Allah, the Victorious, the Perfectly Wise.

We did not create the skies and Earth and all among them without truth and an appointed term. The disbelievers reject that by which they are warned.

Say, "Do you see what you invoke besides Allah? Show me what they have created on Earth, or do they have a share in the skies? Bring me a Book before this one or any remnant of knowledge if you are telling the truth."

Who is more astray than one who invokes any besides Allah? Such [idols] will not answer him/her on the Day of Resurrection, and they are unconscious of his/her call?

When humanity is assembled, (the idols) will be hostile to them and reject their worship.

When Our evident signs are rehearsed to them, the disbelievers say of the truth they hear, "This is evidently enchantment."

Do they claim that he has manufactured it?

[Prophet Muhammed,] say, "If I had manufactured it, then you could not obtain a single blessing for me from Allah. He knows best that about which you talk. He is sufficient for a witness between me and you. He is the Most Forgiving, the Most Merciful.

—QUR'AN 46: 1-8

Daily living tip: People may bully you about your religion. Respond with kindness. Learn how to disarm them with wit and humor. Wait until you're seventy years old to act like a sassy brat. For now, be kind and sweet and easy to get along with.

Today's prayer: O my Lord, grant me wisdom and purity of heart in my responses to bullies.

Allah Will Teach You the Qur'an.

Glorify the name of your Lord the Highest! He has created and proportioned. He has measured and guided. He has brought forth the pasture. And He makes it ruined stubble.

We will teach you [the Qur'an] so that you won't forget. The exception is as Allah wills. Indeed, He knows what is visible and what is hidden.

We will make it easy for you, simple. Therefore, remind in case there is benefit to those reminded. The reminder will be received by those who have reverence. It will be rejected by the wretched ones. They will enter the great fire. There they will neither die nor live.

Prosperity will be for the one who purified him-/herself. [He/she] glorifies the name of his/her Lord and prays.

Ridiculous! You prefer the life of this world. But the hereafter is better and permanent.

Truly, this is in the earlier Scriptures. [They are] the records of Abraham and Moses.

—QUR'AN 87

Daily living tip: Read the Qur'an as if it were written just for you. Personalize it. In that way, you can figure out how to apply it to your own daily life. Make it stick to your heart like spit-out bubblegum sticks to the bottom of your best pair of shoes.

Today's prayer: O my Lord, show me how to make the messages of the Qur'an apply to my own life, and help me to live the Qur'an every day.

The Choice is Yours.

We have presented for people, in this Qur'an, every kind of parable in order that they may take heed. The Qur'an is in Arabic. It contains no distortion so that people may learn righteousness.

Allah presents this parable: A man serves many partners who are at odds with one another. Another man peacefully serves only one master. How do these two compare? Praise Allah! Most people, however, have no knowledge.

Truly, We have revealed the Book to you in truth for the benefit of humanity. The person, then, who receives guidance benefits his/her own soul. The person who strays injures his/her own soul. You, however, are not responsible for their actions.

Say, "O Allah, Creator of Heaven and Earth, Knower of all that is secret and public. You will judge among Your servants concerning those matters about which they differ."

—QUR'AN 39: 27-29, 41, 46

Daily living tip: Be careful to always put Allah first. Do not let others influence you away from Allah's will in your life. Don't be a knucklehead just because the knuckleheads are popular. Someday they won't be so popular, and it will be your turn to shine.

Today's prayer: O my Lord, direct my path so I am not misled by those who do not have correct guidance.

Allah is the Ultimate Planner.

Messengers before you [Prophet Muhammed] were mocked, but I granted respite to the disbelievers until I finally punished them. How terrible was my retribution!

Is He, who monitors every soul and all it does, comparable? Yet they assign partners to Allah. Say, "Okay, name them. Can you really tell Him anything about Earth that He doesn't already know, or are you just a show of words?"

Nonsense! To themselves, the disbelievers' inventions seem pleasing, but they are hindered from the path. Those whom Allah leaves astray cannot be guided by anyone. For them is a penalty in this life, but even harsher is the penalty of the hereafter. They have no defender against Allah.

The example of the garden promised to the righteous is rivers flowing beneath it, fruits that stay fresh, and its shade. Such is the finale for the righteous, but the end for disbelievers is fire.

Those to whom We have given the Book rejoice at what has been revealed to (Prophet Muhammed), but among the clans are those who reject part of it. Say, "I am commanded to worship Allah, and I do not join partners with Him. Unto Him I call, and unto Him is my return."

—QUR'AN 13: 32-36

Daily living tip: Do not reject any verses of the Qur'an. If there is a verse that you do not understand, trust that you will be granted that understanding whenever you need it. Ask someone you trust and don't ask a meathead.

Today's prayer: O my Lord, as I read the Qur'an, grant me understanding and wisdom so I may know how each verse applies to me.

Allah Has Ultimate Dominion.

May whatever is of Heaven and Earth declare the praises and glory of Allah, for He is the Victorious, the Perfectly Wise! To Him belongs the dominion of the skies and the earth. It is He who gives life and death, and He has power over all things. He is the First and the Last, the Evident and the Obscure, and He is the All-knowing concerning everything.

It is He who has created the skies and Earth in six days and is ultimately established on the throne. He knows what penetrates the earth and what emerges from it, and what falls from the sky and what mounts up to it. And He is with you wherever you may be, and Allah observes all that you do.

To Him belongs the dominion of Heaven and Earth, and all affairs are referred back to Allah. He merges night into day, and day into night, and He has full knowledge of the secrets of hearts.

—QUR'AN 57: 1-6

Daily living tip: Spend time in nature and consider how everything in creation is in constant communion with Allah. Join nature in its worship of the Creator. Don't let that squawky little bird outdo you. Squawk praises to Allah in your own way.

Today's prayer: O my Lord, help me see Your glory in nature and be able to look beyond the creation and see Your power present in all things.

Allah Creates as He Will.

To Allah belongs the dominion of Heaven and Earth. He creates what He wills. He gives a male or female child according to His will. Or He gives both male and female children, and He leaves childless whom He will. He truly is filled with knowledge and power.

Allah knows what every female bears [in the womb]. He knows how much the wombs will fall short or exceed [the normal nine months of pregnancy]. Everything is before His sight, in proper perspective. He knows what is concealed and what is publicized. He is the Great, the Most Exalted.

It doesn't matter whether any of you hides his/her thoughts or speaks openly. [It doesn't matter] whether any of you hides at night or strolls freely during the day. For each person, angels trail before and behind and guard him/her by the command of Allah. Truly, Allah will never change the condition of a people until they change it themselves. When Allah wills a people's punishment, however, there can be no avoiding it, and they will find no one to protect them except Him.

—QUR'AN 42: 49-50 AND QUR'AN 13: 8-11

Daily living tip: Don't sneak around doing things that you know are wrong. Even if your parents don't find out, Allah always knows. Remember there are consequences for your actions. If you throw mud into the air, mud comes back to hit you in the head.

Today's prayer: O my Lord, help me to honor You by remembering that everything I do matters and is recorded.

Creation is a Gift for Humanity.

It is He who commands rain from the sky. From it you drink, and because of it exists vegetation on which your cattle feed. With it He produces for you corn, olives, date palms, grapes, and every other kind of fruit. Truly, in this is a sign for those who ponder.

He has made subject to you the night and the day. The sun and moon and stars are under His command. Truly, in this are signs for those with wisdom.

He has multiplied things on this earth in various hues. Truly, in this is a sign for people who take notice.

He made the sea subject to you so you may eat fresh and tender meat and so you may derive ornaments from it to wear. You see the ships that plow the waves so you may seek the bounty of Allah and perhaps be grateful.

He has firmly tied mountains onto the earth so that the earth will not tremble with you. There are rivers and roads so you may guide yourselves. There are landmarks and stars by which people guide themselves.

—Qur'an 16: 10-16

Daily living tip: Always take time to think about even the smallest blessings. Just having a glass of clean water to drink is a major blessing that many people take for granted. Also, don't put muddy water into your soul –only the living water of Allah.

Today's prayer: O my Lord, let me never be oblivious to the multiple blessings around me no matter how small they may seem.

The Blessings of Allah Cannot be Counted.

Is He who creates like the one who cannot create? Will you not consider?

If you were to count the blessings of Allah, you would never be able to number them all.

Allah is the Most Forgiving, the Most Merciful.

To Him is credited the primal origin of the atmosphere and planet Earth. How can He have a [begotten] child when He has no spouse? He has created all things, and He has full knowledge of all things. That is your Lord God! No god is there except Him, the Creator of all things. Worship Him for He has all things in His care.

No vision can grasp Him, but His grasp encompasses all visions. He is beyond our comprehension, but He comprehends all.

"Now evidence has appeared from your Lord. If any will see, the benefit will be to his/her own soul. If any chooses to remain unseeing, the detriment will be his/her own. I [your Prophet] am not appointed to guard you."

—QUR'AN 16: 17-18 AND QUR'AN 6: 101-104

Daily living tip: Whatever you visualize Allah to be, He is always greater. Any drawings or paintings you see of God are just representations of others' thoughts and in no way depict the reality of Allah. Cartoons can be funny, but they are stupid when they try to depict Allah.

Today's prayer: O my Lord, let me not be distracted by those who portray God in the limitations of their own designs.

Nothing Compares to Allah.

To Him belong all things of the skies and Earth. He is the Highest, the Magnificent. The skies above nearly burst as the angels celebrate the praises of their Lord and pray for forgiveness for all beings on Earth. Truly, Allah is the Most Forgiving, the Most Merciful.

As for those who rely on protectors other than Him, Allah watches over them. It's not up to you to be responsible for them.

If Allah had so willed, He could have made (humanity) one single people [with no racial and ethnic diversity]. He admits whom He will to His mercy, and the sinners will have no protector or helper.

The Creator of the skies and Earth has designed you to become mates. He has also made pairs among cattle. By this plan He multiplies you. There is nothing that compares to Him. He is the All-hearing, the All-seeing.

To Him belong the keys to Heaven and Earth. He expounds or limits sustenance as He will, for He is fully aware.

He is the One who accepts repentance from His servants and forgives sins. He knows all that you do.

—Qur'an 42: 4-6, 8, 11-12, 25

Daily living tip: Appreciate the diversity of people just like you would appreciate a field of different colored flowers. Every person is a creation of the same God. Everybody is beautiful in his or her own way, even if he or she has a toothless grin and is bow-legged. Treasure everybody.

Today's prayer: O my Lord, may everyone learn to find beauty in the diversity of all people regardless of skin color, culture, country of origin, or any other aspect of pluralism.

To Him Belong the Most Beautiful Names.

May whatever is in the skies and of the earth declare the praises and glory of Allah. He is the Victorious, the Perfectly Wise!

O Believers, fear Allah, and may every soul observe what he/she has invested for tomorrow. Observe your duty to Allah, for Allah is well acquainted with what you do.

Allah is He besides whom there is no deity. He knows both secrets and proclamations. He is the Most Gracious, the Most Merciful.

Allah is He besides whom there is no deity. He is the Absolute Ruler, the Holy One, the Source of Peace, the Source of Salvation, the Protector, the Victorious, the Compeller, and the Majestic. Glory belongs to Allah who is above any partners attributed to Him! He is God the Creator, the Organizer, the Designer. To Him belong the most beautiful names. All that is of the skies and Earth declare His praises and glory, and He is the Victorious, the Perfectly Wise.

—QUR'AN 59: 1, 18, 22-24

Daily living tip: There are thousands of names for God because of all the different religions, languages, cultures, and the various attributes of God. There is only One God for everyone, however. Nobody has a monopoly on God. Even the pig has the same God as you.

Today's prayer: O my Lord, help me to never dismiss the faith of others by having an attitude that my version of God is the only one that matters.

He Has Blessed Us With the Seven Habitual Lines.

There is nothing without its resources with Us. We bestow whatever is needed in specific measures. We send the pollinating winds, and then cause the rain to descend from the sky. With it, you have water to drink, even though you are not the guardians of its storage.

Truly, your Lord is the Creator, the All-knowing. We have given you the seven repetitions [of Chapter 1] and the amazing Qur'an.

[The habitually repeated lines:]

[1] In the Name of Allah, the Most Gracious, the Most Merciful.

[2] Praise belongs to Allah, the Lord of the Worlds! [3] The Most Gracious, the Most Merciful! [4] Master of the Day of Judgment!

[5] We worship You. We seek Your help. [6] Show us the Straight Way. [7] [Show us] the way of those on whom You have given Your grace. [Show us the way of] those who do not anger You and who do not go the wrong way.

—QUR'AN 15: 21-22, 86-87 AND QUR'AN 1

Daily living tip: Read the Qur'an every day and study its meanings. Trust Allah to help you understand how the Qur'an can guide you personally. You don't have to wander around like a lost puppy. Allah calls you home.

Today's prayer: O my Lord, keep me on the Straight Way and guide me with Your beautiful Word.

Allah Guides Whom He Will to His Light.

Allah is the Light of Heaven and Earth. The parable of His light is as if there were a niche within which is a lamp encased in crystal-clear glass glowing like a brilliant star. The lamp is lit [with oil] from an olive tree from neither east nor west [a universal tree], and the oil is so perfect that it is luminous even without the fire.

Light upon light! Allah guides whom He will to His light.

Allah sets forth such parables for the sake of humanity. Allah does have all knowledge.

[Such light exists] in houses that Allah has permitted to accrue honor because of the celebration within them of His name. In them, He is glorified mornings and evenings by people who will not be distracted by trade or materialism. [They will not be distracted] from the remembrance of Allah, the tradition of prayer, and the practice of routine charity. They fear only the day when hearts and eyes will be transformed. Allah will reward them in accordance with the best of their deeds plus even more for them from His grace. Allah provides for those whom He will, without measure.

—Qur'an 24: 35-38

Daily living tip: Live in such an admirable way that you are a light for others. Let the love and grace of Allah shine through you. Don't act like a drunk monkey. Be someone's inspiration. Be someone's answer to prayer.

Today's prayer: O my Lord, make me a good influence on others. May your light shine in my life so others may find the Straight Way.

Allah is the Cherisher and Sustainer of the Worlds.

Your Lord is Allah who created the skies and Earth in six days, and then established Himself on the [Heavenly] throne. He drags the night across the day as they swiftly run from one another. He created the sun, the moon, and the stars –all subject to His command. Blessed be Allah, the Cherisher and Sustainer of the Worlds!

Call upon your Lord with humility and in privacy. Allah does not love those who transgress beyond boundaries.

Commit no chaos on Earth now that it has been set in order [according to the perfect balance of nature]. Address Allah in reverence and sincerity, for the mercy of Allah is always near to those who live righteously.

He sends the winds like heralds of glad tidings, going before His mercy. When they have carried the heavily laden clouds, We shepherd them to a land that is desiccated. [We] make rain to descend upon it, and produce every kind of harvest from it. Thus, shall We raise the dead. Perhaps you will remember.

From the goodly land, by the will of its Cherisher, fruits and vegetables are produced. From the land that is sour, nothing is produced except spindly plants. This is how we explain the various signs for those who are grateful.

—QUR'AN 7: 54-58

Daily living tip: Humanity has created chaos in the world. Instead of being guardians of the planet, people have abused and exploited natural resources and polluted land and water. Be part of the solution. Find ways that you can be a responsible citizen of the planet. Don't go around like a tornado over a trash heap, leaving a mess.

Today's prayer: O my Lord, make me ever mindful of my duties to safeguard the planet and to do whatever I can to help make the planet a healthy place for all people, plants, animals, and ecosystems.

In All Creation Are Signs of Allah.

Signs are in all creation for wise people. Signs are in the skies and the earth. They are in the alternation of night and day. They are in the ships gliding across the sea for the benefit of humanity. Signs are in the rain that Allah sends from the sky and the life it awakens from a silent earth. They are in the multitudes of creatures Allah has distributed abroad. Signs are in the changing winds, and in the clouds trailing like servants of the sky and earth.

Yet, some people revere others, besides Allah, as equal. They love (their idols) as they should love Allah. But those of faith have lots of love for Allah. If only the unrighteous could understand, they would envision the punishment. They would realize that Allah has all power, and Allah will intensely enforce the punishment.

Then the [sinful] role models will distance themselves from those [fans] who followed. They will see the penalty, and all their relationships will be stopped. Those who followed will say, "If only we had one more chance, we would distance ourselves from them, just as they have now distanced themselves from us." Thus, Allah will reveal to them their deeds as regrets. There will be no way for them to escape the fire [of Hell].

—QUR'AN 2: 164-167

Daily living tip: Nature has messages for you, so spend time in nature. Go camping or hiking in wild lands. If you can't do that, watch nature shows on TV or read books about nature. You haven't lived until you've had to run screaming through the woods because you walked into a spiderweb with the biggest, ugliest spider you can imagine stuck to your forehead.

Today's prayer: O my Lord, may the whole world know Your awesome deeds. Make me one who can read Your words in the miracles of nature.

Creation is to be Observed and Celebrated.

Qaf! Consider the glorious Qur'an!

They wonder that a warner has come to them from among themselves.

The disbelievers say, "Well, this is a fine thing! After we die and turn to dust, we're supposed to live again? That is beyond our understanding."

We know how many of them the earth has already taken [to the graves]. With Us is a secure record.

They who deny the truth when they hear it must surely be in a state of confusion! Do they not look at the sky above them? Do they not consider how We have made and adorned it, and that there are no flaws in it? And the earth? We have spread it broadly and set mountains to anchor it, and have produced every kind of beautiful growth. [These things] are to be observed and celebrated by every repentant worshiper.

From the sky We send rain charged with blessing. We produce gardens and fields for harvest. Tall and stately are the palm trees. Their shoots of fruit stalks are piled one over another as sustenance for devoted servants.

We give new life to land that seems dead. Thus will be the Day of Resurrection.

—QUR'AN 50: 1-11

Daily living tip: Celebrate nature by planting a garden or a tree. If you can't do that, grow houseplants or herbs from seeds or cuttings. Plants can teach you things about life. When you watch the miracle of growth, you realize that your own life has a journey. Plant your feet in good spiritual soil so you won't grow to be useless. Produce fruits of the spirit.

Today's prayer: O my Lord, make me one who is observant of all the splendors of nature. May my celebration of nature bring me closer to You the Creator.

The Creation of Humanity Itself is a Sign.

Among His signs is that He created you from dust, and then, behold, you were human beings, dispersed. Among His signs is that He created for you mates from among yourselves so that you may dwell in tranquility with them, and He has put love and mercy among you. Truly, in this are signs for people who ponder.

Among His signs are the creation of the skies and Earth, and the variations in your languages and your colors. Truly, in this are signs for those of knowledge.

Among His signs are the sleep by night or day and your pursuit of His bounty. Truly, in these are signs for people who listen.

Among His signs are that Heaven and Earth stand by His command and that when He calls you by a single call, behold, you will emerge from the earth.

To Him belongs every being in Heaven and on Earth; all are devoutly obedient to Him.

He is the One who begins creation, and then repeats it, and for Him that is quite easy. For Him are the most meritorious similes in Heaven and on Earth, for He is the Victorious, the Perfectly Wise.

—QUR'AN 30: 20-23, 25-27

Daily living tip: Learn to appreciate the diversity of human beings –the different skin colors, unique facial features, languages, religions, and cultures. Even obnoxious people need a hug. Everybody needs hugs for healing.

Today's prayer: O my Lord, erase hate and bigotry from among people. Help me to be brave if I have an opportunity to speak or act against hateful prejudice.

Allah Created Earth Itself in Two Stages.

Say, "Do you deny He who created Earth in two days? Do you equate others with Him? He is Lord of the Worlds. He set, on (the land), mountains standing firmly, high above it. He bestowed blessings on it, and He measured provisions upon it in four days, in accordance with those who seek.

"He intended the sky, which was like smoke. He said to it and to Earth, 'Come together, willingly or unwillingly.'

"They said, 'We come in obedience.'"

"He completed the skies as seven layers, in two days, and He assigned to each [layer of] sky its purpose. We adorned this world's sky with lights and protection. Such is the decree of the Victorious, the All-knowing."

If they reject, say, "I have warned you of a thunderous disaster like the disaster that overwhelmed the Ad and the Thamud."

—QUR'AN 41: 9-13

Daily living tip: Learn to think of Earth and Sky as artwork by the Master Artist, and you will find beautiful treasures of artistry in every bit of creation you see. Well, maybe not raccoon poop, but you get the idea.

Today's prayer: O my Lord, teach me to appreciate the artworks You have painted into creation.

He is Lord of the Rising Sun.

Consider the arranged ranks. [They] deter by restraint. [They] proclaim the remembrance [of Allah]: "Truly, your God is One! [He is] Lord of Heaven and Earth and all thereof. He is Lord of every point of the rising sun."

Truly, with beautiful stars, We decorated the sky of this universe. [This is] to guard against all obstinate, rebellious demons. [This is] so they could not listen to the Exalted Assembly. Instead, they are repelled from every side. [They are] banished because they are under a perpetual penalty. Some may snatch something [of divine value], but they are pursued by a comet of piercing brightness.

Ask their opinion: Are they more difficult to create or others We have created? Indeed, We created (humanity) from a sticky clay. How you marvel while they mock! And when they are reminded, they still do not pay heed.

—QUR'AN 37: 1-13

Daily living tip: Whether you are dancing under the moonlight or strolling under the rays of the sun, be grateful for the amazing world in which we live. Watch out for that gopher hole while you're dancing in the woods though.

Today's prayer: O my Lord, how wonderful it is to walk in the sun! How amazing is the light of the moon! May the whole world know of your awesome deeds!

Allah Created You as His Representative.

Recall that your Lord announced to the angels, "I will create a representative upon Earth."

They responded, "Why would You create someone who would create evil and shed blood? We celebrate Your praises and glorify Your holiness."

Allah answered, "I know things about which you know nothing."

(Allah) taught Adam the names of all things. He placed (those things) before the angels and said, "Tell Me the names of these if you're so smart."

They answered, "Glory to You! We have no knowledge except what You have taught us. Truly, it is only You who is perfect in knowledge and wisdom."

(Allah) said, "O Adam, tell them the names."

When (Adam) had done so, Allah said [to the angels], "Didn't I tell you that I know secrets of Heaven and Earth, and I know what you reveal and what you conceal?"

—QUR'AN 2: 30-33

Daily living tip: When you wake up every morning, remind yourself that you are Allah's representative on the earth, and you have the responsibility to reflect well of the Creator. If your reflection of Him is like a dirty mirror, clean up your act.

Today's prayer: O my Lord, teach me how to represent You in all that I do whether in interactions with people or in safeguarding Your creation.

Humanity Accepted the Responsibility of Choice.

[Remember] when We arranged a covenant with the prophets, as with (Prophet Muhammed), Noah, Abraham, Moses, and Jesus the son of Mary [for examples]. We arranged a solemn covenant. [That was] so that the truthful may be questioned about their truth. For the disbelievers, He has prepared a horrid punishment.

O Believers, do not be like those who insulted Moses. Allah delivered him from their accusations, and he was honorable in the sight of Allah.

O Believers, fear Allah and say something on behalf of what is right. He will mend your conduct, and He will forgive you of your sins. Whoever obeys Allah and His messenger has already attained the highest achievement [salvation].

Truly, We offered the responsibility to the skies and the earth and the mountains, but they refused to undertake it, being afraid. Humanity, however, accepted it. Truly, he/she was unjust and foolish. Allah must punish the hypocrites –both male and female— and idolaters –both male and female. Allah is forgiving to the believers –both male and female— and Allah is Most Forgiving, Most Merciful.

—QUR'AN 33: 7-8, 69-73

Daily living tip: Humanity has undertaken responsibility, so be sure to take your part of the responsibility seriously, and always do your best. Don't be like a scab for the devil to pick at. Strive to be someone who contributes good things to this world as long as you live.

Today's prayer: O my Lord, help me to walk upon the earth in gentleness, kindness, and humility and ever be mindful of my duties as a citizen of Planet Earth.

Satan Lost His Lofty Position in Heaven.

We created you and gave you form. We beckoned the angels to bow down to Adam. They did so, except Iblis [Satan]. He refused to be among those who bowed.

(Allah) asked, "What prevented you from bowing when I commanded you?"

(Iblis) answered, "I am better than he; You created me from fire, and him from clay."

(Allah) ordered, "Descend [from your lofty position]. You are not permitted to be arrogant here [in the counsel of Allah]. Get out [of Heaven], for you are among the disgraced.

(Iblis) said, "Give me reprieve until the Day of Resurrection."

(Allah) said, "Be among those who are reprieved."

(Iblis) said, "Because you have thwarted me, I will prepare to ambush those along the Straight Way. Then I will assault them from front, back, right side, and left side. You will find no gratitude [for Allah's mercy] in most of them."

(Allah) said, "Get out, disgraced and expelled. If any [spirit-beings or humans] choose to follow you, I will fill Hell with you all."

—QUR'AN 7: 11-18

Daily living tip: Don't lose your position under Allah's grace and mercy. Watch out for those who would mislead you and make you into a nasty so-and-so. Watch your mouth as well as your actions. Picking up vulgar, abrasive talk and ugly actions will make you into a real jerk. Not cool!

Today's prayer: O my Lord, take my heart and guard me from the temptations thrown to me from Satan and his allies.

Do You Hate Truth?

Truly, We have delivered to you the truth, but most of you hate truth. Have (the sinners) come up with their own plan? It is We who have the plan! Do they think that We do not hear their secrets and private counsel? Indeed! And our messengers [the angels] are by them, keeping a record.

It is He who is God in Heaven and God on Earth. He is the sum of all wisdom and knowledge. Blessed is He who governs the skies and the earth and all that is contained therein. With Him is the knowledge of the hour [of judgment] and to Him you shall return.

Those whom are invoked besides Allah have no power of intercession except those who bear witness to the truth and have knowledge.

If you ask (the sinners) who created them, they will certainly say, "God!" Why then are they so perverted?

Consider his lament: "O my Lord, truly these people will never believe!"

Simply ignore them, wishing them, "Peace!" Soon they will know.

—QUR'AN 43:78-80, 84-89

Daily living tip: People around you may hate hearing the truth. Abide by it and state it no matter how unpopular it is. Be brave and patient when confronted by bullies. Sometimes the best response is to walk away, blowing raspberries (phhhhht!). If people hate you because you're Muslim, that's their problem. Leave them to their struggle.

Today's prayer: O my Lord, give me the patience I need to deal with bullies. Help me know the right words to say and how to act around them.

Humanity Lost Its Lofty Position in Heaven.

"O Adam, dwell with your wife in the Garden [of Eden]. Eat from whatever you wish, but do not approach this tree or you would be among sinners."

Then Satan whispered to them in order to reveal to them their shame, which was hidden from them. He said, "Your Lord only forbade you this tree to keep you from becoming angels or immortal beings."

He swore to them both, "Indeed, I am among the sincere advisors." By deceit he brought about their fall. After they had tasted of the tree, they realized their shame. They began to sew together leaves of the garden to cover their bodies.

Their Lord called to them, "Did I not forbid that tree from you and tell you that Satan was an avowed enemy to you?"

They said, "Our Lord, we have wronged our own souls. If You do not forgive us and grant mercy upon us, we will certainly be lost."

(Allah) said [to all human souls], "Get down [from your divine prestige], with enmity among yourselves. On [this physical] Earth will be your dwelling place and your livelihood for a time."

He said, "You will live there and die there, and from it you will be brought forth."

—Qur'an 7: 19-25

Daily living tip: Before you do anything, make sure you can say, "Bism'Allah" (in the name of God). If you don't feel comfortable using God's name before your act, then it is likely something you should not do. Maybe take a nap instead or a bubble bath.

Today's prayer: O my Lord, help me to discern between right and wrong and not to follow the advice of Satan and those who follow him.

Allah Forgave Adam and Eve.

We said to the angels, "Bow down to Adam," and they bowed, except Iblis [Satan]. He refused and was haughty and became one of those who rejected faith.

We said, "O Adam, you and your wife shall dwell in Paradise and eat freely as you desire, but do not approach the tree that will lead you into sin."

Then Satan made them fall from (Paradise). Satan caused them to be cast from that [perfect realm] in which they were.

We said, "All [humanity], get out and abide with bad feelings among yourselves. On Earth will be your dwelling place and your means of survival for a reckoned period of time."

Adam received words [of guidance] from his Lord, and (his Lord) forgave him for He is the Responder, the Most Merciful.

We said, "All of you [all humanity], descend from here [the original Paradise], and, when you receive guidance from Me. If you follow My guidance, you will have no fear or grief [in the hereafter]. Some people will reject faith and disagree with Our signs. They will always be among the people of the fire."

—QUR'AN 2: 34-39

Daily living tip: No matter how hard you try, you will always have times where you fall short in following Allah's will, even if it's just a bad thought about someone. Daily ask for forgiveness for those times and of course for any major sins. Allah will forgive you for being a jerk.

Today's prayer: O my Lord, grant Your mercy and forgiveness to me, my parents, and all believers. Save us from the Hell fire.

Do Not Allow Satan to Deceive You.

O Believers, do not follow Satan's footsteps. Any who follow Satan's footsteps perpetuates corruption and immorality.

If it were not for the grace and mercy of Allah, no one would remain pure, but Allah purifies whom He pleases. Allah is the All-hearing, the All-knowing.

Those among you graced with Allah's favor and prosperity should not neglect helping their relatives, those in need, and those who have been deployed for the service of Allah. Be forgiving and benevolent if you expect Allah to forgive you of your sins. Allah is the Most Forgiving, the Most Merciful.

Say, "I seek refuge with the Lord of the Dawn. [I seek refuge] from the corruption of created things. [I seek refuge] from the corruption of darkness as it spreads. [I seek refuge] from the corruption of those who blow on knots [in practicing black magic]. [I seek refuge] from the corruption of the envious one as he practices envy."

Say, "I seek refuge with the Lord of the People. The King of People! The God of People! [I seek refuge] from the corruption of the whisperer who withdraws. He whispers into the hearts of people. [He whispers] among the spirit-beings and people."

—Qur'an 24: 21-22 and Qur'an 113 and Qur'an 114

Daily living tip: Remember that Satan can only whisper and suggest to you to do what is wrong. It is your choice whether to follow him or do the right thing. Don't blame Satan for your choice. Take responsibility for your own actions when you act like a dork.

Today's prayer: O my Lord, empower me to ignore the suggestions of Satan and to make the best choices in how I live.

Satan's Promises Are False.

(Satan) makes promises and creates vain desires, but Satan's promises are nothing but deception. (For his followers,) Hell will be their quarters, and they will be unable to escape.

But those who believe and live righteously will be admitted to gardens [of Paradise], with underground rivers, and there they will live forever.

Allah's promise is true, and whose word can be more honest than Allah's?

Neither your own desires nor those of the People of the Book are valid. Whoever performs evil will be requited accordingly, and he/she will find no protector or helper other than Allah.

If anyone –male or female— performs deeds of righteousness and has faith, he/she will enter Heaven, and not the least bit of injustice will be done.

Who can be better in religion than one who submits his/her whole self to Allah, lives righteously, and follows the religion of Abraham, who was true in faith? Allah called Abraham His friend.

To Allah belong all things of the skies and Earth, and Allah encompasses all things.

—Qur'an 4: 120-126

Daily living tip: Your friends may offer you what they think is fun; for examples, smoking, drinking alcohol, and listening to music with vulgar lyrics. Be strong and brave enough to turn away from these temptations. Tell your friends, "I have better ways of having fun," and invite them to participate in a healthy activity with you.

Today's prayer: O my Lord, help me to be a good influence on others and to invite them to what is good and pure.

Consider When Humanity Was Not.

Has there not been a time over humanity when he/she was nothing –not even a mention? We created humanity from a union of gametes so that We may test him/her. We gave him/her [the gifts of] hearing and sight. We showed him/her the way, whether he/she is grateful or ungrateful.

We have bestowed upon you the Qur'an in portions. Therefore, be patient for the command of your Lord. Do not heed the sinner or the disbeliever. Remember the Name of your Lord morning and evening. Part of the night, prostrate to Him. Glorify Him all through the night.

Truly, these [sinners] love the present life and disregard the difficult Day [of Judgment]. We created them and made their bodies durable. When We will, we can change their bodies into similar ones.

Truly, this is reminder: Whosoever will come may come to the [Straight] Way of the Lord. But you cannot come except in accordance with Allah's will. Indeed, Allah is the All-knowing, the Perfectly Wise. He will admit to His mercy whom He will, but for the lost He has prepared a dreadful penalty.

—Qur'an 76: 1-3, 23-31

Daily living tip: Before the creation of humanity, the world belonged to animals, plants, water, and soil. Nature can take care of itself without humans, but humanity cannot survive without the creation and forces of nature, so always respect nature. It's not nice to dump on nature. Respect nature and do what you can to preserve and protect it.

Today's prayer: O my Lord, make me a friend of Your creation and not one who pollutes and exploits what the planet offers.

Consider Your Own Creation.

We created you. Why then do you not believe in Me? Do you consider the reproductive sperm and ovum? Are they created by you, or are We the Creator?

We have decreed that death be your shared fate. We will not be frustrated from changing your life form into something new to you. You are certainly familiar with the first form of creation. Why then would you not ponder [the spiritual form]?

Do you consider what you cultivate? Do you cause it to sprout, or do We? If it were Our intention, We could have crumbled (the seeds) to dust, and you would be left bewildered. [You would complain,] "We are burdened with debt. We are deprived!"

Do you consider the water you drink? Do you entice it from the clouds, or do We? If it were Our intention, We could make it salty and bitter. Why then do you not give thanks?

Do you consider the fire you kindle? Do you grow the timber [from which the fire is fed], or do We? We have made it a token [of Our gifts] and a thing of comfort and ease for campers in the wilderness.

Glorify, then, the Name of your Lord the Supreme Being.

—Qur'an 56: 57-7

Daily living tip: Even in the 21st century, many people all over the world, including the USA, live without electricity, plumbing, clean drinking water, housing, and other things that most people take for granted. Don't overlook even the tiniest blessing that makes your life easier.

Today's prayer: O my Lord, make me ever mindful of every blessing, privilege, and opportunity I have.

Allah Did Not Create the World for Sport.

We did not create the skies and Earth and all among them simply as a sport. If it had been Our desire to indulge in fun, We would have done so on Our own, if We acted so.

Instead [of playing sport], We hurl truth against deceit in order to destroy (deceit), and then deception perishes. Beware of incurring misery because of your [false] descriptions [of God].

To Him belong all that is of the skies and Earth. Even those [angels] in His very presence are not too proud to serve Him, and neither do they tire. They celebrate [His glory] night and day, without pause.

Do the disbelievers not understand that the skies and Earth were massed together before we split them apart? We made every living thing from water! Will they not believe?

We established, on the earth, mountains standing firmly to prevent (the earth) from trembling with them. We made mountain passes so that perhaps they will be guided.

We made the sky as a canopy, well-guarded. Still, they reject the signs of such things.

He created the night and the day and the sun and the moon. They all swim, each to its own path.

—Qur'an 21: 16-20, 30-33

Daily living tip: Allah has a purpose for everything He created. Sometimes, we may not understand the reason for a created thing; for examples, fleas, ticks, and lice. People trying to understand Allah, however, is like a pet trying to understand what the veterinarian is doing. Remember that Allah knows best, and our brains are no match for His wisdom. You don't have to hug a bug; just realize it belongs on this planet just as much as you do.

Today's prayer: O my Lord, help me to appreciate the value of every created thing whether or not I understand its value.

Allah Created the World for a Reason.

Do (the disbelievers) not ponder in their own minds? Only for good cause and for a determined time did Allah create the skies and the earth and all among them. Yet, certainly there are many among people who deny their meeting with their Lord.

Do they not travel throughout the earth and see what was the end of those before them? They were superior to them in strength, and they tilled the soil. They populated in greater numbers than these [disbelievers] have done. Their messengers came to them with evidence, which they rejected. Allah did not wrong them, but they wronged their own souls.

In the long run, evil in the extreme will be the end of those who do evil, because they rejected the signs of Allah and displayed them for ridicule.

Allah alone begins creation and then repeats it. You shall then be returned to Him. On the day that the hour [of judgment] happens, the guilty will be dumbstruck with despair. No intercessor will be among their partners, and they will reject their partners.

—QUR'AN 30: 8-13

Daily living tip: Natural disasters –floods, tornadoes, hurricanes, earthquakes, etc.— are reminders that this world has an appointed time for its existence. Although this creation will eventually come to an end, you are still responsible to safeguard it. Try to live your whole life without being a blockhead.

Today's prayer: O my Lord, may Your help and mercy come to all those in the paths of natural disasters. Accept the victims into Paradise and help the survivors to recover.

The Purpose of This Life
is to Attain the Eternal Life.

Every soul will taste death, and only on the Day of Judgment will you be paid your full recompense. Whoever is far removed from the fire and admitted into Paradise will have attained the purpose of life. The life of this world is nothing but enjoyment of delusion.

You will certainly be tested in your possessions and in your personal selves. You will certainly hear much that will grieve you from those who received the (Scriptures) before you and from those who worship many gods. If you are patient and reverent, then that indeed will be a determining factor in all affairs.

Surely, in the creation of the skies and Earth, in the alternation of night and day, signs are there for people of understanding. [They are] people who celebrate Allah, whether standing, sitting, or lying on their sides. [They] think about the creation of the skies and the earth: "Our Lord, You have not created this for nothing. Glory to You! Grant us salvation from the penalty of the fire. Our Lord, any whom You do admit to the fire, You will certainly cover with shame, and never will the sinners find any helpers."

—QUR'AN 3: 185-186, 190-192

Daily living tip: All throughout your life, you will be confronted with problems and challenges. Realize these are opportunities for you to stand strong in the face of adversity and that you will be rewarded for passing each test of faith. Don't be a jerk to other people. They are struggling with their problems too.

Today's prayer: O my Lord, help me to face every obstacle with faith, strength, bravery, and resilience.

Day
40

True Religion is Complete Submission to Allah.

Say, "Shall I give you the good news of things far better than those [possessions of this present life]? For those who remain conscious of their Lord are gardens with rivers flowing beneath. They will abide forever with holy companions. They will have the acceptance of Allah. In Allah's sight are His servants. [They are] those who say, 'Our Lord, we have indeed believed, so forgive us our sins and save us from the agonizing fire.' [They are] those who are patient, truthful, and humbly obedient, those who spend (for charity), and those who seek forgiveness in the early hours of morning.

"Allah bears witness that no deity is there except Him. So do His angels [bear witness] and those endued with knowledge and perseverance for justice. No god is there except Him, the Victorious, the Perfectly Wise.

"Truly, the religion near Allah is complete submission to His will. The People of the Book did not differ from that except through spite of one another after they had received knowledge. If any deny the verses of Allah, then truly Allah is swift in accountability."

—QUR'AN 3: 15-19

Daily living tip: When people ask you about Islam, tell them, "When God created humanity, He did not leave them without a religion. The original religion He gave was peace with God through complete submission to Him. In Arabic, that religion is called Islam." That is a good starting point for explaining the religion.

Today's prayer: O my Lord, grant me the peace that comes from living in complete submission to Your will.

Submission to Allah Was the Religion of Noah.

He decrees for you the same religion that He ordained for Noah, which is what We have inspired to you [Prophet Muhammed]. We also ordained [this religion] for Abraham, Moses, and Jesus. Specifically, that you should remain faithful in religion and create no divisions therein.

As for those who worship other things besides Allah, you [Prophet Muhammed] call them to dreadful accountability. Allah chooses who comes to Him, as He pleases. He guides to Himself those who repent.

(The religious sects) became divided only after knowledge had come to them, due to sinfulness among them. If it had not been for a prior Word sent forth from your Lord, concerning an appointed term, the matter would have been resolved among them. Truly, those who have inherited the Book from them are suspicious about it.

Because of that, give the call and stand faithfully as you are commanded. Do not follow their vain desire, but say, "I believe in the Book Allah has bestowed, and I am commanded to judge justly among you. Allah is our Lord and your Lord. We are responsible for our deeds, and you are responsible for your deeds. No contention is between you and us. Allah will bring us all together, and to Him is our destiny."

—QUR'AN 42: 13-15

Daily living tip: Instead of arguing about differences among religions, try focusing on the consonant values because all those values came from the same original religion. Those values include such things as peace, love, charity, compassion, goodwill, honesty, justice, and fairness. Don't be a religious supremacist acting like your religion is the only one that matters.

Today's prayer: O my Lord, help me to refrain from arguing about religious matters and find the agreeable things instead.

Allah Sent Messengers with Evidence.

Have you not heard the story of those before you —of the people of Noah, Ad, and Thamud— and of those after them? No one knows them except Allah.

Messengers came to them with evidence, but they put their hands to their mouths and shouted, "We reject what you bring, and we are suspicious of what you offer!"

Their messengers answered, "Is there any doubt about Allah, the Creator of the skies and Earth? It is He who invites you so that He may forgive you of your sins and give you reprieve for an appointed term."

They said, "You are no more than human, just like us! You want to turn us away from that which our fathers worshiped. So then, bring us definite proof."

Their messengers said to them, "It's true that we are human like you, but Allah grants His grace to those of His servants as He pleases. It is not our job to provide proof except as Allah permits. On Allah, may all people of faith put their trust. There is no reason why we should not put our trust in Allah. He has guided us to our ways. We shall certainly bear with patience all the hurt you may cause us. On Allah should the reliant depend."

—QUR'AN 14: 9-12

Daily living tip: When your non-Muslim friends ask you about Islam, tell them, "Muslims believe in all the prophets, including Moses and Jesus, as well as Muhammed (peace upon them)." Islam is cool because we have more prophets than most other religions. Rap about that!

Today's prayer: O my Lord, help me defend my religion in the most beautiful ways.

Remember the Story of Cain and Able.

Recite to (the masses) the true story of the two sons of Adam. They each presented a sacrifice [to God]. It was accepted from one, but not from the other.

(Cain) said [to Abel], "You can be sure that I will kill you."

(Abel) said, "Allah accepts the sacrifices of those who are righteous. If you lay your hand against me to kill me, I will not lay my hand against you to kill you, because I do fear Allah, the Lord of the Worlds. I intend to allow you to mount upon yourself my error [of not using self-defense] as well as your own [sin]. You will be among the companions of the fire, which is the reward of those who commit evil."

(Cain's) ego urged him toward the killing of his brother. He murdered (Abel) and became one of the lost ones.

Then Allah sent a raven, which scratched upon the ground to show (Cain) how to hide the appalling corpse of his brother. "So miserable am I!" he said. "Was I not even able to be as this raven in hiding the disgrace of my brother?" Then he was filled with regret.

—QUR'AN 5: 27-31

Daily living tip: Nature has messengers for people. Look deep into nature and see what you can learn about yourself. For example, the squirrels teach us to save and prepare when they store nuts for the winter. The birds teach us to be happy and sing with joy. Cats teach us how to relax and just chill.

Today's prayer: O my Lord, tend to the wildlife and ease their struggle as they try to survive in a world where wild lands have been polluted and diminished.

To Kill One Person is to Kill an Entire Population.

Because of the account [of Cain and Abel], We ordained for the Children of Israel that if anyone killed a person –unless it is [punishment] for murder or spreading evil throughout the land— it would be as if he/she had killed all humanity. And if anyone saved a life, it would be as if he/she saved all humanity.

Although there came to them Our messengers with obvious signs –even after all that— many of then continued in unrestrained behavior throughout the land.

The payment for those [terrorists] who wage war against Allah and His messenger and strive to proliferate evil [eg, rape, pedophilia] throughout the land is their being executed or crucified. [Another option is] their having alternating hands and feet amputated [ie, right hand and left foot]. [Another option is] their being exiled from the country. [Consider which is most appropriate for the hideousness of each crime.] That is their disgrace in this world, but an intense torment will be theirs in the hereafter. The exception is those who repent before you overpower them. In that case, realize that Allah is the Most Forgiving, the Most Merciful.

—Qur'an 5: 32-33

Daily living tip: Society has to have strict laws and punishments to control the evil that some people do. If you are in a situation where someone is about to break the law (for example, underage drinking or using drugs), speak up to let that person know the law and the consequences. Yeah, some people will ridicule you. So what! Suck it up, buttercup; things are going to get a lot tougher in this world. You have to get used to it.

Today's prayer: O my Lord, make me brave and smart enough to know how to handle difficult decisions.

Noah Witnessed to His People.

We sent Noah to his people: "Warn your people before a grievous penalty comes to them."

(Noah) said, "O my people, I am an explicit and open advisor to you. [This is] so you may worship and revere Allah and obey me [as His servant]. He will forgive you for your sins and give you respite for a definite term. When a decided term is completed by Allah, it cannot be delayed, if you only knew."

(Noah) said, "O my Lord, I have called to my people day and night. But my call only increases their flight. Every time I have called to them so You might forgive them, they have thrust their fingers into their ears. [They have] pulled their garments over themselves, become obstinate, and acquired arrogance. I have called to them aloud. I have spoken to them publicly and privately. (I have said), 'Ask forgiveness from your Lord, for He is Most Forgiving. He will send rain abundantly. [He will] increase your wealth and sons and bestow on you gardens and running water. What is the matter with you that you do not place your hope for kindness and patience in Allah?'"

—QUR'AN 71: 1-13

Daily living tip: Take the warnings of the Qur'an seriously but also take seriously the mercy and grace of Allah. He is always available and willing to hear your prayer of repentance. You're going to mess up. Just try not to goof up your whole life. Do the best you can and trust in Allah to take up your slack.

Today's prayer: O my Lord, forgive me for any sins large or small and help me do better.

Noah Obeyed Allah,
But Most Other People Were Lost.

It was revealed to Noah, "None of your people will believe except those who have already believed. Do not grieve over their deeds any longer. Build an ark under Our eyes and according to Our inspiration. No longer speak to Me on behalf of those lost in sin. They will surely be drowned."

(Noah) began construction of the ark. Whenever leaders of his people passed, they ridiculed him [and his family], but he said, "Taunt us now, but we scoff at you even as you ridicule us. Soon you will realize on whom will descend a penalty that will shame and on whom will be unleashed a lasting penalty."

Finally, Our command emerged, and the earthen oven boiled over. We commanded [Noah], "Embark, along with a pair [male and female] of each creature, and with your family, except those [family members] against whom the Word has already gone against, and with other believers." But only a few believed with him.

(Noah) then ordered, "Board the ark! In the Name of Allah are its passage and its anchoring. My Lord is surely the Most Forgiving, the Most Merciful."

(The ark) floated with them on mountainous waves, and Noah called out to his son who had estranged himself, "O my son, come on board with us and do not be among the disbelievers."

(The son) replied, "I will take refuge on some mountain where I will be safe from the [rising] waters."

(Noah) said, "This day there is no harbor from the command of Allah except for those on whom He has shown mercy."

Then the waves swelled between them, and (the son) became among those who drowned.

—QUR'AN 11: 36-43

Daily living tip: Whenever you hear of any disaster, be sure to pray for the victims and the survivors. You never know when tragedy may strike you, and then you will need the blessing of your own prayers. Life is tough. You have to be tougher.

Today's prayer: O my Lord, let me not go astray but lead me in the way that will keep me within your mercy and grace.

The Ark Was a Sign for Humanity.

A sign for (humanity) is that We carried their descendants [humanity's DNA] in the loaded ark [of Noah]. We have created for them similar (vessels), which they ride. If it were Our will, We could drown them, and no responder would come for their deliverance. The exception would be as a mercy from Us, and for accommodation for a time.

Can a person not understand that We created him/her from [male and female] gametes? Yet, he/she is openly adverse. He/she compares Us [to created things] and forgets his/her own origin. He/she says, "Who can revive decomposed bones?"

Say, "He who created them in the first place will give them life again, for He is capable in every form of creating. [He is] the same who produces for you fire from the green tree, which you use for kindling. Is it not possible for the One who created the heavens and Earth to create anew? Yes, indeed, for He is the Creator, the All-knowing. Truly, when He intends something, He just says, 'Be!' and it is. So glory to Him in whose hands is the dominion of all things, and to Him you will return."

—QUR'AN 36: 41-44, 77-83

Daily living tip: Sometimes such difficulties arise that you may wish for a miracle. Miracles do occur; it's a miracle that you even exist. Sometimes the miracle is simply that you are able to overcome a difficulty so hard that it breaks your heart into a million pieces. Stay strong. Don't wimp out.

Today's prayer: O my Lord, relieve me of severe difficulties and help me overcome the difficulties life does hold for me.

Follow the Religion of Abraham.

An excellent example for you to follow is that of Abraham and those with him.

They said to their people, "We are distinct from you and whatever you worship besides Allah. We have rejected you, and animosity and disgust have arisen between us and you forever unless you believe in Allah alone."

But Abraham said to his father, "I will pray for forgiveness for you, although I have no power to get anything on your behalf from Allah."

"Our Lord, in You we trust, and to You we repent. To You is our final goal. Our Lord, do not make us a trial for the disbelievers, but forgive us, our Lord. Truly, You are the Victorious, the Perfectly Wise."

Certainly, in them [Abraham's family] was an excellent example for you to follow as those whose hope is in Allah and in the last day.

If any resist, truly Allah is Independent, the Praised One.

Say, "Allah speaks the truth. Follow the religion of Abraham the honorable. He was not one of the idolaters."

—QUR'AN 60: 4-6 AND QUR'AN 3: 95

Daily living tip: Anything that comes between you and the grace and mercy of Allah is an idol. Do not let anything prevent you from being true in faith. It's okay to have fun and enjoy life. Just don't leave Allah out of your fun as well as your worship.

Today's prayer: O my Lord, help me to not be distracted by the things of this world but help me to remember my duties to You.

Abraham Discovered the Truth.

Recall that Abraham said to his father Azar, "Do you acknowledge idols for gods? I see you and your people in obvious error."

We showed Abraham the splendor of the skies and Earth so he may have assurance.

When the night enveloped him, he saw a star and said, "This is my Lord." When it set, he said, "I cannot love something that disappears."

When he saw the moon rise, he said, "This is my Lord." When the moon set, he said, "Unless my Lord guides me, I shall surely be among those who are lost."

When he saw the sun rise, he said, "This is my Lord; this is the most awesome of all." But when the sun set, he said, "O my people, I am indeed free from your assigning partners to Allah. I am firmly focused on He who created the skies and Earth; I am dedicated, and I am not of those who believe in idols."

—QUR'AN 6: 74-79

Daily living tip: When you look at the splendor of the skies and the earth, be in awe of the Creator and remember His blessings upon you. Realize the world has a Creator. It doesn't exist by accident. Allah may have used some forms of evolution, but that doesn't take away from the fact He was in control of it.

Today's prayer: O my Lord, do not let me take anything for granted but remind me to always be grateful for all the wonders of Your creation.

Abraham Witnessed to His Family.

Mention Abraham in the Book. He was a man of truth –a prophet. He said to his father, "O my father, why do you worship that which cannot hear or see and which cannot profit you anything? O my father, knowledge has come to me that has not come to you. Follow me; I will guide you to a way that is even and straight. O my father, do not serve Satan for Satan is a rebel against the Most Gracious. O my father, I fear that a penalty may afflict you from the Most Gracious because you have befriended Satan."

(The father) replied, "Do you hate my gods, O Abraham? If you don't stop, I will indeed stone you. Now get away from me for a long time."

Abraham said, "Peace to you. I will pray to my Lord for your forgiveness, for He is to me Most Gracious. I will ignore you and those whom you invoke besides Allah. I will call on my Lord. Perhaps, by my prayer to my Lord, I will not be unblessed."

When he turned away from them and from those whom they worshiped besides Allah, We bestowed on him Isaac and Jacob. Each one of them We made a prophet. We bestowed Our mercy on them. We granted them lofty honor on the tongue of truth.

—Qur'an 19: 41-50

Daily living tip: We are commanded to obey our parents in all but one thing: worshiping a god other than the true God of all creation. Be obedient and honorable to your parents or guardians, but do not allow any error of theirs to misguide you. You are responsible whether you're a winner or a goofball.

Today's prayer: O my Lord, help my parents in faith and keep them on the Straight Way.

Invite Others to the True Religion.

Abraham was indeed a model devoutly obedient to Allah, sincere in faith, and not assigning gods with Allah. He was grateful for the blessings of Allah who chose him and guided him to the Straight Way. We gave him goodness in this world, and he will truly be among the righteous in the hereafter.

We have inspired you to follow the ways of Abraham, the true in faith; he never assigned gods with Allah.

Invite all to the way of your Lord by using wisdom and beautiful witnessing. Make your persuasion in ways most gracious. Your Lord knows who has strayed from His path and who has received guidance.

If you expose them [by pointing out their faults], expose them no worse than they have embarrassed you [in denigrating your religion]. Instead, show patience; that is indeed the way of tolerance. And do be tolerant, for patience is a virtue from Allah. And do not grieve over (the disbelievers), nor be distressed over their plots. Allah is with those who restrain themselves and act appropriately.

—QUR'AN 16: 120-123, 125-128

Daily living tip: Don't just tell others about Islam; show Islam by being a kind person in both words and deeds. Do not condemn the religions of others. You don't have to make Islam look good by trying to make other religions look bad. Islam will look good if you look good in how you interact with others.

Today's prayer: O my Lord, give me proper conduct and proper words with all those with whom I interact.

Remember Ishmael, Abraham's First Son.

Mention Ishmael in the Book. He was certainly true to what he promised. He was a messenger, a prophet. He encouraged his people in prayer and charity. He was acceptable in the sight of his Lord.

Mention Enoch in the Book. He certainly was a man of truth, a prophet. We raised him to a higher plane.

They were among the prophets on whom Allah bestowed his grace. [They were] from the posterity of Adam and of those We preserved with Noah. [They were] of the posterity of Abraham and Israel. We guided and chose all those. Whenever the signs of the Most Gracious were recited to them, they would fall prostrating and weeping.

After them, however, there followed a posterity who missed prayers and followed lustful desires. Soon, then, they will face destruction. The exceptions are those who repent and believe, and perform deeds of righteousness. They will enter Paradise, and they will not be slighted in the least.

—QUR'AN 19: 54-60

Daily living tip: Muslims believe in all the prophets. They shared the same message of submitting to the will of Allah and living righteously. When people defame Prophet Muhammed (peace upon him) we cannot respond by ridiculing the prophets they follow because we follow those prophets too. Defend the Prophet by reflecting his kindness and patience.

Today's prayer: O my Lord, make me wise enough to know how to respond to every hateful person that insults me because of my religion.

Abraham Was Prepared to Sacrifice His Child.

[Abraham prayed,] "O my Lord, grant me [a child] from among the righteous."

So We gave him the good news of a pleasant son.

When (the son) had attained an accountable age, (Abraham) told him, "O my son, I have seen a vision in which I offer you in sacrifice. What is your opinion?"

"O my father, do as you are commanded. You will discover, Allah willing, that I will be loyal."

After they had both peacefully agreed, and Abraham had laid the son face down, We called to him, "O Abraham, you have already fulfilled the vision!"

This is how We reward those who do right. This was obviously a test. We ransomed (the son) with a substantial sacrifice. And We instituted for him among later generations, "May peace be upon Abraham!"

This is how We reward those who do right. He truly was one of Our believing servants. We gave him the good news of Isaac, a prophet and one of the righteous. We blessed (Abraham) and Isaac. Of their descendants are those that do right and those that do obvious wrong to their own souls.

—Qur'an 37: 100-113

Daily living tip: Everyday, commit yourself to doing Allah's will and being obedient to His commandments. Find guidance in the Qur'an for how best to live your life. Allah is not going to dump on you anything you can't handle as long as you trust in Him to see you through it.

Today's prayer: O my Lord, peace and blessings upon every child who died young for whatever reason. May all children make many wonderful friends in Heaven.

Abraham and Sarah Received Good News of a Son.

Our messengers certainly came to Abraham with good news. They said, "Peace!"

He answered, "Peace!"

He hurried to offer them a roasted calf. When he saw that they did not touch it, he became suspicious and fearful of them.

They said, "Have no fear. Indeed, we have been sent against the people of Lot."

(Abraham's) wife was standing. She laughed when We gave her the good news of Isaac and, after him, Jacob.

She said, "Oh, me! Shall I bear a child now that I am an old woman and my husband an old man? That would certainly be amazing!"

They said, "Do you marvel at Allah's command? The grace of Allah and His blessings are upon you, O people of this house. He is indeed the Most Praiseworthy, the Majestic."

—QUR'AN 11: 69-73

Daily living tip: A miracle is a surprising and welcome event that cannot be explained by science or nature. If you believe in miracles, you may find them happening in your life. Even when things go whack, Allah can use that situation to make something good happen.

Today's prayer: O my Lord, provide for me a future that is blessed with divine wonders.

Abraham Was a Model for All Nations.

O Children of Israel, remember the favor I bestowed upon you and that I chose you over all other people. Then guard yourselves against a day when one soul cannot comfort another. There will be no compensation, intercession, or assistance.

Remember that Abraham was tested by his Lord with certain commands, which he fulfilled.

(Allah) said, "I will make you a model for the nations."

(Abraham) pleaded, "And also my children?"

He answered, "My covenant will not embrace the sinners."

Remember that We made the House [of Prayer, the Kabah in Meccah] a place of congregation for people and a place of sanctuary. Take the example of Abraham as a position of prayer.

We made a pact with Abraham and Ishmael. We wanted them to bless My House for those who walk around it, use it as a retreat, and bow and prostrate [in prayer].

Remember that Abraham said, "My Lord, make (Mecca) a City of Peace. Provide fruits for those inhabitants who believe in Allah and the Last Day."

(Allah) said, "For those who reject faith, I will allow them their pleasure for a while. Soon I will drive them to the torment of fire –an evil destination.

—Qur'an 2: 122-126

Daily living tip: Hajj (the journey to Mecca during the hajj month) is required for every Muslim who can afford it. This trip is getting more and more expensive. Start saving for it today. Get a piggy bank or other container for saving money. Try finding some chores you can do to earn money and put some of it into your hajj savings.

Today's prayer: O my Lord, if it is Your will, please bless my future with hajj, and also bless my future spouse and children with hajj.

Jacob and His Children Followed Abraham.

Remember that Abraham and Ishmael raised the foundations of the House.

[Their prayer:] "Our Lord, accept our service. You are the All-hearing, the All-knowing. Our Lord, make us those in submission to You. Of our descendants, make a people who submit to You. Teach us our rituals of worship. Accept our repentance, for You are the Most Forgiving, the Most Merciful.

"Our Lord, send a messenger from among their own people. [May the messenger] be one who will recite Your signs to them, instruct them in Scripture and wisdom, and purify them. You are the Exalted in Might and Wisdom."

Who shuns the religion of Abraham except one who fools him-/herself? We chose (Abraham) [for purity] in this world, and he will be among the righteous in the hereafter.

Recall when his Lord said to him, "Surrender your life to Me."

(Abraham) answered, "I surrender to the Lord of All the Worlds."

Abraham left this legacy for his children. Jacob also said, "O my children, Allah has chosen to reveal the true faith to you. Do not die without having submitted to Allah."

Can you testify about when death appeared before Jacob? He said to his children, "What will you worship after I am gone?"

They answered, "We will worship your God and the God of your fathers –Abraham, Ishmael, and Isaac. He is the only God, and we submit ourselves to Him."

These were people who have passed. They will be accountable for what they did, just as you will of what you do. You won't be given credit for what they did.

—QUR'AN 2: 127-134

Daily living tip: The religion of Abraham was simply to submit his whole self to Allah and live righteously. If someone asks you about religion, point them to the religion of Abraham and then trust Allah to help them interpret what that means for him or her.

Today's prayer: O my Lord, help me surrender my life completely to You, Lord of All the Worlds.

Abraham Was Not a Jew or a Christian.

Why do you People of the Book argue about Abraham [eg, his role in Judaism and Christianity] when neither the Torah nor the Gospel [of Jesus] was revealed until after him? Don't you have any sense? You are always arguing about things of which you have some knowledge. Why would you argue about something unknown to you? Allah knows, and you do not know. Abraham was not a Jew or a Christian. He was true in faith and submitted to Allah. He was not one of the idolaters.

The people most worthy to be counted with Abraham are those who follow him, as do this Prophet [Muhammed] and those who believe [with him]. Allah is the Guardian of all those who have faith.

Some of the People of the Book would like to lead you astray [away from Islam]. They lead only themselves astray and don't even realize it.

People of the Book, why do you reject the signs of Allah, which you witness? People of the Book, why do you cloak truth with fabrication, thereby concealing the truth, when you do have sense?

—QUR'AN 3: 65-71

Daily living tip: Although Jews are more tolerant in religious differences, many Christians feel it is their duty to "save" you. Ask them, "What religion did God give to Adam and Eve?" Most people never thought of that. It will be a good way to start a discussion.

Today's prayer: O my Lord, help me in my interactions with non-Muslims to be able to have intelligent conversations without conflict.

No One Has a Monopoly Over Allah's Grace.

We certainly sent Noah and Abraham. We established within their descendants the family of prophets and the Book. Among them were those rightly guided, but most of them were defiantly disobedient.

We sent Our messengers after their footsteps. We followed them with Jesus the son of Mary and bestowed on him the Gospel. We ordained within the hearts of his followers compassion and mercy, but (certain) followers made up the idea of monasticism [eg, celibacy and self-denial]. We did not prescribe that for them. We only commanded seeking the contentment of Allah, but they failed to observe that as they should have. Still, We rewarded the believers appropriately, but many are defiantly disobedient.

O Believers, be conscious of Allah and believe in His messenger [Muhammed, in addition to Jesus], and He will bestow on you a double portion of His mercy. He will provide a light by which you can walk, and He will forgive you. Allah is the Most Forgiving, the Most Merciful.

The People of the Book should know that they have no monopoly over the grace of Allah. Grace is in Allah's hand; He bestows it on whomever He will. Allah is the Lord of Abundant Grace.

—QUR'AN 57: 26-29

Daily living tip: The Qur'an is for everybody. Although the passage above is directed mostly to Christians, we Muslims can also learn from it. Muslims also invent ideas and tack them onto the religion without any basis. Before you accept any idea as being true Islam, make sure it conforms to what the Qur'an says. Put Qur'an first.

Today's prayer: O my Lord, do not allow me to be misled by ideas and opinions that have no basis in the Qur'an.

Shu'ayb Witnessed to His People.

To the Midian people, We sent Jethro, one of their own people. He said, "O my people, worship Allah. You have no god except Him. Do not slight in measure or weight. I see you in prosperity, but I fear for you the penalty of a day that will overwhelm you.

"O my people, give correct measure and weight, and do not withhold from people what they are due. Do not sin in the land with intent to do evil. That which is left for you by Allah is best for you. If only you believed! I am not assigned to keep watch over you, however."

(The Midian people) said, "O Jethro, does your religion tell you that we must abandon the religion of our fathers or that we abandon what we will with our own property? For sure, you are the one tolerant of faults and rightly guided!"

He answered, "O my people, see if I have evidence from my Lord, and He has provided me with ample sustenance as from Himself. I do not wish to oppose you, doing that which I forbid you to do. I only want to improve you to the best of my power, and my success can come only from Allah. In Him I trust, and to Him I turn."

—QUR'AN 11: 84-88

Daily living tip: Living in submission to Allah means more than just prayer and worship. Every aspect of your life must be good, honorable, and trustworthy. For examples, cheating on a test or lying about who ate the last cookie are outside what Allah intends for you.

Today's prayer: O my Lord, make every part of my life in keeping with Your honor and glory.

Most of Jethro's People Rejected His Message.

[Prophet Jethro said,] "O my people, just because I alienate myself from you [because of your lifestyle], do not let that cause you to sin. [You could] then to suffer a fate similar to that of the people of Noah or of Heber or of Salih. You are not far removed from the people of Lot [of the infamous cities of Sodom and Gomorrah]. Ask forgiveness of your Lord, turning to Him in repentance. My Lord is indeed flowing with mercy and loving kindness."

(The Midian people) said, "O Jethro, we do not understand most of what you are saying. In fact, nobody here sees that you have any strengths! If it were not for your [prestigious] family, we would already have stoned you. Among us, you have no honorable position."

He responded, "O my people, is my family of more concern to you than Allah? You cast Him aside, behind your backs, but, truly, my Lord surrounds all that you do.

"O my people, do whatever you can, and I also. Soon you will know on whom descends the penalty of shame and who is a liar. Watch, and I too am watching with you."

—QUR'AN 11: 89-93

Daily living tip: It is extremely difficult for someone raised in a religion to give up the only religion he or she has ever known. Be gentle and understanding when presenting Islam to anyone of another religion. It's harder for someone to change his or her religion than it is to dye his or her hair purple. It's not a flippant decision, so take it easy.

Today's prayer: O my Lord, when I am surrounded by non-Muslims, help me to represent Islam in the best manner and not be arrogant or abusive.

Salih Witnessed to His People.

When Our command went forth, We saved Jethro and those believers with him, by Our grace. The mighty blast, however, seized the sinners, and they lay flattened in their homes. It was as if they had never lived there. Away with Midian, as with the Thamud!

To the Thamud people, We sent Salih, one of their own brothers. He said, "O my people, worship Allah. You have no god except Him. Now evidence from your Lord has come to you. This female camel from Allah is a sign for you, so allow her to graze upon Allah's earth, and allow no harm to come upon her. Otherwise, you will be seized with a horrid punishment.

"Remember how He made you inheritors after the Ad people and gave you occupancy in the land. You built palaces and mansions on the plains and carved houses in the mountainsides. Remember the blessings from Allah, and refrain from sin and wickedness on the earth."

The arrogant aristocrats among the [Thamud] people said to those they considered weak, which were the believers, "How do you know that Salih is a messenger from his Lord?"

They answered, "We believe in the revelation sent through him."

—QUR'AN 11: 94-95 AND QUR'AN 7: 73-75

Daily living tip: When people condemn your religion, just say, "I believe in the revelation sent to Prophet Muhammed (peace upon him). If you knew the truth about it, you would believe in it too instead of believing the lies told about it." The problem is: some people love their hate more than they love the truth.

Today's prayer: O my Lord, keep me strong and wise when my faith is challenged.

The Thamud Rejected Salih's Message.

Consider the sun and its splendor. Consider the moon as it follows. Consider the day as it displays its glory. Consider the night as it conceals! Consider the sky and its structure. Consider the earth and its expanse. Consider the soul and the design given to it. [Consider] its enlightenment as to wrong and right. Truly he/she succeeds who purifies it. He/she fails who corrupts it.

The Thamud were in rejection through their sinfulness. The most wicked person among them was delegated.

But the messenger of Allah said to them, "A female camel of Allah has come, so let her drink."

They rejected him. They butchered (the camel). Because of their crimes, their Lord destroyed them and razed them. For Him is no fear of its consequences.

We offered guidance to the Thamud, but they preferred blindness to guidance. The stunning punishment of humiliation seized them because of what they earned. However, We delivered those few who did believe and lived righteously.

—QUR'AN 91 AND QUR'AN 41: 17-18

Daily living tip: If you ever feel that your belief in Allah is in doubt, try to go wilderness camping in a tent. If you can't do that, do you have a backyard where you can camp? If not, then at least watch some nature shows on TV or read a book about nature. Nature has messages for you about the reality of Allah.

Today's prayer: O my Lord, show me the lessons You have prepared for me in the wonders of Your creation.

Lot Witnessed to His People.

The arrogant aristocrats said, "As far as we are concerned, we reject your faith."

Next, they hamstrung the female camel in insolent defiance of their Lord. They said, "O Salih, bring about your threats if you really are a messenger."

An earthquake took them before they knew what was happening, and they were left flattened in their homes.

Salih left them, saying, "O my people, I did warn you with the message given to me by my Lord. I gave you good counsel, but you do not appreciate good advisors."

We also sent Lot. He said to his people, "Do you commit such immoral acts as no other people in creation committed before you? You practice homosexuality in preference to [marital relations with] women. You are indeed a people transgressing far beyond boundaries."

We saved (Lot) and his family, except for his wife. She was among those who lagged behind.

—QUR'AN 7: 76-81, 83

Daily living tip: Sinful lifestyles are not confined to the LGBTQ+ community; straight people mess up too. Sex outside marriage and sodomy are wrong for everybody. Don't target any person or group for hate and disgust. You don't have to agree with someone's lifestyle in order to show that person kindness and respect.

Today's prayer: O my Lord, keep me safe from temptations to engage in what you have declared forbidden.

Lot's People Would Not Forsake Their Evil.

Our messengers [angels] came to Lot. He was grieved because of them and felt anxiety over them. He said, "This is a dreadful day."

(Lot's) people mobbed towards him [and expressed an interest in his guests]. They had long been in the habit of practicing perversions. He said, "O my people, here are my daughters. They are decent for you [to have in marriage]. Now fear Allah, and do not make me ashamed in front of my guests. Is there not among you a single man with moral character?"

They replied, "You know full well that we have no desire for your daughters. You know perfectly what we want."

He said, "I would overpower you if I could, or I would take refuge with a strong ally."

(The angels) said, "O Lot, we are messengers from your Lord. By no means will (the evil men) get to you. Now travel with your family while a part of the night still remains, and do not let anyone look back. But your wife will, and she will suffer the fate of the people. Morning is their appointed time. Is the morning not very near?"

—QUR'AN 11: 77-81

Daily living tip: You will hear much about "gay rights" and "gay pride." You can respond by saying, "I respect everyone's right to fair and equal treatment, but the gay lifestyle is not allowed in my religion." Don't get dragged into an argument about it.

Today's prayer: O my Lord, help me to speak truth and avoid arguments.

Sodom and Gomorrah Were Condemned.

When Our command went forth, We toppled (the cities of Sodom and Gomorrah). We showered them with brimstones as hard as baked clay, layer upon layer.

[The shower of brimstones] became the mark of your Lord [for sinful cities]. (That calamity) is never very far from the sinners.

The people of Lot rejected the messengers. Their brother Lot said to them, "Will you have no fear? I am to you a messenger worthy of all trust. So fear Allah and obey me. I do not ask any reward from you for it. My reward is only from the Lord of the Worlds.

"Will you [men] go to other men of the world [for sex]? [Will you] leave those whom Allah has created for you to be your mates? You are a sinful people."

They said, "If you do not stop, O Lot, you will certainly be thrown out!"

He said, "I truly hate what you do."

[Lot prayed,] "O my Lord, deliver me and my family from such activities as that in which they engage."

So We delivered him and all his family, except for an old woman [Lot's wife] who lingered behind. We destroyed all the others. We rained on them a shower [of brimstones] until it became the ruinous downpour of those warned.

—QUR'AN 11: 82-83 AND QUR'AN 26: 160-173

Daily living tip: Do not be hateful to LGBTQ+ people. Some of those conditions are due to genetic disorders. Some are trauma related, and some may even be due to mental problems. It's not up to you to judge. As you can see in today's Qur'an passage, Allah is able to take action against a people if He so chooses.

Today's prayer: O my Lord, grant proper guidance to people suffering from LGBTQ+ conditions and provide healing and a means for them to live acceptable lifestyles.

Hud Witnessed to His People.

To the Ad people, We sent Heber, one of their own brothers. He said, "O my people, worship Allah. You have no god except Him. Will you not fear Him?"

The leaders among the disbelievers said, "You must be an imbecile, and we think you are a liar."

He said, "O my people, I am not an imbecile, but a messenger from the Lord and Sustainer of the Worlds. I am simply fulfilling for you the duties of my Lord's mission. I am to you a sincere and trustworthy advisor. Do you wonder about a message to you from your Lord through a man of your own people? Remember that He made you inheritors after the people of Noah and gave you prestige among nations. Remember the blessings from Allah so you may prosper."

They said, "Do you approach us, expecting us to worship Allah alone and forsake the religion of our fathers? Bring about what you threatened if you're telling the truth.

He said, "Punishment and wrath are already upon you from your Lord. Will you argue with me over names [of gods] that you and your fathers have devised without authority from Allah? Wait, then, and I too am waiting."

We saved (Heber) and those who followed him, by Our mercy. We cut the roots of those who rejected Our signs and would not believe.

—QUR'AN 7: 65-72

Daily living tip: Don't take information for granted. Just because you are taught something all your life does not make it true. Research information for yourself and discover the truth. Many people have come to Islam because they did their own research and found Islam to be the true religion.

Today's prayer: O my Lord, help me discern between what is true and what I have been misled to believe is true.

Populations Are Held Accountable.

Whenever We sent a prophet to a town, We took its people into suffering and adversity in order that they might learn humility. We then changed their suffering into prosperity until they grew and multiplied and claimed, "Our fathers were touched by suffering and affluence."

Behold, We called them to account all of a sudden without their suspecting it.

If the people of the towns had believed and feared Allah, We certainly would have lent them blessings from the sky and the earth. They refused, however, so We made them accountable for their errors.

Did the people of the towns feel secure against the coming of Our wrath by night while they slept? Did they feel secure against its coming in broad daylight while they entertained themselves? Did they feel secure against Allah's plans? Only those left to ruin can feel secure from Allah's plans.

—QUR'AN 7: 94-99

Daily living tip: We are born into a world of struggle to learn humility and patience; however, sometimes we make the struggle harder than it was meant to be. Try to make choices in your life that will bring you blessings and not adversity. Try not to make stupid decisions that make a mess of your life.

Today's prayer: O my Lord, give me wisdom to choose correctly whenever I am faced with choices and temptations.

Humanity Originally Was One Nation.

Ask the Children of Israel how much evidence We sent them.

Allah strictly punishes whoever finds a substitute [for Allah's Word] after Allah's favor has come to him/her.

The life of this world is alluring to those who reject faith. They scoff at the believers. The righteous will be above them on the Day of Resurrection. Allah provides without measure to those He will.

Humanity was one single nation. Allah sent prophets with glad tidings and warnings. With them, He sent the Book in truth. With it, people can learn about things about which they differ. After the clear signs had come to them, people differed only because of jealousy. Allah, by His grace, guided the believers to the truth concerning that about which they disagreed. Allah guides whom He will to a path that is straight.

Do you think that you should enter Paradise without difficulties like what came to those who passed this way before you? They faced suffering and adversity. They were so shaken that even the messenger and those who joined him in faith cried, "When will Allah's help come?" Truly, the help of Allah is near!

—Qur'an 2: 211-214

Daily living tip: Don't get dragged into arguments about religion. If someone tries to argue with you about matters of faith, try to steer the conversation into focusing on the things that all religions have in common; for examples, honesty, charity, goodwill, compassion, and justice. Debates only push people farther apart.

Today's prayer: O my Lord, help me to focus on the consonant values of all religions of light while respecting the differences.

Job Kept His Faith Despite Afflictions.

Honor Our Servant Job.

He cried to his Lord, "Satan has afflicted me with distress and suffering!"

[He was commanded:] "Strike your foot!" [A spring was uncovered.] "Now here is cool water for washing and drinking."

We restored his family for him and doubled its number [from the number of family members he had lost]. This was a grace from Us and a thing for commemoration for all who have understanding.

[Job's wife lost patience, and Job had vowed to punish her for her. Allah commanded:] "Take just a little handful of grass and whisk [her] with it, so you will not fault on your vow."

Truly We found (Job) full of patience. How excellent a servant! He was truly repentant.

Honor our servants Abraham, Isaac, and Jacob –endowed with strength and vision. We purified them with excellent thoughts of the [Heavenly] home. They were with Us and from among the chosen and honorable.

Honor Ishmael, Elijah, and he [Elisha] who took the pledge of the cloak. Each of them was from among the honorable.

This is a reminder, and, truly, for the righteous there is a beautiful place of return –Gardens of Eden, which will have open doors for them. Therein they will relax, and they can order abundant fruit and drink. Along with them will be [others] who are not flirtatious, of the same age. Such is the promise made to you for the Day of Accounting! That will be Our gift, which will never decay.

—QUR'AN 38: 41-54

Daily living tip: One thing that makes Islam unique is that we believe in all the prophets. Try to learn their stories and how they added to the message of Islam. Read the Book of Job in the Bible. It's a dynamite story!

Today's prayer: O my Lord, peace and blessings to all the prophets and to all the children of Abraham.

Consider the Story of Joseph.

Truly, in the story of Joseph and his brothers are signs for seekers [of truth].

(His brothers) said, "Certainly, Joseph and his brother [Benjamin] are loved more by our father than we are, but we are a tough group, and our father is clearly mistaken."

So they took (Joseph) away, and they agreed to throw him to the bottom of a well. We inspired (Joseph), "Certainly, you will someday confront them with the truth of this situation, when they are unaware."

(The brothers) claimed, "O our father, we went racing with one another and left Joseph with our things. A wolf devoured him, but you will never believe us, even though we are telling the truth."

They had stained his shirt with blood.

(Their father) said, "No, your minds have concocted this tale, but there is grace in patience. I will seek Allah's help against your plot."

A caravan dispatched its water-bearer, and he let down his bucket. He said, "What luck! A young man!" (The caravan) secretly kept (Joseph) as a fortune, but Allah was well aware of what was happening.

(The caravan) sold him for a pitiful price –a few silver coins. That is how much they underestimated him.

—QUR'AN 12: 7- 8, 15, 17-20

Daily living tip: You will no doubt have challenges in your life for which the solution seems hopeless. Keep patient and believe that somehow, sometime Allah will make things right. Many lessons are in the story of Joseph (peace upon him). Make the prophets your role models. They've already shown you what's rocking.

Today's prayer: O my Lord, increase me in patience, faith, and strength of character.

By Allah's Grace,
Joseph Interpreted the King's Dream.

The king [of Egypt] said, "I saw [in a dream] seven fat cows devoured by seven lean ones, and seven green ears of corn and another [seven] withered. O Chiefs, explain my dream if you are able to interpret dreams."

They said, "It is a confused medley of dreams, and we are not skilled in such interpretation."

[A man in the king's court, however, sought Joseph's advice.]

(Joseph) explained, "For seven years you should plant diligently. At harvest time, you should preserve the ears except the least amount for eating. Then there will be seven harsh years in which you will devour what you have stored except a little to remain preserved. After that there will be a year in which the people will have abundant rain and during which they may press [grapes and olives]."

So the king said, "Bring him to me, and I will put him directly under my service."

After he had spoken to Joseph, he said, "Certainly on this day you are, before the court's presence, established with rank and reliability fully proven."

—QUR'AN 12: 43-44, 47-49, 54

Daily living tip: No matter how awful your situation is, be patient. Allah is able to bring goodness out of terrible situations caused by other people. When you're in a mess, don't lose hope. You are an amazing person, and you're stronger than you think.

Today's prayer: O my Lord, when life puts me in difficult situations, help me to endure until Your help comes, and help me to trust that surely Your help will come.

By Allah's Grace,
Joseph's Brothers Came to Him for Help.

(Joseph) said, "Set me over the storehouses of the land. I will guard them as one with knowledge."

This is how We established power to Joseph in the land, to exercise authority and do as he pleased.

We bestow Our mercy on whom We please, and We do not allow the reward of those who do good to be lost. Truly, however, the reward of the hereafter is better for those who believe and are loyal in righteousness.

Finally, Joseph's brothers came before him [seeking provisions because of the drought]. He recognized them, but they did not recognize him.

When they came before Joseph, they said to him, "O mighty ruler, hardship has come upon our family, and we now have little to offer in trade. We ask that you give us full measure [of grain] and consider it charity. Allah rewards the charitable."

(Joseph) said, "Do you remember how you treated Joseph and his [younger] brother [Benjamin] without realizing your ignorance?"

They said, "Are you indeed Joseph?"

He answered, "I am Joseph, and this is my brother [Benjamin]. Allah has indeed been gracious to us. For one who is righteous and patient, Allah will not allow the reward to be lost from those who do right."

—QUR'AN 12: 55-58, 88-90

Daily living tip: Forgiveness is often a process. Sometimes the hurt is so bad that you can't forgive someone right away. You may experience a time of anger, but soon you can come to a point where your neither forgive nor not forgive; you just leave it in Allah's trust. Eventually, you can forgive. It is hard when the offender never apologizes or makes amends. Forgive anyway.

Today's prayer: O my Lord, help me to become more forgiving of those who wrong me as You are the Most Forgiving.

By Allah's Grace, Joseph Was Reunited with His Parents.

(Joseph's brothers) said, "Indeed Allah has preferred you over us, and we certainly have been guilty of sin."

He said, "This day, may there be no accusation against you. Allah will forgive you, and He is the Most Merciful among those who show mercy."

When the bearer of the good news came, he cast [Joseph's] shirt over (Jacob's) face, and (Jacob) regained his sight. (Jacob) said [to the brothers], "Did I not say to you that I know from Allah that which you do not know?"

They said, "O our father, ask for forgiveness for us because of our sins, for we were truly at fault."

He said, "I will ask my Lord to forgive you, and He the Most Merciful of those who show mercy."

[Later] they presented themselves before Joseph. He extended his home to his parents, and he invited, "Enter Egypt in safety, if it pleases Allah."

[Joseph's prayer:] "My Lord, You have indeed bestowed on me some power and taught me something of the interpretations of dreams. Creator of Heaven and Earth, You are my protector in this world and in the hereafter. Accept my soul as one in complete submission to Your will, and unite me with the righteous."

—Qur'an 12: 91-92, 96-99, 101

Daily living tip: Whether you made a minor slip or committed a horrible act, come to Allah every day with a repentant heart. Confess your sins and ask for forgiveness. You can't screw up too much for Allah. He is bigger than your screw-ups.

Today's prayer: O my Lord, forgive me for all my sins, great and small, and help me to live more righteously day by day.

Day
74

Most People Ignore the Dynamics of Such Stories.

[The story of Joseph] is one [of the stories] that happened unseen [by you], which We convey to you. You were not with them as (Joseph's brothers) unanimously agreed to their conniving plan. Yet most people will have no faith no matter how passionately you desire it. You ask no reward of them for this; it is no less than a message to benefit all creatures.

How many signs of the skies and Earth do they pass? Yet, they ignore them. Most of them do not believe in Allah without making associations. Do they then feel secure from the coming disaster of the wrath of Allah, or from the hour [of the final end]? It will come all of a sudden while they are not expecting it?

Say, "This is my way. I and my followers invite to Allah on the basis of undeniable evidence. Glory to Allah! I am not one of the idolaters."

We never sent anyone before you except people whom We inspired, who were of the common people. Do they not travel throughout the land and wonder what became of those before them? The home of the hereafter is best for those who live righteously. Will you not understand?

—Qur'an 12: 102-109

Daily living tip: When you read the stories of the people of faith, learn what you can from their lives so that you can apply those lessons to your own life. You are unique. There is nobody else like you. Make your uniqueness count by applying the lessons of the Qur'an. That's how you make your life great.

Today's prayer: O my Lord, increase my faith and wisdom and give me guidance from the stories of the people of faith.

Muhammed Was a Common Man, Just as Joseph Was.

Was it so amazing to people that We inspired a man among men so that he would warn humanity? He proclaimed the good news to those who would believe that the glorious truth stands before their Lord.

The disbelievers responded, "This is simply some kind of sorcery."

Your Lord is God who created the skies and Earth in six days. He established Himself on a throne from where He would govern all creation. There can be no intercessor except as He allows. Your Lord God is He whom you should serve. Will you consider yourself warned?

To Him will you all return. The promise of Allah is true and certain. It is He who initiates [the process of] creation and then repeats it. [He did this] so He may reward with justice those who believe and who perform righteous deeds. But those who reject Him will have nothing but scalding water to drink and a dreadful penalty because of their rejection of Him.

—QUR'AN 10: 2-4

Daily living tip: Prophet Muhammed (peace upon him) fulfilled a prophecy in the Torah (Deuteronomy 18: 15-19). Look this up and be prepared to use it in defense of Prophet Muhammed. Some people won't believe you. It doesn't matter. That's their struggle.

Today's prayer: O my Lord, when people question the reality of Muhammed being a prophet, help me find the right words to defend him.

All the Prophets Faced Opposition.

We did not allow any person before you to live forever. If you [Prophet Muhammed] die, would they live forever? Every soul shall have a taste of death, and We test you by evil and by goodness as a trial [so you may have opportunities to prove yourselves deserving of Paradise]. To Us you must return.

When the disbelievers see you [Prophet Muhammed], they don't show you anything but disrespect: "Is this the one who runs his mouth about your gods?" They scoff at the mention of the Most Gracious.

Humanity is a creature of haste. Soon I will show You My signs [of the end times], but don't rush Me!

They say, "When will this promise come to pass, if you are telling the truth?"

If the disbelievers only knew when they will not be able to deflect the fire from their faces or from their backs, when no help can come to them! It will come upon them suddenly and overwhelm them. They will have no power to avert it, and they will get no reprieve.

Messengers before (Prophet Muhammed) were mocked, but their scoffers were contained by their own contempt.

—Qur'an 21: 34-41

Daily living tip: When you are faced with adversity, don't panic. Start trying to think of a solution or how to manage the difficulty. Be a problem-solver, not a problem-worrier.

Today's prayer: O my Lord, help me to become independent enough that I can face problems with determination and patience.

All the Prophets Were Common People.

Closer and closer to humanity the reckoning comes, yet they are oblivious and remain obstinate. Every time a new reminder comes to them from their Lord, they listen to it in jest. Their minds are frivolously distracted. In secret counsel, the unjust discuss, "Is this [the Prophet] not only a mortal like any of you? Will you wittingly yield to [his] magical charm?"

Say, "My Lord knows every word spoken throughout Heaven and Earth. He is the Listener and the Omniscient."

"Bunk!" they say. "Medleys of dreams! Bunk! He forged it. Bunk! He is only a poet. He must produce a sign like those [miracles] of the past [by the earlier prophets]."

Before them were populations, none of which believed before We destroyed them. Will these [contemporary populations] believe?

Before (Prophet Muhammed), messengers We sent were mere men to whom We granted inspiration. If you doubt that, ask those [Jews] who remember [the Word]. We did not give (the messengers) bodies with no need of food, and they were not exempt from death.

Eventually, We fulfilled Our promise to them, and We saved them and those whom We pleased, but We destroyed those who sinned without boundaries.

We have revealed for you a Book in which is a reminder for you. Will you not understand?

—QUR'AN 21: 1-10

Daily living tip: All the prophets (peace upon them) were people who shared the same message: repent of your sins, submit yourself to Allah, and live righteously. Do not join hypocrites who try to keep people divided by honoring one prophet above all other prophets when every prophet's mission was important to the overall message.

Today's prayer: O my Lord, keep me focused on the united message, goodwill, and harmony of all the prophets.

The God of the Torah is the God of the Qur'an.

They did not fairly appraise Allah when they said, "Allah does not reveal anything to any human being."

Say, "Who then bestowed the Book that Moses brought, which was a light and guidance for the people? You made it into scrolls disclosing some [Scriptures] while concealing many. [Through the Torah,] you were taught that which you never knew, neither you nor your ancestors." Say, "Allah!" and then leave them plunged into vain discourse.

This is a Book that We have bestowed, bringing blessings and confirming (the Book), which came before it so that you [Prophet Muhammed] may warn the Mother of Cities [Mecca] and all around her. Those who believe in the hereafter believe in this [Book], and they are observant of prayers.

Who is more unjust than one who invents a lie against Allah, or who has said, "I have received inspiration," when he/she has not received it, or who has said, "I can reveal something like what Allah has revealed"?

If you could only see how the wicked fare in the agonies of death! The angels stretch forth their hands: "Yield your souls! This day you will receive your reward –a penalty of shame for the lies you used to tell against Allah instead of truth and for scornfully rejecting His signs."

—Qur'an 6: 91-93

Daily living tip: Ignorant people will claim that Allah is Satan. Explain to them that Allah is the Arabic word for God and that it is similar to a Hebrew word for God in the Torah and the Aramaic word for God that Jesus spoke. After that, leave them to their delusions; otherwise, they will drag you into their vain and ignorant talk. If they do believe you, that opens a door for rational discussion.

Today's prayer: O my Lord, bless me with words of wisdom and keep me from vain arguments with hypocrites.

Prophet Muhammed
Sealed the Messages of All the Prophets.

You have, in the messenger of Allah, a beautiful pattern for anyone whose hope is in Allah and the last day and who habitually remembers Allah.

No difficulty can affect the Prophet in what Allah has appointed for him [as his mission]. That was the practice of Allah for those [prophets] of old, who are now in the past. The command of Allah is a determined decree. [It is] for those who preach the messages of Allah and fear Him. They fear no one but Allah, and Allah is sufficient to call to accountability.

Muhammed is not the father of any of your men, but he is the messenger of Allah and the Seal of the Prophets. Allah has full knowledge of all things.

Truly, Allah and His angels bestow blessings upon the Prophet. O Believers, pray for blessings upon him and greet him respectfully. Those who exasperate Allah and His messenger have been condemned by Allah in this world and the next. Allah has prepared a humiliating punishment for them. Those who, without cause, aggravate believing men and women carry the burden of a slur and a glaring sin.

—QUR'AN 33: 21, 38-40, 56-58

Daily living tip: The definition of prophet may be different in Islam than it is in other religions. Even among Muslims, some may have a different interpretation of "Seal of the Prophets." Be able to respect others' views while being true to your own.

Today's prayer: O my Lord, give me the proper understanding of what Your Word means and help me share that with others in a respectful manner.

Every Prophet Spoke
the Common Language of the Time and Place.

Alif Lam Ra! A Book is revealed unto you [Prophet Muhammed] so that you may lead humanity from the depths of darkness into light. That is in accordance to the will of their Lord. Lead them to the way of the Exalted in Power, Worthy of all Praise. Lead them to the way of Allah to whom belong all things of the skies and of Earth.

Woe to the disbelievers because of a terrible penalty!

Those who treasure the life of this world more than that of the hereafter, who hinder others from seeking the path of Allah, and who seek in (the path) something negative are off course by a long shot.

We never sent a messenger except in the language of the common people, in order to clarify for them. Now Allah allows those whom He will to remain straying, and He guides whom He will. He is the Victorious, the Perfectly Wise.

We sent Moses with our signs: "Bring your people from the depths of darkness into light and remind them of the days of Allah." Truly in this [story of Moses] are signs for those who are steadfastly patient and appreciative.

—Qur'an 14: 1-5

Daily living tip: There is one Qur'an, which is in classical Arabic; however, there are many translations. Try to get several translations and focus on the best interpretations. If you can learn the original Arabic, that will be even better. An Arabic dictionary will also help you find the best meanings to apply to each verse.

Today's prayer: O my Lord, teach me the best interpretations of Your holy Word.

Consider the Story of Moses.

Ta Seen Meem. These are verses of the Book that clarifies. We recite to you some of the story of Moses and Pharaoh truthfully for people of faith.

Pharaoh exalted himself in the land and made its people into castes. He oppressed a small group [the Hebrew nation] among them; he killed their sons but kept their girls alive. He was indeed among the corrupt.

We intended to be gracious to those who were oppressed in the land to make them leaders and heirs. [We intended] to empower them in the land and to show Pharaoh, [his prime minister] Haman, and their troops under them what they had feared.

We sent this inspiration to the mother of Moses: "Breastfeed until you have fear for him; cast him into the river [in a basket sealed with pitch], but have no fear or grief. We will restore him to you, and We will make Him one of the [divine] messengers."

The family of Pharaoh unwittingly pulled him [from the river] so that (Moses) would become to them an adversary and a sorrow, for Pharaoh and Haman and their troops were sinful.

Pharaoh's wife said, "A joy to the eye for me and for you! Do not kill him. It may be that he will be a blessing to us, or we may adopt him as a son."

And they didn't have a clue.

—QUR'AN 28: 1-9

Daily living tip: Imagine the faith that Moses' mother had to put her little baby into a basket and place it in a river infested with snakes and crocodiles! Your faith will likely never require that great a test, but pray that your faith will become that immense.

Today's prayer: O my Lord, increase my faith daily throughout my life until it becomes as great as the faith of Moses' mother.

By Allah's Grace,
Moses Had Wisdom and Knowledge.

An empty feeling came into the heart of Moses' mother. She was about to disclose the matter if We had not strengthened her heart so she would remain a believer. She said to the sister [of Moses, Miriam], "Follow him," so she watched him from a distance, while they [the family of Pharaoh] had no suspicion.

We ordained that he refused breast milk [from a nursemaid appointed by the household of Pharaoh]. (Miriam) approached and said, "Shall I point out to you the people of a house, who will nurture him for you and be sincere to him?"

In this way, We restored (Moses) to his mother so that her eye would be comforted and that she would not grieve and that she would know that the promise of Allah is true. Most people, however, do not understand.

When (Moses) reached accountable age and was mature, We bestowed on him wisdom and knowledge. That is the way We reward those who live righteously.

—QUR'AN 28: 10-14

Daily living tip: Notice that even Moses' mother began to have doubt and to worry. Allah used her worry to make something good happen. The message here is that you should always do the best you can to keep your faith up and then trust Allah to take up your slack.

Today's prayer: O my Lord, even when my faith fails me, use me to make good things happen.

Allah Spoke Directly to Moses.

Have you heard the story of Moses?

When he saw a fire [in the distance], he said to his family, "Stay here. I see a fire. Perhaps I can bring back a stick of flame from it or find some guidance there."

When he approached the fire [which was a burning bush, unconsumed], a voice was heard. "O Moses, truly, I am your Lord; remove your shoes, for you are in the sacred valley of Tuwa [below Mount Sinai]. I have chosen you, so listen to inspiration.

"Truly, I am God. No god is there except Me, so worship Me and establish prayers in remembrance of Me.

"Truly, the hour (of judgment) is coming –which I plan to keep secret— when every soul will receive its reward by the measure of its endeavor. Therefore, do not let the disbelievers, who follow their own desires, divert you or you will perish."

—QUR'AN 20: 9-16

Daily living tip: Approach your prayer rug as if it is your burning bush in the wilderness. It is your personal space to escape the darkness of this world and commune with your Creator. That's a blessing not everyone realizes.

Today's prayer: O my Lord, still my heart and help me to hear the small, still voice of Your guidance.

Allah Sent Moses to Challenge Pharaoh.

[God said to Moses:] "Go to Pharaoh for he has indeed transgressed all boundaries."

(Moses) said, "O my Lord, expand my breast [with the breath of God's wisdom]. Ease my task for me. Remove my speech impediment so that what I say may be understood. Give me a priest from my family –Aaron, my brother. Strengthen me through him, and make him my partner in my task. In this way, we may greatly praise You and greatly remember You. You are He who watches over us."

(God) said, "Granted is your prayer, O Moses.

"I have prepared You for Myself. You and your brother shall go with My signs, and falter not in keeping Me in remembrance.

"Go to Pharaoh for he has indeed transgressed all boundaries. Speak gently to him in the chance that he may take heed and fear."

They said, "Our Lord, we fear that he may abuse us or that he will continue sinning."

He said, "Fear not for I am with you. I hear and I see."

—QUR'AN 20: 24-36, 41-46

Daily living tip: Notice that, even though Pharoah was cruel and sinful, Allah told Moses and Aaron to speak gently to him. Allah never wants us to be harsh, critical, and judgmental in witnessing for Him. Don't come at people like a mad hornet. Be nice.

Today's prayer: O my Lord, as I interact with others, help me to always be polite, considerate, and kind.

Despite the Signs, Pharaoh Was Unconvinced.

[The Lord said to Moses and Aaron,] "Both of you go to (Pharaoh) and say, 'We two are messengers sent by your Lord. Set free the Children of Israel to go with us, and do not afflict them. With a sign, we come from your Lord. Peace to all who follow guidance! It has been revealed to us of the penalty for those who reject and ignore.'"

(Pharaoh) responded, "Who then, O Moses, is the Lord of you two?"

(Moses) answered, "Our Lord is He who gave each thing its creation and then its direction."

(Pharaoh) asked, "So, what do you make of the previous generations [who did not worship the One God]?"

(Moses) replied, "The knowledge concerning that is with my Lord in a Book. My Lord never errs and never forgets."

We showed Pharaoh Our signs [miracles], but he denied and rebuffed.

He said, "Have you come to drive us out of our land with your magic, O Moses? We can certainly perform magic to match yours. Plan a meeting between us and yourself, and neither we nor you shall fail to attend, and have it in a place where all is fair."

(Moses) said, "Your meeting will be on the Day of the Festival; let the people assemble when the sun is high."

—QUR'AN 20: 47-52, 56-59

Daily living tip: The prophets (peace upon them) were called to complete difficult and hazardous missions; however, Allah empowered them to succeed. Trust that Allah will also help you to succeed in whatever plans He has for you. You are amazing. You can do whatever needs to be done. Just don't wimp out.

Today's prayer: O my Lord, help me to know what Your will is for my life and then help me to achieve all that You have planned for me to do.

Pharaoh's Magicians Became Convinced.

[On that day,] (Pharaoh's magicians) said, "Moses, do you want to throw first, or do you want us to throw first?"

He said, "You go ahead and be first."

[The magicians threw down ropes and rods.]

Their ropes and their rods, as it seemed to (Moses) because of their magic, were animated [like snakes].

Moses panicked and felt afraid.

We said, "Fear not! You have the advantage." Throw that [staff] which is in your right hand. It will immediately swallow that which they have faked, which is merely a magician's illusion. The sorcerer will not flourish no matter where he goes."

[After Moses' feat,] the magicians threw themselves into prostration and said, "We believe in the Lord of Aaron and Moses."

(Pharaoh) said, "Are you going to believe in Him without my permission? Surely this must be your leader who taught you magic! I will certainly cut off your hands and feet on opposite sides [ie, one left hand, one right foot], and I will have you crucified on trunks of palm trees. Then you will realize which of us can give the most severe and most enduring punishment."

—QUR'AN 20: 65-71

Daily living tip: Sometimes you may panic and feel afraid when you see that evil seems to be more successful than righteousness. Sometimes it seems like wicked people have more success than good people who are always struggling. It doesn't seem fair. Know that Allah has everything all figured out, and, though you may not see it now, somehow, sometime, He will make everything right.

Today's prayer: O my Lord, help me to see beyond this realm of injustices and find the truths of Your perfect plan.

Pharaoh's Magicians
Would Not Forsake Their New Belief.

(Pharaoh's magicians) answered, "We will never regard you as greater than the proven signs we have seen or greater than Him who created us. So decree whatever you want, for your decrees only pertain to the life of this world. We believe in our Lord. May He forgive us our faults and the sorcery you compelled us to do. Allah is the best and the Most Abiding."

Truly, the one who comes [after death] to his/her Lord as a sinner faces Hell, wherein he/she shall neither die nor live.

Those who come to Him as believers having worked righteousness will join exalted ranks. [They will have] gardens of eternity beneath which rivers flow. They will dwell therein forever. That is the reward of those who purify themselves.

O Children of Israel, We delivered you from your enemy. We made a covenant with you on the right side of Mount (Sinai). We sent manna and quail to you: "Eat of the humane/ethical things We have provided for you, but commit no excess, lest My wrath should descend upon you. Those upon whom My wrath descend really do perish! I am Most Forgiving for those who repent, believe, live righteously, and are receptive to guidance.

—QUR'AN 20: 72-76, 80-82

Daily living tip: At some point in your life, you may have friends who try to tempt you away from what you know to be true. They may sound convincing. Be sure of your faith and make a commitment to yourself not to forsake it. Don't be a lamebrain.

Today's prayer: O my Lord, keep me strong in my faith when others try to persuade me away from it.

Plagues Were Sent Upon the People of Pharaoh.

We punished the people of Pharaoh with years [of drought] and scarce crops, so perhaps they would take heed. When things were good, they would say, "We deserve this!" When calamity seized them, they ascribed it to evil omens connected with Moses and those with him. Actually, the omens of evil were their own, by Allah's decree. Most of them, however, never understood.

They said [to Moses], "No matter what signs you bring in performing your sorcery upon us, we will never believe in you."

As a result, We heaped upon them death and destruction, locusts, lice, frogs, blood [from water], and other signs that were well explained. These people, however, were mired in ignorance and committed to sin.

Every time the penalty fell upon them, they said, "O Moses, on our behalf, call upon your Lord in virtue of His promise to you. If you will remove the penalty from us, we will certainly believe in you, and we will let the Children of Israel go with you.

Every time We removed the penalty from them for a determined time, which they had to fulfill, they broke their promise.

Finally, We demanded justice of them, and We drowned them in the sea, because they rejected Our signs and failed to heed their warning.

—QUR'AN 7: 130-136

Daily living tip: In your life, people will break their promises, break their trust with you. You will learn to be cautious of such people. Forgive them and let Allah either punish them or guide them. You're not in this struggle alone. Allah is on your side when you are in the right.

Today's prayer: O my Lord, forgive those who do wrong to me and grant them proper guidance.

Pharaoh and His Soldiers Were Drowned.

We took the Children of Israel across the sea. Pharaoh and his soldiers followed them, with insolence and spite.

Finally, when ((Pharaoh) was overcome by drowning, he said, "I believe that no god is there except Him in whom the Children of Israel believe. I am among those who submit."

"Too late! Just a little while ago, you were rebellious and committing criminal acts. Today We will save only your body as a sign to your successors. Many among Humanity are heedless of Our signs."

Repentance will not be accepted from those who sin until they are dying and then say, "Now I truly repent." [Repentance will not be accepted from] those who die as disbelievers. We have prepared a horrible punishment for these.

Wherever you are, be sure that death will find you, even if you are in mighty, towering castles.

If some good befalls (the idolaters), they say, "This is from Allah!" If a crisis comes, they say, "This is (the Prophet's) fault!"

Say, "All things are from Allah."

What is wrong with people that they scarcely understand a single thing?

—QUR'AN 10: 90-92 AND QUR'AN 4: 18, 78

Daily living tip: In a beautiful, Jewish parable, the angels are cheering when Pharoah and his soldiers are drowning in the sea. Allah says to the angels, "Don't you realize those are My children too?" Allah does not take pleasure in the horrific demise even of wicked people, so you shouldn't either.

Today's prayer: O my Lord, make my heart so pure and gentle that I am even sad when bad things happen to bad people.

The Children of Israel
Were Blessed Because of Their Patience.

To Moses, We gave nine evident signs.

Ask the Children of Israel about when he came to them. Pharaoh said to him, "O Moses, I consider you to be possessed."

(Moses) said, "You know full well that these things have been sent down by none other than the Lord of the skies and Earth as evidence. I consider you, O Pharaoh, doomed to destruction."

So (Pharaoh) resolved to remove (the Children of Israel) from the face of the earth, but We drowned him and all those with him.

After that, We said to the Children of Israel, "Live in the land. When the promise of the hereafter comes to pass, We will assemble you in a diverse crowd."

We made those who had been oppressed to inherit the eastern and western parts of the land that We had blessed. The best promise of your Lord was fulfilled to the Children of Israel because of their patience, and We destroyed what Pharaoh and his people had built and erected.

—QUR'AN 17: 101-104 AND QUR'AN 7: 137

Daily living tip: When things are not going your way and all seems bleak, be patient. Eventually, your life will brighten, and good things will happen. Sometimes it's hard to stay positive. Don't give up. Life is not always easy, but you got this.

Today's prayer: O my Lord, grant me patience. No matter how rotten things get, help me to remember that something good is on its way.

Jews Must Remember Their Heritage.

O Children of Israel, remember My favor that I showed you. Remember that I preferred you above all others. Guard yourselves against a day when one soul cannot help another. No one can stand up for him/her. No payment can be accepted. No help will be available.

Remember how We delivered you from the people of Pharaoh. They gave you difficult work. They were mean to you. They killed your sons while allowing your girls to live. In that, the Lord allowed you to have a big test.

Remember that We divided the sea to save you. We drowned Pharaoh's people within your very sight.

Remember that We gave Moses forty nights. In his absence, you worshiped a calf and made ugly sins. Even then, We forgave you so you could show your gratitude.

Remember that We gave Moses the Book [of the Torah] and the criterion [the Ten Commandments] so you may be guided.

—QUR'AN 2: 47-53

Daily living tip: The Qur'an is for everybody, including the Jews. It does not require the Jews to forsake the Torah (the Judaic law books) in order to accept the message of the Qur'an. When you talk to Jews or anyone else about Islam, first accept them as they are and respect their religious beliefs.

Today's prayer: O my Lord, may everyone find his or her personal message you have presented in the Qur'an.

Jews Must Learn
from the Mistakes of Their Ancestry.

Remember that Moses said to his people, "O my people, you have deceived yourselves by worshiping the calf. Repent to your Creator and punish by death (those who do not repent). This is necessary in the sight of your Creator." Then He accepted your repentance. Indeed, He is the Responsive, the Most Merciful.

Remember that you said, "O Moses, we shall not believe in you until Allah shows Himself to us." You were seized as you beheld the lightning [of the Divine Presence]. Then We revived you from your death and gave you the opportunity to be grateful.

We provided for you the shade of clouds and sent you manna and quail. We said, "Eat of the good things We have provided you." (Your rebellion) did Us no harm, but they [who complained] harmed their own souls.

Remember that We said, "Enter this town and enjoy what you find there as you desire. Enter the gate with humility expressed in your manner and words. We shall forgive your faults and magnify those who act properly."

Sinners changed the command that had been given them. We punished them with a plague from Heaven because of their consistent rebellion.

—QUR'AN 2: 54-59

Daily living tip: Don't be like those who rebelled against God even after He proved His favors to them. Realize your blessings and always show gratitude in the way that you live. The older you get, the more blessings you will rack up. Remembering those blessings will help you face challenges.

Today's prayer: O my Lord, do not let me take Your favors for granted but help me to be grateful for all blessings great and small.

Consider the Value of All the Prophets.

Those who believe and do not confound their beliefs with error are saved, for they are guided. Such was the reasoning about Us that We gave to Abraham to confront his people. We elevate whom We will, degree by degree. Your Lord is Perfectly Wise, the All-knowing.

We blessed (Abraham) with Isaac and Jacob. We guided them as We had previously guided Noah. Among (Abraham's) descendants were David, Solomon, Job, Joseph, Moses, and Aaron. Thus do We reward those who live righteously.

Also, Zachariah, John, Jesus, and Elijah are all in the ranks of the righteous, as well as Ishmael, Elisha, Jonah, and Lot. To all these We gave favor above nations. We chose them, their fathers, descendants, and brothers and guided them to the Straight Way.

This indicates the guidance of Allah. He gives guidance to whom He pleases among His worshipers. If any were to acknowledge other gods with Him, however, all the good they did would have been in vain.

—Qur'an 6: 82-88

Daily living tip: Realize the importance of every prophet as each one contributed to the overall mission of bringing people closer to the grace and mercy of Allah. Now it's your turn. You're not a prophet, but you are a representative of the prophets' message. Don't blow it by creeping on people. Be gentle in your speech.

Today's prayer: O my Lord, may peace and blessings be upon all the prophets.

Allah Bestowed His Favor on the Prophets.

We bestowed Our favor on Moses and Aaron. We delivered them and their people from great calamity. We helped them overcome and become victors. We gave them the Book that clarifies. We guided them to the Straight Way.

We provided for them, through later generations, [this blessing]: "Peace to Moses and Aaron!"

This is how We reward those who do right. They were among our believing servants.

Elijah was also among the messengers. He said to his people, "Will you not have fear? Will you call upon Baal and forsake the Best of Creators? Allah [is] your Lord and the Lord of your ancestors."

But they rejected him, and they will certainly be held accountable. The exception is the devoted servants of Allah.

We provided for him, through later generations, [this blessing]: "Peace to Elijah!"

This is how We reward those who do right. He was one of our believing servants.

—QUR'AN 37: 114-132

Daily living tip: While others may hold up Hollywood actors, athletes, musicians, and other celebrities as their role models, you should look to the lives of the prophets in how to model your life. Other people will let you down. Don't be a sucker.

Today's prayer: O my Lord, set my eyes upon the lives of the prophets so that I may learn how best to conduct myself and practice my faith.

Muhammed Submitted to the One God.

Say [on Allah's behalf], "O My believing servants, fear and obey your Lord. For those who live righteously in this world, there is beauty. Spacious is Allah's earth! Those who patiently persevere will truly receive a reward without measure."

Say, "I [Muhammed] am commanded to serve Allah with devoted faith. I am commanded to be the first among Muslims [of the Qur'anically organized religion]."

Say, "I fear, if I disobeyed my Lord, the penalty of a mighty day [of judgment]."

Say, "I worship Allah alone with sincere faith. You serve whatever you want besides Him!"

Say, "The losers will lose their own souls and their families [who follow in sin], on the Day of Judgment. Isn't that a real loss! They shall have layers of fire above them and layers below them. With this, Allah warns His servants: 'O My Servants, fear and obey Me!'"

For those who abstain from the worship of idols and repent to Allah, there is the good news. Announce the good news to My servants. [They are] those who listen to the Word and follow the best in it [without distortions and misinterpretations]. They are the ones whom Allah has guided. They are among those of understanding.

—QUR'AN 39: 10-18

Daily living tip: Walk upon the earth with humility, but also be brave enough to speak out against what is wrong whenever you are confronted with it. You may be bullied, but you can take it. The people bullying you are not important enough to lose your faith over. Persevere.

Today's prayer: O my Lord, help me to be brave when it is Your will that I speak up and proclaim my faith and defend what is right.

Believe in All the Messengers.

[Remember] Job. He called to his Lord, "Truly distress has seized me, but You are the Most Merciful of the merciful."

So We listened to him, We removed the distress that was upon him. We restored his people to him and multiplied them. {This was] all as a grace from Us and a tribute for the worshipers.

Remember Ishmael, Enoch, and Ezekiel. All were among the patient. We admitted them into Our mercy, for they were among the righteous ones.

Allah bears witness that what He has sent to (Prophet Muhammed) He has sent from His knowledge. The angels also bear witness, although Allah is enough for a witness.

Those who reject faith and obstruct the way of Allah have wandered far astray. Allah will not forgive those who reject faith and continue to sin. He will not guide them on a path, except the path to Hell to dwell therein continuously. This is easy for Allah!

O Humanity, the messenger has come to you with truth from Allah. It is best for you to believe. If you reject faith, to Allah belong all things of Heaven and Earth, and Allah is the All-knowing, the Perfectly Wise.

—QUR'AN 21: 83-86 AND QUR'AN 4: 166-170

Daily living tip: Learn all you can from all the messengers and prophets. All knowledge is from Allah, so do not too arrogant to accept knowledge from any reliable sources. All truth is Allah's truth. Just filter everything through the Qur'an to test if it's true.

Today's prayer: O my Lord, fill me with a desire to seek and find all the knowledge available to me.

Consider the Story of Jonah.

[Remember] the man of the fish [Jonah]! When he left angrily, he thought that We had no power over him. In depths of darkness, he cried, "No god is there but You! Glory to You! I was wrong."

We listened to him and delivered him from distress. Thus do We deliver those of faith.

He ran away to a loaded ship. He cast lots [with the other seafarers], and he was condemned [and cast into the sea]. The big fish swallowed him. He had committed acts worthy of blame. If he had not been among those who glorify [Allah], then he would certainly have remained inside (the fish's) belly until the Day of Resurrection.

We cast him onto the barren shore in a state of sickness. We caused a spreading gourd plant to grow over him [to shade him].

We sent him to over a hundred thousand people. They believed, so We allowed them to have joy for a while.

—QUR'AN 21: 87-88 AND QUR'AN 37: 140-148

Daily living tip: Always trust that, no matter what the obstacles, Allah is able to fulfill what He has planned for your life. Believe that your life will be awesome. It won't be stress-free, but you'll be able to handle whatever comes. Strive for success and believe in yourself.

Today's prayer: O my Lord, open my eyes that I may see Your wondrous acts as You keep me on the path You have paved for my future.

Jonah's People Were Blessed
Because They Believed.

Patiently wait for the judgment of your Lord, and do not be like [Jonah] the companion of the fish when he called in distress. If it had not been for the arrival of the grace of his Lord, he would certainly have been cast onto the barren shore, disgraced. His Lord chose him and made him among the righteous.

Why did not a single community believe so that its faith would do it some good, except the people of Jonah? When they believed, We removed from them the penalty of disgrace in this world. We permitted them enjoyment for a while.

We have sent to you [Prophet Muhammed] inspiration just as We sent it to Noah and the prophets after him. We sent inspiration to Abraham, Ishmael, Isaac, Jacob and the [Judaic] tribes, Jesus, Job, Jonah, Aaron, and Solomon. To David We gave the Psalms. We have already told you about some messengers but not about others. To Moses, Allah spoke directly. There were messengers who gave good news as well as warning that humanity, after arrival of the messengers, would have no claim against Allah. Allah is Victorious, Perfectly Wise.

—QUR'AN 68: 48-50 AND QUR'AN 10: 98 AND QUR'AN 4: 163-165

Daily living tip: Jews have the Tanakh (Jewish Bible). Christians have the Protestant Bible, the Catholic Bible, and the Orthodox Bible. Muslims are the most blessed! We have those plus the splendor of the Qur'an. Learn all you can from all religious books but filter the information through the Qur'an.

Today's prayer: O my Lord, help me discern the truth by always putting Qur'an first.

Luqman Was Blessed with Wisdom.

We bestowed this wisdom on Luqman [an Arab sage of old]: "Show gratitude to Allah. Whoever is grateful is so to the benefit of his/her own soul. As for one who is ungrateful, truly, Allah is Independent, the Praised One."

Luqman instructed his son, "O my son, do not associate others with Allah. Truly, associating partners [in worship] is surely a great injustice.

"O my son, if there were the weight of a mustard seed within a rock or in the sky or in the earth, Allah will reveal it. Allah is the Subtle One, Fully Aware.

"O my son, establish routine prayers, enforce what is just, and prohibit what is wrong. Bear with patient faithfulness whatever befalls you. Truly, such matters require determination.

"Do not turn your cheek [in arrogance] from people. Do not walk proudly over the earth. Truly, Allah does not like every self-conceited braggart.

"Be moderate in your pace and speak softly. Truly, the harshest of sounds, without a doubt, is the braying of donkeys."

—QUR'AN 31: 12-13, 16-19

Daily living tip: No matter what successes you have in life, do not let them make you arrogant. It is by Allah's grace that you were allowed to succeed. Stay humble and gracious. You have talents and skills by Allah's favor on you. Use them wisely.

Today's prayer: O my Lord, help me to succeed in whatever I attempt, in accordance with Your will, but do not let my successes make me arrogant and boastful.

The Children of Israel
Were Given a Book of Scriptures.

We previously granted to the Children of Israel the Book, wisdom, and the gift of prophecy. We provided fine things for sustenance, and We favored them above all other nations. We provided obvious signs in matters. They did not differ until after knowledge had been imparted to them, [and they divided into sects] because of the jealousies among themselves. Truly, the Lord will judge among them on the Day of Judgment concerning the matters about which they differ.

Have you considered the leaders who were over the Children of Israel after the time of Moses? They said to a prophet [Samuel] who was among them, "Appoint a king for us so we may fight in the way of Allah."

He said, "If you were commanded to fight, is it possible that you would refuse to fight?"

They answered, "How could we refuse to fight in the way of Allah, now that our homes and our families have been disrupted!"

But when they were commanded to fight, they retreated, except for a small brigade. Allah has full knowledge of those who are wrong.

—QUR'AN 45: 16-17 AND QUR'AN 2: 246

Daily living tip: The stories of the Children of Israel are in the Qur'an so that we may learn from their experiences –not so that we may judge them. Read the Qur'an for its lessons and leave the judgment to Allah.

Today's prayer: O my Lord, put the lessons of the Qur'an into my heart so I may receive proper guidance.

Saul Was Appointed King Over the Israelites.

Their prophet [Samuel] announced to them, "Allah has appointed Saul as king over you."

(The Israelites) said, "How can he exercise authority over us when we are better suited than him to exercise authority? He does not even have the gift of abundant wealth.

He replied, "Allah has chosen him above you. Allah has generously given him the gifts of knowledge and physical prowess. Allah grants His authority to whom He pleases. Allah is All-embracing, the All-knowing.

Also, their prophet said to them, "Surely, a sign of his authority is that the Ark [of the Covenant] shall be returned to you. With it is tranquility from your Lord. You will get bac the relics left by the family of Moses and the family of Aaron. It will be carried by angels. Indeed, in this is a sure sign for you if you have faith."

Saul set forth with the brigades. He said, "Allah will certainly test you at the river. Whoever drinks from it [like an animal] will not proceed with me. Only those who do not taste it will go, plus those who sip from the hand."

They all drank [like animals] except a few.

—Qur'an 2: 247-249A

Daily living tip: People will often underestimate you and tell you that you are not good enough, strong enough, smart enough. Don't listen to them. If it is Allah's will, you will achieve your goals. Just keep doing the best you can. Be your own super hero.

Today's prayer: O my Lord, help me to set and achieve goals in my life that are according to Your will.

Saul's Army Defeated the Philistines.

After (Saul) and the faithful ones with him had crossed the river, some of them decided, "No, this day we will not be able to cope with Goliath [the giant] and his forces."

Some were convinced that they must meet Allah that day [through their deaths]. They said, "How often, by Allah's will, has a small force vanquished a larger one? Allah is with those who patiently persevere."

When they advanced to meet Goliath and his forces, they prayed, "Our Lord, pour loyalty upon us and make our tread certain. Help us against the unbelieving people."

By Allah's will, (Saul's army) defeated them, and David slew Goliath. Allah gave (David) power and wisdom and taught him whatsoever He willed.

If Allah had not curbed one set of people by means of another, the earth would indeed be filled with wickedness. Allah is filled with bounty for all the worlds.

Such as these are the verses of Allah. We recite them to you in truth. Truly, you [Prophet Muhammed] are one of the messengers.

—QUR'AN 2: 249B-252

Daily living tip: You will have Goliaths in your life –problems that seem too big to handle. Know that Allah will empower you and give you whatever you need to conquer your problems. Just don't give up. Keep on going strong.

Today's prayer: O my Lord, inspire me with bravery and conviction so that I may be successful in overcoming any problems I may encounter.

Allah Blessed David and Solomon.

We bestowed grace aforetime on David from Us. O Mountains, sing praises with him! Also, you birds!

We made iron pliable for him. Make coats of mail, carefully measuring the links, and work righteousness, for be sure that I see all that you do."

We gave Solomon to David. [He was] an excellent servant. Indeed, he always turned [to Us].

For Solomon, We gave [the speed of] wind. Its early morning was a month, and its evening was a month. We made a fount of molten metal to flow for him, and spirit-beings worked for him, by the will of his Lord. If any of them neglected Our command, We made him taste the penalty of the blazing fire. They worked for him as he desired –arches, [artistic] images, basins as large as reservoirs, and cauldrons built in place. Work, O Family of David, with gratitude! But few of my servants are grateful.

—QUR'AN 34: 10-11 AND QUR'AN 38: 30 AND QUR'AN 34: 12-13

Daily living tip: Whether a person is a student, an employee, or an entrepreneur, our work is something for which we should be grateful. Our brains and bodies were built to be put to good use, so stay active. Don't waste the skills and talents Allah has given you.

Today's prayer: O my Lord, bless my brain and my body so that I can always be productive.

Yemen Ignored the Signs of Allah.

For Sheba [Yemen], a sign was in the land –two gardens, one on the right and one on the left. "Eat of the sustenance provided by your Lord, and be grateful to Him for a fair and happy territory and a Lord Most Forgiving."

They disregarded, however, and We sent a flood from the dams against them. We changed their two plots into gardens producing bitter fruit and tamarisks and a few lote trees. That was the repayment We gave them because they disbelieved. We never give such repayment to any except the ungrateful.

Between (Sheba) and the cities that We blessed, We placed cities in strategic locations, and among them We appointed fair mileage. "Travel therein, safely, by night and by day."

But they said, "Our Lord, place longer distances for our journeys," but they wronged themselves. Eventually, We made them as a fable, and We dispersed them all in scattered fragments. Truly, in this are signs for every patient and grateful person.

To them, Iblis [Satan] proved true his idea, and they followed him –all except a few that believed. He had no authority over them except to recognize the person who believes in the hereafter from he/she who is in doubt concerning it. Your Lord watches over everything.

—QUR'AN 34: 15-21

Daily living tip: Trust Allah to provide what is intended for you, and then be happy with what He has provided. You will always be sad if you look for greater blessings without being grateful for the blessings you already have.

Today's prayer: O my Lord, help me to achieve all that You have planned for Me, but also help me to be grateful for every achievement I attain.

Solomon Had the Gift of Understanding Creatures.

We gave knowledge to David and Solomon. They said, "Praise to Allah, who has shown us favor above many of His believing servants."

Solomon, David's heir, said, "O People, we have been taught the language of birds, and we have been given benefit from all things. This is indeed a real blessing."

Assembled for Solomon were armies of spirit-beings and men and birds, readied to be mobilized.

When they came to a valley of ants, one of the ants communicated, "All ants, retreat to your tunnels; otherwise, Solomon and his armies may unwittingly crush you."

(Solomon) [perceiving the ant's communication] smiled, amused at its speech. He said, "O my Lord, inspire me to be always grateful for Your blessing, which You have bestowed on me and my parents. [Inspire me] to perform such righteous deeds as will please You. Admit me, by Your grace, to be among Your righteous servants."

—QUR'AN 27: 15-19

Daily living tip: The animals and other creatures were created before people. They are able to communicate with the Creator in a way we cannot understand. Study all creatures and appreciate them as if they are our brothers and sisters in faith. They belong on this planet just as much as you do.

Today's prayer: O my Lord, make me one who has sincere appreciation, respect, and love for all Your creatures.

David Was Tested.

Have you heard the story of the plaintiffs? They climbed over the wall into the prayer room. They entered the presence of David; he was frightened by them.

They said, "Don't be afraid. We are two plaintiffs. One of us is wrong; decide between us with truth, and do not treat us unjustly, but guide us to the right way."

[One testified:] "This is my brother. He has ninety-nine ewes, and I have one ewe. Yet he says, 'Give her unto my care,' and he demanded harshly."

(David) said, "He has undoubtedly wronged you by demanding that your ewe be added to his ewes. Many partners betray one another –but not those who believe and perform righteous deeds. How few they are!"

David realized, however, that We had tested him, and he asked forgiveness from his Lord [for his own sin of betrayal]. He fell down, bowed, and repented. We forgave him for that, and he had closeness with Us and a beautiful return.

—QUR'AN 38: 21-25

Daily living tip: David (peace upon him) was put in a position of judging between the plaintiffs even though he had committed a similar error. This story is in the Qur'an to remind us not to be hypocrites. Don't waste your time judging others when you have your own errors for which to atone.

Today's prayer: O my Lord, if I have sinned, lift the veil from my eyes and let me see the error of my own ways so I may repent and do better in the future.

The Believers Will Have the Help They Need.

We will undoubtedly help Our messengers and other believers, both in this world's life and in the day when the witnesses will approach. On that day, excuses will be of no use to the wicked; they will have the curse and abode of wretchedness.

Certainly, We gave Moses the guidance [of the Torah], and We gave the Book as an inheritance for the Children of Israel. It is a guide and a reminder for people of understanding.

Certainly be patient, for the promise of Allah is true. Ask forgiveness for your sin, and celebrate the praises of your Lord in the evening and in the morning.

Not equal are the unseeing and the seeing or the believers who live righteously and those who live wickedly. You don't heed much.

The hour [of dread] will certainly come. Do not doubt it, even though most people do not believe.

Your Lord says, "Call on Me; I will answer you.

"Truly, those too arrogant to serve Me, however, will find themselves mortified in Hell."

—QUR'AN 40: 51-55, 58-60

Daily living tip: One of the benefits of believing in Allah is knowing that you are never alone. Even in dark times, try to remember Allah is there, and He is on your side. Take time away from electronic devices and other distractions. Be still. Be alone. Just be.

Today's prayer: O my Lord, help me to keep my faith even when I fail to sense Your presence in my life.

Jesus Confirmed the Torah.

In the footsteps of (Moses, the Jewish prophets, rabbis, and doctors of law), We sent Jesus the son of Mary to confirm the Torah revealed before him. We gave him the Gospel wherein was guidance and light, confirmation of the preceding Torah, and direction and warning for those who revere Allah.

May the people of the Gospel discern by what Allah has revealed in it. Those who fail to recognize what Allah has revealed are rebellious.

To you [Muhammed] We sent the Book in truth, confirming and guarding (the Scriptures) that came previously. Differentiate among them [the People of the Gospel] by what Allah has revealed. Do not follow their vain desires [to convert to their sects], which would be a departure from the truth that has come to you.

To each [society] among you We have prescribed a law and an evident way. If Allah had so willed, He would have made you a single society, except to test you in what He has given you. Therefore, strive as in a race in all virtues. The goal of you all is to Allah. He will eventually settle all your disputes.

—Qur'an 5: 46-48

Daily living tip: The differences in religious views are a test for us. You can pass the test by not arguing with people about their faith. Instead, simply share your own beliefs in a respectful manner. Learn how to have a nice conversation without acting like a jackass.

Today's prayer: O my Lord, help me to avoid vain arguments about religion and give me the right words and actions to shut down such arguments.

The Torah is Still Valid for the Jews.

Why would (the scoffing Jews) come to (Prophet Muhammed) for judgment when they have the Torah before them? Therein is the command of Allah, yet, even after that, (these specific Jews) would backslide because they are not people of faith.

It was We who revealed the [Mosaic] law wherein was guidance and light. The Jews are evaluated by its standards, and by the prophets who submitted to Allah's will. [The Jews are evaluated] by the rabbis and doctors of law who were entrusted with the protection of Allah's Book [the Jewish Bible] and who were witnesses for it. Therefore, do not fear people, but fear Me. Do not trade My signs [ie, Scriptures] for a miserable profit. Any who fail to discern by what Allah has revealed are disbelievers.

We ordained therein [in the Jewish Bible], "Life for life, eye for eye, nose for nose, ear for ear, tooth for tooth, and the punishment should fit the crime. If anyone should relinquish punishment [as an act of kindness], however, this would be an act of atonement for oneself. Any who fail to discern by what Allah has revealed are sinners.

—QUR'AN 5: 43-45

Daily living tip: Most of the Jews of the Qur'an were Sadducees, a Jewish sect which no longer exists. The Qur'an is for everybody, however. Jews do not have to abandon their faith in order to accept Prophet Muhammed (peace upon him) and the revelation of the Qur'an. Invite Jews to the message of Islam without saying anything bad about Judaism.

Today's prayer: O my Lord, help me to find the beauty of Islam within the beauties of other religions.

John the Baptist Was Prophesied to Zechariah.

Remember the mercy of your Lord to His Servant Zechariah when he cried to his Lord a secret petition. He said, "My Lord, frail indeed are my bones, and the hair of my head shines white. Nevertheless, I am never unblessed, my Lord, in my prayer to You. Indeed, I am concerned about my successors following me, and my wife is barren. However, grant me an heir as from You to represent me and represent the family of Jacob. Make him, my Lord, pleasing."

"O Zechariah, indeed, We give you good news of a son. His name shall be John; on no other by that name have We already granted distinction."

He said, "My Lord, how shall I have a son when my wife is barren, and I have grown quite feeble in my old age?"

(The angel of God) said, "Albeit. Your Lord says, 'That is as easy for me as when I created you when you had been nothing.'"

—QUR'AN 19: 2-9

Daily living tip: When Allah has a plan for you, trust that He will see you through no matter how impossible it may seem. You are smarter and tougher than you think. Don't let people put you down and make you feel stupid. Take charge of your life and don't let other people mess you up.

Today's prayer: O my Lord, help me to set goals in keeping with Your will in my life and help me to attain all You have planned for me.

John the Baptist Was Blessed with Wisdom.

[Remember] Zechariah when he cried to his Lord, "My Lord, do not leave me without children, although You are the best of inheritors."

We listened to him, and We granted him John [the Baptist]. We cured his wife [of her infertility].

(Ishmael, Enoch, Elisha, Jonah, and Zechariah) were quick to perform good deeds. They always called on Us with love and reverence and humbled themselves before Us.

(Zechariah) said, "My Lord, give me a sign."

He said, "Your sign will be that you cannot speak to anyone for three straight nights."

(Zachariah) appeared to his people from his prayer chamber, and he told them by signs to glorify Allah in the morning and in the evening.

[After John's birth:] "O John, secure the Book with valor."

We gave him wisdom even as a youth, and compassion as from Us, and purity. He was devout. He was kind to his parents, and he was never arrogant or rebellious.

Peace on him the day he was born, the day that he died, and the day that he will be resurrected to life.

—QUR'AN 21: 89-90 AND QUR'AN 19: 10-15

Daily living tip: Always be kind and respectful to your parent or parents or guardian. Realize that he, she, or they are struggling too and are likely doing the best even if mistakes are made. Adults screw up sometimes too. Give them a break.

Today's prayer: O my Lord, bless my parents (or single parent) with good health and wisdom in caring for the family.

Jesus Was Prophesied to Virgin Mary.

Recall in the Book [of Qur'an] [the story of] Mary when she withdrew from her family to a place of the East. She screened herself from them [for the purpose of prayer and meditation]. We sent Our Spirit to her, and he appeared before her as a man in all respects.

She said, "Indeed I seek protection with the Most Gracious from you, if you fear Allah."

He said, "I am simply a messenger from your Lord announcing to you the gift of a holy son."

She asked, "How shall I have a son when no man has touched me. I am not unchaste!"

He said, "Albeit. Your Lord says, 'That is easy for Me, and to appoint him as a sign for all people and a mercy from Us is a matter decreed!"

(Mary) conceived him, and she isolated herself with him to a remote place. The discomfort of bearing a child drove her to the trunk of a palm tree. She cried, "O, I would rather have died and been forgotten and out of sight!"

—QUR'AN 19: 16-23

Daily living tip: Sometimes Allah calls us to do things that take bravery. Always look to Mary (peace upon her) as an example of how to be brave and dignified no matter what you have to do. She was one tough cookie. Try to be awesome like she was.

Today's prayer: O my Lord, help me to face all challenges with the grace and courage that Mary had (peace upon her).

Mary Was Vindicated Against Slander.

Then [a voice] came to (Mary) from beneath her, "Do not grieve. Truly, your Lord has opened a spring beneath you. Also, shake toward you the trunk of the palm tree, and fresh, ripe dates will fall for you. Eat and drink and freshen your eyes. If you see anyone, say, 'I have vowed a fast to the Most Gracious that I will not converse with any person this day.'"

Finally (Mary) returned to her people, carrying the infant.

They said, "O Mary, truly you have brought an astonishing thing! O sister of Aaron [in the family of priests], your father was not an evil man, and your mother was not unchaste!"

She pointed to (the baby) [as if to say, "Ask him"].

They said, "How can we talk with an infant from the cradle?"

[The baby Jesus] said, "I am indeed a servant of Allah. He has given me Scriptures and made me a prophet. He has made me blessed wherever I am and has instilled in me prayer and charity as long as I live. He has made me kind to my mother and not arrogant or rebellious. Peace was upon me the day I was born, and will be upon me the day that I die and the day I shall be resurrected."

—QUR'AN 19: 24-33

Daily living tip: Gossip is a hurtful thing. When anyone tells lies about you, remember Mary (peace upon her). Some people claimed that she had gotten pregnant by a Roman soldier. She faced the gossipers, and Allah vindicated her. Trust that He will do the same for you.

Today's prayer: O my Lord, if someone tells lies about me, help me to hold my head high until the truth is proven.

Despite Proof, People Made Incredulous Claims and Requests.

People of the Book ask you [O Muhammed] to cause a Book to descend from Heaven. They asked Moses for an even greater thing when they said, "Show us Allah unveiled." They were dazed by thunder and lightning because of their offense. They worshiped the calf even after obvious signs had appeared to them. We forgave them, and We gave Moses evidence of authority.

They rejected faith when they uttered against Mary a serious false charge.

They also said that they killed Jesus the Messiah, son of Mary, Allah's messenger. But they did not kill him or crucify him, although such was made apparent to them. Those who differ about this are full of doubts about it with no authentic knowledge, but only conjecture to follow. For certain, they did not kill him! Rather, Allah raised him to Himself. Allah is the Victorious, the Perfectly Wise.

—QUR'AN 4: 153, 156-158

Daily living tip: The Qur'an says that the crucifixion appeared real. The Christian Bible tells what the world saw: a defeated and humiliated man on the cross. The Qur'an tells what Allah saw: victory over the cross. No need to argue about it.

Today's prayer: O my Lord, help me to find the proper balance of truths instead of finding conflicts in different beliefs.

Jesus is Not God.

They blaspheme who say that Allah is indeed the Messiah the son of Mary. Messiah said, "O Children of Israel, worship Allah my Lord and your Lord."

Concerning anyone who associates partners with Allah, Allah will indeed forbid Paradise to him/her. The fire will be his/her abode. There will be no one to help the sinners.

They blaspheme who say that Allah is indeed third of a Trinity. No god is there except One God. If they do not desist from what they are saying, truly, a horrendous punishment will afflict the disbelievers among them.

Why do they not turn to Allah and seek His forgiveness? Allah is Most Forgiving, Most Merciful.

Messiah the son of Mary was only a messenger [not the incarnation of God]. Certainly, messengers came and went before him. His mother was truthful. They both had to eat food [like everybody else].

See how We make His Signs clear to them [the misguided]. Yet look at how they are deluded.

—QUR'AN 5: 72-75

Daily living tip: Church doctrine smothered the real Jesus (peace upon him). The Qur'an brought him back. That is something to be excited about. Offer to present Jesus to others but do it in a respectful manner.

Today's prayer: O my Lord, help me to be such a good follower of Jesus (peace upon him) that others will want to follow him also and not follow a false representation of him.

Jesus' Creation Was Similar to Adam's Creation.

That [story of] Jesus, son of Mary, is a statement of truth about which they dispute.

It is not befitting of Allah that He would beget a son. Glory to Him! When He decrees a matter, He only says to it, "Be!" and it is.

Truly, Allah is my Lord and your Lord; therefore, serve Him; this is the Straight Way.

The simile of Jesus, in relation to Allah, is the same as Adam: He created (Adam) from dust, and then He said to him, "Be!" and he was.

The truth is from your Lord, so do not be among those who doubt.

If anyone argues about this matter with you, now that knowledge has come to you, say, "Come. We shall assemble our sons and your sons, our women and your women, ourselves and yourselves. We shall humbly pray and invoke the condemnation of Allah on whoever is lying."

This is surely the true account. No god is there except Allah. Allah is certainly He who is Victorious, the Perfectly Wise.

If they backslide, Allah is aware of the sinners.

—QUR'AN 19: 34-36 AND QUR'AN 3: 59-63

Daily living tip: The doctrine of most Christian churches is that Jesus (peace upon him) is God and the literal Son of God. If there is to be any condemnation, it should come from Allah alone –not from you. Your duty is only to share what you believe –that Jesus is a spirit emanating from God but not God.

Today's prayer: O my Lord, give me a kind and loving spirit so I may be friends with people of all religions.

Allah Will Confirm Jesus' Miraculous Life.

One day Allah will assemble the messengers and ask, "What response did you receive?"

They will say, "We have no knowledge; indeed, You are the Intellect of what is hidden."

Allah will then say, "O Jesus son of Mary, recall my favor to you and to your mother when I strengthened you with the Holy Spirit. You spoke to people in infancy as well as in maturity. I taught you the Book and Wisdom, the Torah and the Gospel. You made from clay the figure of a bird, by My will. You breathed into it, and it became a [living] bird, by My will.

"You healed those born blind and the lepers, by My will. You brought forth the dead, by My will.

"I restrained the Children of Israel from you when you showed them obvious signs. The disbelievers among them said, 'This is nothing but evident magic.'

"I inspired the disciples to have faith in Me and My messenger. They said, 'We believe, so bear witness that we indeed are Muslims [ie, in submission to God].'"

—QUR'AN 5: 109-111

Daily living tip: The Gospel is Jesus' message to repent of one's sins, submit oneself to Allah, and live righteously. Follow Jesus' true teachings and do not let non-Muslims confuse you. They may try to knock you off your game. Be patient with them and hope they will be properly guided.

Today's prayer: O my Lord, help me to be an ambassador for Jesus by keeping his message pure and simple.

Jesus Will Testify That He Did Not Claim Divinity.

Allah will say, "O Jesus son of Mary, did you say to people, 'Worship me and my mother as divinities, detracting from Allah'?"

(Jesus) will say, "Glory to You! I could never say such a thing! If I had said anything like that, You surely would have known it. You know what is in my heart, though I do not know all that is in Yours. Truly, You know fully all that is hidden.

"I never said anything to them other than what You commanded me to say, which was, 'Worship Allah, my Lord and your Lord.' I was a witness for them while I lived among them. After You raised me [to Heaven], You were the Watcher over them. You witnessed everything."

"If you decide to punish them, they are still Your servants; if You decide to forgive them, You are the Victorious, the Perfectly Wise."

Allah will say, "This is a day on which the truthful will profit from their truth."

They will have gardens, with underground rivers, which is their eternal home. Allah will be pleased with them, and they with Allah. That is the awesome salvation!

To Allah belongs the dominion of Heaven and Earth and all therein. He has power over all things!

—QUR'AN 5: 116-120

Daily living tip: Notice that in today's passage, Jesus (peace upon him) leaves the judgment to Allah whether to punish or forgive those who revere Mary and Jesus as divinities. If Jesus leaves that judgment to Allah, then certainly you should too. It's not your job to decide who is going to Heaven or Hell.

Today's prayer: O my Lord, keep my worship pure from any associations with You.

Jesus Was Created by, Not Begotten of, Allah.

They say, "The Most Gracious has begotten a son."

This is indeed a monstrous thing to say. The skies are ready to burst, the earth to split asunder, and the mountains to crash in utter ruin from their invoking a son for the Most Gracious! It is not consonant with the majesty of the Most Gracious that He should beget a son.

No one of Heaven or Earth escapes coming to the Most Gracious as a servant. Truly, He does take account of all and has numbered them completely. Every one of them will come to Him individually on the Day of Judgment. Truly, on those who believe and perform deeds of righteousness, the Most Gracious will bestow affection.

We have made (the Word) accessible in your own language, so that with it you may give good news to the righteous and warning to people of conflict.

—Qur'an 19: 88-97

Daily living tip: When you research what the Qur'an says, you will find that it is always correct. In this case, it is correcting the King James Version of the Bible where Jesus is referred to as God's "only begotten son" (John 3: 16). This is a false translation as the word *begotten* was added. The Greek word used was *monogenes*. It literally means 'one of a kind' or it could be translated to 'unique'. In a spiritual sense, we are all children of the Creator, and Jesus (peace upon him) is unique in several ways.

Today's prayer: O my Lord, thank you for the gift of the Qur'an so that we will not fall prey to false teachings.

Jesus Worshiped Allah Alone.

When [Jesus] the son of Mary is presented as an example, look how your people jest! They say, "Is he any better than our gods?" They ask you this only for the sake of argument, because they are a contentious people.

(Jesus) was merely a servant [not a god]. We granted Our favor to him, and We made him an example for the Children of Israel. If it had been Our will, We could have made angels from among you, succeeding over the earth.

(Jesus) shall be a sign of the hour [of judgment]; therefore, have no doubt about this, but follow Me. This is the Straight Way.

Do not allow Satan to hinder you; truly, he is your avowed enemy.

Jesus came with obvious signs. He said, "Truly, I have come to you with wisdom in order to clarify some of that about which you dispute; therefore, fear Allah and obey me.

"Truly, Allah is my Lord and your Lord, so worship Him. This is the Straight Way."

—QUR'AN 43: 57-64

Daily living tip: The best way to follow Jesus is to worship the God he worshiped. Allah is God of all the prophets, including Jesus (peace upon him). There is One God for everyone, and we worship Him best when we worship Him together.

Today's prayer: O my Lord, may the hour of judgment find me worshiping You alone.

Do Not Attribute Divinity to Anyone.

The Jews call Ezra a son of Allah, and the Christians call Messiah the son of Allah. That is a saying from their own mouths, but they simply imitate what the disbelievers of old used to say. Allah may destroy them. How they are deluded!

They take their priests and their saints to be their lords, instead of Allah, as well as Messiah, the son of Mary. Yet they were commanded to worship only One God. No god is there except Him. Glory to Him from having the partners they associate.

They want to extinguish Allah's light with their mouths, but Allah will not allow anything except that His light be perfected, even though the unbelievers detest it.

He is the One who has sent His messenger with guidance and the religion of truth to prevail it over all other religions, even though the idolaters detest it.

O Believers, many among the priests and other religious leaders falsely devour the substance of people and hinder from the way of Allah. Among them are those who hoard gold and silver and do not use it in the way of Allah. Announce to them a grievous penalty.

—QUR'AN 9: 30-34

Daily living tip: Not only must you not put any religious person on a pedestal, but also do not engage in hero worship –modeling your life after a celebrity. It's fine to look up to someone as a role model, but you still must put Allah first. Role models can let you down, so don't place them too high.

Today's prayer: O my Lord, let me not place anyone in such a superior place that I would even allow that person to lead me astray.

All True Believers Will Be Rewarded in Paradise.

O Messenger, proclaim that which has been sent to you from your Lord. If you did not, you would not have fulfilled His message. Allah will defend you from the others. Allah does not guide those who reject faith.

Say, "O People of the Book, you have no foundation unless you stand firmly by the Torah, the Gospel, and what else has descended to you from your Lord"

What has been revealed to you [Muhammed], from your Lord, increases rebellion and unbelief in most of them. Do not fret over people without faith.

Indeed, those who believe [in the Qur'an], those who are [practicing] Jews, the Sabeans, the Christians, and any others who believe in Allah and the last day and who perform righteous deeds will have neither fear nor grief.

—QUR'AN 5: 67-69

Daily living tip: There are thousands of religions all over the world. Try to focus on their consonant values of peace, love, compassion, goodwill, justice, kindness, charity, and fairness while respecting the differences. Believers of all religions are stronger when we unite for peace instead of being divided.

Today's prayer: O my Lord, bless people of all religions and help them find ways for religion to unite us instead of divide us.

The Concept of the Trinity Compromises the Oneness of Allah.

O People of the Book, do not commit excesses in your religion. Do not say things about Allah other than the truth.

Jesus the Messiah, the son of Mary, was Allah's messenger, His Word breathed into Mary, and a spirit emanating from Him. Believe in Allah and His messengers. Stop talking about "the Trinity"! That would be better for you. God is One God. Glory to Him! He is above begetting a child. To Him belong all things of Heaven and Earth. Allah is all you need to settle accounts.

Messiah does not refuse to be Allah's servant. Neither do the angels who are near [to God]. Those who do refuse to worship Him and are arrogant will be congregated before Him [to give account].

To those who believe and perform righteous deeds, Allah will grant their earned rewards and will give them even more blessings. As for those who are scornful and arrogant, He will punish them with a grievous penalty. Beyond Allah, they will find no protector or savior.

—QUR'AN 4: 171-173

Daily living tip: The Qur'an is for people of all religions, and it corrects some mistakes that people made in religion. Invite people of all religions to find what guidance the Qur'an has just for them. You don't have to try to convert people. Just share truth and leave the rest to Allah.

Today's prayer: O my Lord, do not let me be judgmental of others but help me to share the message of the Qur'an in a loving way.

All Beings Are Humbled in the Presence of Allah.

It is He who shows you lightning, both for dread [of potential danger] and optimism [for the promise of rain]. It is He who causes clouds to form and become heavy. Thunder repeats His praises, as do the angels filled with awe. He flings the thundering bolts of lightning, and He allows them to strike whomever He wills. Yet people dare to argue about Allah and the measure of His power.

To Him belong all honest prayers. Any others upon whom are depended besides Him give no better response than if someone were to extend his/her hands [into a deep well] for water but cannot reach the water and get it to his/her mouth. The prayer of one without faith is nothing but stray wandering.

All beings of the skies and Earth prostrate themselves to Allah either willingly or unwillingly, as [is illustrated by] their shadows in the mornings and in the evenings.

Say, "Who is the Lord and Sustainer of Heaven and Earth?"

Say, "Allah!"

Say, "Do you then rely on others besides Him –others who have no power either for good or for harm even for themselves?"

Say, "Are the unseeing equal to the seeing? Are the depths of darkness equal to light?"

Do they assign partners to Allah, claiming they created as He created, so that their creation was equal to His?

Say, "Allah is the Creator of all things! He is the One, the Prevailing Force!"

—Qur'an 13: 12-16

Daily living tip: Whether it's a fierce lightning strike or the gentle crawl of a tiny bug, try to see the power of the Creator in all things. Don't walk around like an airhead, not seeing the small wonders around you.

Today's prayer: O my Lord, how awesome is your creation! Make me one who always shows respect to all created things.

Faithful Servants Are Those Who Submit to Allah.

O Humanity, here is offered a parable. Pay attention to it.

Those upon whom you call besides Allah cannot create even a fly, even if they all met together just for that purpose. And if a fly should snatch away anything [for example, a morsel of bread], they would have no power to get it back. That is how feeble the petitioners and the petitioned [idols] are. They have made no fair estimate of Allah, for truly Allah is strong and powerful.

Allah chooses messengers from among angels and from among people. Allah listens and understands. He knows what is before them and what is behind them. All queries are finally referred to Allah.

O Believers, bow and prostrate yourselves and adore your Lord. Perform goodness so that you may prosper.

Also, strive in His cause as you should strive. He has chosen you and has imposed no difficulties on you in religion. It is the same religion of your father Abraham. He called you "those who submit to Allah" [Muslims], both before and in this Book, so that the messenger [Prophet Muhammed] may witness to you, and you may witness to Humanity.

Establish routine prayers, give regularly to charity, and be faithful to Allah. He is your Protector –the best to protect and the best to help.

—QUR'AN 22: 73-78

Daily living tip: Worship is not only prayer and charity, but also being faithful to Allah in every part of your life. Always try to do your best whether as a student, a friend, an athlete, an artist, or in whatever activity you participate. Putting forth your best effort is also a form of worship.

Today's prayer: O my Lord, help me to be the best I can be in every part of my life as I dedicate my life to You.

Heaven and Earth Glorify Allah.

Whatever is of Heaven and Earth glorifies Allah. Dominion is His, and to Him all praise is due. He has power over all things. It is He who has created you. Among you are believers and disbelievers. Know that Allah is fully aware of all that you do.

He created the skies and Earth with truth. He has given you form and made the human body a beautiful shape. To Him is the ultimate goal.

He knows all that is in Heaven and throughout Earth. He knows all that is concealed as well as what is revealed. Allah has full knowledge of what is in the hearts.

Have you not heard the story of those who previously rejected faith? They tasted the evil result of their conduct, and they had a horrid punishment. That was because, after their messengers presented obvious signs, they said, "You, mere humans, are trying to tell us how to live?" They rejected and turned away, but Allah can do without them. Allah is Independent, the Praised One.

—QUR'AN 64: 1-6

Daily living tip: When you glorify Allah, think about how awesome it is that all of nature is joining you in your praises. Your voice joins all the praises arising from the earth and spirals to Allah in one beautiful sonnet of the planet.

Today's prayer: O my Lord, how amazing You are! Your splendor fills Heaven and Earth! All glory, honor, and praise belong to You!

Publicly Claim the Religion of Abraham.

Say, "Truly, my Lord has guided me to a way that is straight, a religion of righteousness. It is the religion of Abraham who was true in faith. He did not add gods [with God]."

Say, "Truly, my prayer, my service of sacrifice, my life, and my death are for Allah, the Cherisher of the Worlds. No partner does He have: this I am commanded, and I [Muhammed] am the first of those to bow to His will."

Say, "Should I seek, as my Lord, another besides Allah when He is Lord of all? Every soul earns only for itself, and no bearer of burdens can bear the burden of another. Your final goal is to your Lord. He will inform you of the things about which you dispute.

"It is He who has made you representatives, inheritors of Earth. He has raised you in ranks, some above others so that He may test you in the gifts He has given you. Your Lord is quick in punishment, yet He is indeed Most Forgiving, Most Merciful.

—Qur'an 6: 161-165

Daily living tip: Sometimes people will entice you to join them in things that are wrong. Be brave enough to say, "No, thank you. I am a Muslim, and I don't do that." They may make fun of you, but just shrug it off and find better friends.

Today's prayer: O my Lord, do not let me be tempted to do the wrong things, but help me to be brave enough to stand up for what is right.

Allow No Coercion in Religion.

Allah! No deity is there except Him –the Living, the Eternal, the independent One. Rest and sleep cannot appeal to Him. All things of Heaven and Earth are His. Who can intercede in His presence except in accordance with His will? He understands situations past, present, and future. No one grasps any of His knowledge except as He permits.

His throne extends over the skies and the earth. He feels no fatigue in guarding and preserving them. He is the Highest, the Magnificent.

Allow no coercion in religion. Truth is evident from error. Whoever rejects evil and believes in Allah has latched onto the most dependable grip that never breaks. And Allah hears and knows all.

Allah is the Protector of those who have faith. From the depths of darkness, He will guide them into light.

Those who reject faith are patrons of the evil ones who divert from the light and lead into the depths of darkness. They will all be companions of the fire wherein they will continuously dwell.

We know best what (the disbelievers) say, and you are not to be a tyrant over them [forcing them to accept Islam]. Admonish with the Qur'an anyone who fears My warning.

—QUR'AN 2: 255-257 AND QUR'AN 50: 45

Daily living tip: The most important thing a person can do is to submit his or her whole self to God. Once he or she has done that, trust God to lead that person in the way of religion. Share what you believe, but don't try to force your views on anyone.

Today's prayer: O my Lord, help me to attract others to Islam in the way that I live.

You Can't Force People
to Believe Against Their Will.

Whatever good happens to you is from Allah. Whatever evil happens is from your own soul.

We have sent you [Prophet Muhammed] as a messenger for humanity. Allah is a sufficient witness.

Surely those who have earned your Lord's word against them will never believe, even if every sign was revealed to them, until they see the horrible punishment.

If it had been your Lord's will, all people would have believed. Would you then force people to become believers?

No soul can believe except by the will of Allah. He will allow doubt from those who refuse to try to understand.

Say, "Behold all that is in the skies and on the earth, but neither signs nor warnings will benefit those who do not believe."

Do they expect other than that of the days of people who passed before them?

Say, "Go ahead and wait, and I will wait also."

We will deliver Our messengers and those who believe. It is proper for Us to save the believers.

—Qur'an 4: 79 and Qur'an 10: 96-97, 99-103

Daily living tip: You will meet people who do not believe in God at all. It is enough for you to let them know that you do believe. Sometimes just stating your faith is enough to make a difference. You don't have to be obnoxious about it.

Today's prayer: O my Lord, grant guidance to those who will believe and choose me to help provide that guidance.

Some People Will Never Believe.

We could send angels to them. We could make the dead speak to them. We could assemble things before them face to face. Even if we did those things, they would still not believe unless Allah so willed. Most of them are ignorant.

For every messenger, We have appointed satanic enemies from among people and spirit-beings. They inspire one another with believable dialog with deception. If your Lord had so planned, they could not have done so. Leave them alone with their inventions.

May the hearts of those who deny the hereafter incline to such (deceit). May they be pleased with it. May they earn from it what they can.

Say, "Should I seek a judge other than Allah? It is He who sent down to you the Book that is clear.

"Those to whom We have given the Book know that it was revealed from your Lord in truth. Therefore, do not be among the disputants."

The Word of your Lord is fulfilled in truth and justice. No one can change His words. He is the All-hearing, the All-knowing.

—QUR'AN 6: 111-115

Daily living tip: Sometimes you may be disappointed and disillusioned at the lack of belief among people. Know that Allah is well aware of their disbelief, and He is still in control. Stay strong in your faith and just do the best you can when you have to be around such people. Don't let them drag you down.

Today's prayer: O my Lord, help me face the struggles of this world with dignity and self-respect.

Allah's Guidance is the Only True Guidance.

Say, "Who delivers you from the dark recesses of land and sea when you call upon Him in humility and silence? [You claim,] 'If only He will deliver us from danger, we will show our gratitude.'"

Say, "Allah delivers you from such danger and other calamities, and still, you worship false gods."

Say, "Should we call on others besides Allah –others that can neither benefit nor harm us? Should we regress after receiving guidance from Allah? Should we then be like one whom the demons have misled? He/she is left to wander aimlessly across the wilderness while his/her friends, trying to guide him/her, beg, 'Follow us.'"

Say, "Allah's guidance is the only guidance. We are commanded to surrender to the Lord of the Worlds. [We are commanded] to be consistent in ritual prayers, and to fear Allah. It is to Him that we shall be assembled."

It is He who created the skies and Earth in accordance with truth. Whenever He says, "Be!" it is. His Word is truth. Dominion is His on the day the trumpet will be blown [on the Day of Resurrection]. He knows the unseen as well as that which is publicized. He is the Perfectly Wise, the All-aware.

—Qur'an 6: 63-64, 71-73

Daily living tip: It's okay to ask others for advice when you need help, but make sure their advice is in keeping with Allah's will in your life. Allah is always the best advisor. If someone gives you rotten advice, be wise enough to recognize it. Just be cool.

Today's prayer: O my Lord, help me to make decisions that best follow Your will.

Truth is Sealed from Those Who Choose Disbelief.

We have given a variety of explanations in the Qur'an so that (the idolaters) may be advised, but only their rebellion increases.

Say, "If there had been gods besides Him, as (the polytheists) claim, then (the lesser gods) would still have to come before the [Heavenly] Throne."

Glory to Him! He is exalted far above their loftiest claims.

The seven skies and Earth and all beings thereof declare His glory. There is nothing that does not celebrate His praises, but you do not understand such praise.

Truly, He is Most Tolerant, Most Forgiving.

When you recite the Qur'an, We put, between you and those who deny the afterlife, an invisible veil. We cover their hearts so they cannot understand (the Qur'an), and We block their ears. When you honor your Lord only, through the Qur'an, they turn their backs in aversion. We know best why they listen when they listen to you and when they meet privately.

The wicked say, "You believe in a man who is possessed!" See what similes they conjure for you [in denigrating Islam], but they have gone astray and will never find their way.

—QUR'AN 17: 41-48

Daily living tip: Islam means 'peace with Allah through complete submission to Him.' It was the original religion given to humanity. All other religions are manifestations of humanity's search to return to that original religion. Praise Allah everyday if you have found that original peace. Most people are frustrated, angry, and confused. If you are among those blessed with peace, that is major.

Today's prayer: O my Lord, thank you for choosing me to understand the message of Islam and have peace with You.

Don't Ignore Allah's Impact on Your Life.

Is one who walks headlong, with his/her face groveling, better guided or one who walks evenly on the Straight Way?

Say, "He created you and provided for you the senses of hearing, seeing, feeling, and perceiving. You give little thanks."

Say, "He multiplied you across the earth, and to Him you will be assembled."

(Scoffers) ask, "When will the promise [of the Day of Judgment] be realized, if you are telling the truth?"

Say, "Such knowledge is with Allah alone. I am only one who gives fair warning."

When they see it quickly approaching, the faces of the disbelievers will show distress, and it will be said, "This is it –what you beckoned!"

Say, "Consider this: Whether Allah destroys me and those with me or bestows His mercy on us, who can deliver the disbelievers from a horrendous penalty?"

Say, "He is the Most Gracious; we have believed in Him, and on Him we have put our trust. Soon you will know who of us [believers or disbelievers] are wrong."

Say, "Don't you understand? If some morning your water supply is suddenly lost into the earth, who then can restore your flow of water?"

—Qur'an 67: 22-30

Daily living tip: Don't take anything for granted. Even simple things like clean water, a comfortable bed, and clothes that fit are actually major blessings. When you're feeling bummed out, try to think of all the good things you have going for you.

Today's prayer: O my Lord, keep me reminded and grateful for every blessing in my life.

The Clothing of Righteousness is Best.

O Children of Adam, truly We have bestowed clothing upon you to cover your shame. It is also an adornment, but the clothing of righteousness is best. Such are among the signs of Allah so that they may remember.

O Children of Adam, do not let Satan seduce you as he seduced your parents from Paradise. He stripped them of their clothing [of divine light] to expose their shame. Indeed, he and his tribe watch you from where you cannot see them. Indeed, We made the evil spirits buddies to those without faith.

When (the disbelievers) commit immorality, they say "We saw our elders doing so," and, "Allah commanded us thus."

Say, "Allah most certainly does not order immorality! Do you say of Allah what you do not know?"

Say, "My Lord has commanded justice and that you set your faces at every place of prayer, and call upon Him, being sincere to Him in religion. As He created you in the beginning, so shall you return."

He has guided some; others have deserved to be astray. Indeed, they took the evil spirits, in preference to Allah, as their buddies. They think they are on the right track.

—Qur'an 7: 26-30

Daily living tip: Having nice clothes is a blessing that many do not have. Everyone, however, can have the beautiful clothes of righteousness. Live a life of kindness and compassion, and you will always be a beautiful person.

Today's prayer: O my Lord, dress me in spiritual clothes of goodness and righteousness.

Remember the Grace of Allah.

Praise Allah, the Originator of the skies and Earth, who made the angels as messengers with wings of two, three, or four [sets]. He adds to creation as He pleases, for truly Allah has power over all things.

What Allah, from mercy, bestows on humanity cannot be withheld by anyone. What He withholds, no one else can grant. He is the Victorious, the Perfectly Wise.

O Humanity, remember the grace of Allah to you. Is there a creator other than Allah to provide for you from Heaven or Earth? No deity is there except Him; how then are you deluded from the truth?

If people reject you [Prophet Muhammed], it is the same rejection suffered by messengers before you. All accounts are returned to Allah.

O Humanity, certainly the promise of Allah is true. Do not let this present life deceive you, and do not let the deceiver [Satan] betray you about Allah. Truly, Satan is an enemy to you, so treat him as your adversary. He only invites his advocates so they may become companions of the blaze.

For the disbelievers, there is a terrible penalty. For those who believe and perform righteous deeds, there is forgiveness and a magnificent reward.

—QUR'AN 35: 1-7

Daily living tip: Grace is the free and unmerited favor of Allah. It is manifested in His forgiveness and salvation. Learn to reflect His grace by being merciful and kind to all people and animals and all creation. Don't be a lowlife loser.

Today's prayer: O my Lord, as You have grace and mercy on me, may I also show grace and mercy to others.

Who Can Dye Better Than Allah?

They say, "In order to be guided, you must become Jews," or, "…Christians."

Say, "No, [I choose] the faith of Abraham the upright. He was not of those who idolized [false] gods."

Say, "We believe in Allah and the revelation given to us [in the Qur'an], and we believe in the revelations given to Abraham, Ishmael, Isaac, Jacob and his descendants, Moses, Jesus, and the other prophets, from their Lord. We do not elevate one above another, and we submit to Allah."

If (the People of the Bible) believe as you believe [that there is One God and that one must submit his/her whole self to God], then they are on the right track. If they decline, however, then they are only in opposition. Allah is enough for you against them. He is the Listener and the Intellect.

Our dye is of Allah, and who can dye better than Allah? We worship Him.

Say, "Will you argue with us about Allah even though He is our Lord and yours as well? We are each responsible for our own deeds, and we are loyal to Him. Or do you claim that Abraham, Ishmael, Isaac, Jacob and his descendants were Jews or Christians? Do you know more than Allah? Who is more unjust than those who fail to share the testimony they have from Allah? Allah knows exactly what you do.

—QUR'AN 2: 135-140

Daily living tip: All religions have beautiful traditions. When Allah's love is the dye for our souls, He gives us an appreciation for all people just like we appreciate all the colors of a flower garden. Learn to love and respect all people regardless of religion, culture, country of origin, or any other aspect of pluralism.

Today's prayer: O my Lord, may all people become united in a spirit of love, respect, and goodwill.

Allah Has Revealed a Beautiful Message.

For those who fear and obey their Lord, lofty mansions have been built with multiple floors. Beneath them, rivers flow. This is the promise of Allah. Allah never fails to keep a promise.

Do you not understand that Allah sends rain from the sky and channels it through springs in the earth? He then uses it to yield crops of various colors. They dry and turn yellow, as you can see, and then He causes them to crumble. In all this is a reminder for people of understanding.

Is one whose heart Allah has opened to submission [to God] receiving enlightenment from his/her Lord? Calamity approaches those whose minds are hardened against the remembrance of Allah. They are obviously misguided.

Allah has revealed the most beautiful message in the form of a Book consistent with itself and repetitious [as liturgy]. The skins of those who fear their Lord tremble [with reverence], and then their skins and hearts soften in remembrance of Allah. Such is the guidance of Allah. He guides with (the Qur'an) whom He pleases, but those whom Allah leaves astray will have no guide.

—QUR'AN 39: 20-23

Daily living tip: Even though today's situations are often different from the time of the Prophet (peace upon him), when you read the Qur'an, try to figure out how you can apply each verse to your own life. The Qur'an was revealed for you. Don't neglect such a magnificent gift.

Today's prayer: O my Lord, teach me how to apply the Qur'an to my daily life.

Differences in Understanding
Caused Divisions Among the Jews.

We gave the Book [of the Torah] to Moses, but differences arose concerning it [among the Pharisees and Sadducees and other Jewish sects]. If it had not been for a Word going forth from your Lord, the matter would have been decided among them. (The various Jewish and Christian sects) are in suspicious doubt about it. Certainly, your Lord will repay them for their deeds. Truly, He is Fully Aware of what they do.

You and those with you should stand firmly as you are commanded. Repent and do not sin. He is All-seeing of all that you do.

Do not tend toward those who sin, or the fire will seize you. You have no protectors except Allah, and you will not be helped.

Establish ritual prayers at both ends of the day and at the approach of night. Truly, good deeds repel evil deeds. May that be a reminder for those who will remember!

Be patient. Truly, Allah will not allow the reward of the righteous to perish.

—QUR'AN 11: 110-115

Daily living tip: The faults of others are not given to us so we may be judgmental. They are given to us as lessons so we may learn from those faults. The message we must take away is to not let sectarian differences divide us Muslims. Embrace other Muslims regardless of what sects or schools of Islam they follow.

Today's prayer: O my Lord, bless the Muslim ummah (faith community) to be united in faith, love, and peace. Make us one faith family.

The Qur'an Can Help the Jews.

Truly, this Qur'an explains for the Children of Israel many things about which they are confused. It is certainly a guide and a mercy to those who believe.

Truly, your Lord will decide among them by His decree. He is the Victorious, the All-knowing. So put your trust in Allah, for now you have found manifest truth.

Truly, you cannot cause the [spiritually] dead to listen or cause the [spiritually] deaf to hear the call if they insist on retreating. You cannot be a guide to the unseeing to keep them from straying. Only those who believe in Our signs will listen, and they will bow in submission to Allah.

When the Word is fulfilled against them, We shall bring forth for them from the earth a beast. He will be able to speak to them because humanity did not believe with assurance in Our signs.

—QUR'AN 27: 76-82

Daily living tip: Share the message of the Qur'an with all who will listen and then trust Allah to give them proper direction. Your duty is only to speak truth. Even if your voice is weak and feeble and unsure, Allah can add His power to it. Trust the power!

Today's prayer: O my Lord, may all who will listen be exposed to the message of the Qur'an and gain understanding.

The Qur'an Confirms the Torah

[Prophet Muhammed,] say, "I am not a bringer of some new-fangled doctrine from among the messengers. I do not know what will be done with me or with you. I follow only that which is revealed to me by inspiration. I am only a lucid warner."

Say, "Understand! If this is from Allah, and you reject it, and a witness from among the Children of Israel testifies to its similarity [to the Jewish Bible] and has believed while you are arrogant, truly Allah does not guide unjust people."

The disbelievers say of the believers, "If this [message] were a good thing, such people would not have gone to it first, before us!" If they are not guided by it, they will say, "This is an old fabrication."

Before this was the Book of Moses [the Torah] as a guide and a mercy. This Book confirms [the Torah] in the Arabic language to admonish the unjust and as good news to those who live righteously.

Truly those who say, "Our Lord is Allah," and remain faithful will have upon them no fear or grief. Such will be companions of the garden, eternally dwelling therein –a recompense for their deeds.

—QUR'AN 46: 9-14

Daily living tip: Respect the Torah (the first five books of the Bible) and respect those who live by it. Don't criticize other people's religious literature. That would be stupid. All truth comes from the same God.

Today's prayer: O my Lord, bless those who follow the Torah and help them to be good and faithful servants of You.

The Qur'an Confirms the Previous Scriptures.

This Qur'an could not possibly have been produced by anyone other than Allah. It confirms that [Torah] which came before it. It is an explanation of the Book in which there is no doubt. It is from the Lord of the Worlds.

Do they claim, "(Muhammed) has made it up"?

Say, "Produce a chapter like it and call on anyone you can besides Allah, if you're telling the truth."

Nonsense! They reject what they cannot understand even before its interpretation has come to them. Those who came before them did the same thing. Look at what happened to those who did wrong.

Among them are some who will come to believe in (this Qur'an) and some who will not. Your Lord knows best those who tend to commit evil.

—QUR'AN 10: 37-40

Daily living tip: Even though the Scriptures contained in the Bible are not in their original form, you can still read them for whatever benefit you can find there. Just filter everything through the Qur'an. Don't be afraid to learn from whatever knowledge is available. People who ridicule the Bible are not helping anything. They only cause trouble.

Today's prayer: O my Lord, help me to appreciate the religious texts of others.

People Still Argue About It.

You were not on the side of the mountain [with Moses] when We beckoned. You are a mercy from your Lord to warn people to whom no previous mentor had been sent so that perhaps they may remember. Without such [warning], a calamity would strike them for what their hands have achieved. They would then say, "Our Lord, why did You not send a messenger? We would have followed Your Scriptures and been among the believers."

But now that truth has come from Us, they say, "Why does he not have signs like Moses had?" But don't they reject what was given to Moses? They say, "It's just two kinds of sorcery supporting one another [the Torah and the Qur'an]." And they say, "We'll just dismiss them all!"

Say, "Bring a Book from Allah that is a better guide than either of them, and I will follow it, if you are so honest!"

And when they are not responsive to you, know that they only follow their own desires. Who is more astray than one who follows his/her own desires and is devoid of guidance from Allah? Allah does not guide people given over to sin.

—QUR'AN 28: 46-50

Daily living tip: Some people will never believe no matter how convincing you are to them. Just do the best you can, and don't give up. Your intentions will be rewarded.

Today's prayer: O my Lord, help me to endure and stay strong in my faith no matter how others may ridicule me.

People Forgot Parts of the Scriptures.

Allah made a covenant with the Children of Israel, and We appointed twelve leaders among them. Allah said, "Surely I am with you if you establish routine prayers, practice consistent charity, believe in My messengers and assist them, and loan to Allah a beautiful loan. Truly, I will wipe from you your sins and admit you to gardens with rivers flowing beneath them. If any of you, after this, resists faith, he/she has certainly wandered from the path of decency."

Because of their breach of the covenant, We condemned (the backslidden Israelites) and made their hearts grow hard. They take words out of context and forget a part of the message sent to them, and you will not cease to find them –except for the few— always bent on deceit. But forgive them and ignore [their faults]. Indeed, Allah loves those who are kind.

Also, from among those who call themselves true Christians, We made a covenant. They forgot a part of the message sent to them, so we aroused enmity and hatred among them until the Day of Resurrection. Soon Allah will show them what they have done.

—QUR'AN 5: 12-14

Daily living tip: The Qur'an often teaches by examples of what other people did. Don't be guilty of forgetting any part of the message that Allah has sent. Learn all you can about the Scriptures and live by their commandments. That will make you a winner!

Today's prayer: O my Lord, bless all believers everywhere and help us all to remember and follow Your teachings.

The Qur'an Can Help the Christians.

O People of the Book, surely Our messenger has come to you, revealing to you much that you concealed in the (Bible) while neglecting some. Surely, there has come to you from Allah a light and a clarifying Book. Allah guides with it all who seek His pleasure in ways of peace that lead them from layers of darkness, by His will, into the light, guiding them to the Straight Way.

Blasphemous indeed is the saying that Allah is the Messiah, the son of Mary. Say, "Who then has the least power against Allah if He decided to destroy the Messiah the son of Mary, his mother and everyone else on the earth? To Allah belongs the dominion of the skies and Earth and all that is among them. He creates what He pleases. Allah is Most Capable over all things.

O People of the Book, Our messenger has surely come to you, clarifying for you after a lull in Our messengers, lest you should say, "No bearer of good news has come to us and no warner."

Surely a bearer of good news and a warner has come to you. Allah is Most Capable over all things.

—QUR'AN 5: 15-17, 19

Daily living tip: Bible-believing people have made some mistakes in their doctrine. The Qur'an gives guidance to correct those errors. Be gentle in your witness as you try to explain the Qur'an to non-Muslims. Don't be a jerk about it.

Today's prayer: O my Lord, open the hearts and minds of all people to the beautiful truths of the Qur'an.

The Qur'an Can Reconcile Christians and Jews.

The Jews say, "The Christians have no basis."

The Christians say, "The Jews have no basis."

Yet they study the same (Scriptures)! They sound similar to those who don't know anything. Allah will judge among them in their disagreements on the Day of Judgment.

Who is worse than someone who tries to get people not to celebrate Allah's name in the places of worship of Allah and who tries to ruin (the places of worship)? People are not supposed to enter (the places of worship) except in reverence. For them, there is nothing but disgrace in this world and an exceeding torment in the world to come.

To Allah belong the east and the west. Wherever you turn, Allah's countenance is there. Truly, Allah is All-embracing, the All-knowing.

They say, "Allah has begotten a son." Glory to Him! Nonsense! To Him belongs all that is of Heaven and Earth. Everything renders worship to Him.

He is the Originator of the skies and Earth. When He decrees a matter, He says to it, "Be!" and it is.

—QUR'AN 2: 113-117

Daily living tip: People criticizing one another's religion is not helpful. It only drives people farther apart. Try to find what people have in common in religion and focus on those things. If a person is not part of your faith, he or she is still part of the family of humanity.

Today's prayer: O my Lord, may all people learn to come together as members of the family of humanity.

Allah Alone Will Judge
Among the Various Religions.

Indeed, as for those who believe [in the Qur'an], those who follow Judaism, and the Sabeans, the Christians, the Magians, and the polytheists, Allah will judge among them on the Day of Resurrection. Indeed, Allah is witness over everything.

Do you not see that to Allah bow down in worship all things that are of Heaven and Earth –the sun, the moon, the stars, the mountains, the trees, the animals, and many people? Many [people] are justly due for punishment. Whomever Allah humiliates cannot become bestowed with honor. Indeed, Allah does what He wills.

Two opposing groups [believers and disbelievers] dispute with each other about their Lord. For those who disbelieve, garments of fire will be cut for them; over their heads will be poured scalding water. With it will be scalded what is within their bodies as well as skins. In addition, there will be rods of iron for them. Every time they want to get away from anguish, they will be forced back: "Taste the penalty of the burning fire."

—QUR'AN 22: 17-22

Daily living tip: It's not up to you to decide who is going to Heaven or Hell. Avoid people who put themselves as equal to Allah in deciding the fate of others. Only Allah is in charge of the judgment. He never put up a "Help Wanted" sign.

Today's prayer: O my Lord, may all believers come together in a spirit of mutual respect and appreciation and stop condemning one another.

Muhammed Brought Good News for Everyone.

We have sent you [Prophet Muhammed] as a witness, as a bringer of good news, and as a warner. [This is] so that (humanity) may believe in Allah and His messenger. [This is so that you] may assist and honor Him, and glorify Him morning and evening.

Truly, those who pledge their allegiance to you [Prophet Muhammed] in actuality pledge their allegiance to Allah. The hand of Allah is over their hands. Anyone who violates his/her oath does so to the harm of his/her own soul. Anyone who fulfills what he/she has covenanted with Allah will soon be granted a great reward from Allah.

To Allah belongs the dominion of Heaven and Earth. He forgives whom He will, and He punishes whom He will. Allah is Most Forgiving, Most Merciful.

He has sent His messenger with guidance and the religion of truth to cause it to prevail over all other religions. Enough is Allah for a witness.

—QUR'AN 48: 8-10, 14, 28

Daily living tip: Consider yourself a representative of Prophet Muhammed (peace upon him). If you are unkind, rude, and obnoxious, you are telling a lie about the Prophet.

Today's prayer: O my Lord, help me to be a good representative of Prophet Muhammed by being a kind and peaceful person.

Some Who Claim to Believe Cannot Be Trusted.

Among humanity are some who say, "We believe in Allah and the last day," but they are not true believers. They seek to trick Allah and those who truly believe. They are only tricking themselves, and they don't even realize it. Their hearts are sick, and Allah makes their sickness worse. A great punishment awaits them because of their dishonesty.

When they are told, "Do not make trouble upon the earth," they say, "We are making things better!" Be careful; they really are the ones who cause trouble, and they don't even realize it.

When they are told, "Believe as others believe," they answer, "Should we believe as the ignorant believe?" Truly, they are the ignorant ones, but they don't know it.

When they meet true believers, they say, "We believe." When they are alone with their unbelieving friends, they say, "We're really part of this crowd; we were just fooling around."

Allah mocks them and allows them to wander blindly in their sin. They have traded guidance for error. They do not profit from their devices, and they are not guided.

—QUR'AN 2: 8-16

Daily living tip: Some people who call themselves Muslims are hateful and have extreme views. Islam is a religion of moderation. Be cautious of those who spout extremist ideas and who seem to hate everyone that does not believe exactly as they believe.

Today's prayer: O my Lord, guide all Muslims to the Straight Way, which is a moderate path, and help them avoid extremism.

"We Have Heard the Call."

[The believers say,] "Our Lord, we certainly have heard the call of one calling to faith, 'Believe in your Lord,' and we have believed. Our Lord, forgive us our sins, blot out our iniquities, and allow us to die among the righteous.

"Our Lord, grant us what You promised through Your messengers, and do not disgrace us on the Day of Resurrection. You certainly never break a promise."

Their Lord responded to them, "Indeed, I will never squander the deeds of any of you, whether male or female. You are each among the others. As for those who have left their homes, were driven from their homes, suffered harm in My cause, fought and were slain, certainly, I will erase their sins from them. I will admit them into gardens with rivers flowing beneath –a reward from the presence of Allah, and with Him is the best reward."

—QUR'AN 3: 193-195

Daily living tip: Every day that you wake up, you are called to serve Allah. Make the best of every day by being a friend to everyone you meet and doing good deeds. If you claim to believe in Allah, and then act like a snot, that's a lie about Allah.

Today's prayer: O my Lord, do not let me forget to be kind, friendly, and helpful to everyone.

Many People Who Believed in the Bible
Also Believed in the Qur'an.

We bestowed (the Qur'an) in truth, and in truth has it descended. We sent you [Prophet Muhammed] only to give good news and to warn. A Qur'an, which We have divided so you may recite to people at intervals, is what We have revealed in parts.

Say, "Whether you believe in it or not, indeed those who were given knowledge before (this Qur'an) fall on their faces in prostration when it is recited to them. They say, 'Glory to our Lord! Truly, the promise of our Lord has been fulfilled.'

"They fall on their faces in tears, and it increases their humility."

Say, "Call upon Allah or call upon the Most Gracious, or by whatever name you call upon Him, for to Him belong the most beautiful names. Do not speak your prayers too loudly or too softly, but seek a moderate tone."

Say, "Praise Allah, the One who begets no son and has no partner in dominion and needs none to protect Him from humiliation. Magnify Him for His magnificence."

—QUR'AN 17: 105-111

Daily living tip: When Bible-believers understand the message of the Qur'an, they will accept it. Learn to present the message without criticizing the Bible. If you criticize the Bible, you will just push people farther away, and they won't want to hear about the Qur'an.

Today's prayer: O my Lord, may more people hear and understand the message of the Qur'an and accept it into their hearts.

Danger is in Rejecting the Scriptures.

Those who reject Our Scriptures, however, and treat them with arrogance are companions of the fire to dwell therein continuously.

Who is more unjust than one who invents a lie against Allah or rejects His Scriptures? For such, their share must reach them from the Book [of Decrees]. Finally, Our messengers [of death] arrive and take their souls. (Those messengers) will ask, "Where are those you used to invoke besides Allah?"

They will answer, "They have left us." They will testify against themselves about being disbelievers.

He will say, "Enter among the generations –of people and spirit-beings who passed away before you— into the fire." Every time a community enters, it curses its sister community until they follow each other, all into the fire.

The last group will say about the first, "Our Lord, these people misled us. Give them a double penalty in the fire."

He will say, "It's double for everybody!" This, however, is beyond your understanding.

Then the first will say to the last, "You have no advantage over us, so taste the penalty for all that you did!"

—QUR'AN 7: 36-39

Daily living tip: How can you know the Scriptures are true? If you live by them, you will find that they work, and your life will be successful. When you depart from the message of the prophets, that's when you mess up.

Today's prayer: O my Lord, thank you for the Scriptures that provide guidance for my life, and thank you for all the prophets who brought the Scriptures.

Every Disbeliever Will Be Questioned.

One day We shall congregate from all people a crowd of those who reject our verses, and they will be held in rows. They will arrive [before God]. (Allah) will say, "Did you reject My signs without comprehension or what?" And the Word will be fulfilled against them because of their sin, and they will be unable to speak.

Do they not see that We have designed the night for their rest and the day for light? Truly, in this alone are signs for any people who will believe.

On the day that the trumpet will sound, those of Heaven and Earth will be smitten with terror. The exception is for those whom Allah has exempted [through His salvation]. All shall come before Him, humiliated.

You see the mountains and think that they are immoveable, but someday they will be gone, just as clouds dissipate by an act of Allah, who perfected everything. He is well aware of all that you do.

—QUR'AN 27: 83-88

Daily living tip: Make the best of this life that Allah has given you, but always remember that this life is temporary. Live your life in such a way that, on the Day of Judgment, Allah will grant you His grace and mercy and salvation.

Today's prayer: O my Lord, bless me and my family and all believers with Your guidance so we may be safe on the Day of Judgment.

No Excuse Will Be Acceptable
on the Day of Judgment.

One day We will raise from each people a witness, and then there will be no excuse acceptable from the disbelievers, and they will not be given the opportunity to repent. When the sinners see the penalty, then it will in no way be mitigated, and they will receive no respite.

When those who added partners to Allah see their partners, they will say, "O Lord, these are our partners whom we used to invoke besides You."

(The idols) will respond to them, "Truly, you are liars!"

That day they will show submission to Allah, and all their inventions will be annulled.

As for the disbelievers who hindered from the path of Allah, We will increase punishment on top of punishment because they had spread corruption.

One day We will raise from each people a witness from among themselves. We will bring (Prophet Muhammed) as a witness over (his contemporaries). We bestowed upon you a Book explaining everything –a guide, a mercy, and good news for those who submit to Allah.

—QUR'AN 16: 84-89

Daily living tip: Don't make excuses for your mistakes. If you are wrong, admit it and apologize if you should. People will respect you more when you acknowledge your mistakes.

Today's prayer: O my Lord, forgive me for any errors I make in my life and help me to be strong enough to make amends.

Entire Communities May Be Punished.

How many communities rebelled against the command of their Lord and of His messengers so that We called each to stern accountability? We imposed on (each rebellious community) exemplary punishment. It experienced the consequences of its conduct, and the end of its conduct was perdition.

Allah has prepared for (such communities) a severe punishment; therefore, fear and obey Allah, you who have understanding and have believed. Allah has indeed bestowed upon you a reminder. [It came by] a messenger [Prophet Muhammed] reciting to you the verses of Allah. Obviously, this is so that He may lead those who believe and perform righteous deeds, from dark shadows into light. Those who believe in Allah and perform righteous deeds will be admitted by Him into gardens beneath which rivers flow, where they will live forever. Allah has indeed granted each one an excellent provision.

Allah is He who created seven skies and also layers of Earth. His command descends throughout so you may know that Allah has power over everything and that Allah comprehends everything with intellect.

—QUR'AN 65: 8-12

Daily living tip: If a community engages in ugly activities, such as cursing, vulgar music, alcoholism, and drugs, it affects everyone. Do your part in helping to maintain a community that provides a healthy environment for everyone.

Today's prayer: O my Lord, bless my community so it may be a place of safety and goodness.

Allah Will Not Destroy a Community if Its Members Will Repent.

Why were there, among generations before you, no people with enough common sense to prohibit evil upon the earth, except for those few people We saved? The sinners pursued the enjoyment of the good things of life, which were given to them, and persisted in sin.

Your Lord would never destroy a community for a single sin if its members were likely to mend.

If your Lord had so willed, He could have made Humanity one people, but they will never cease to argue. The exceptions are those on whom your Lord has bestowed His mercy, and for this reason He created them. The Word of your Lord will be fulfilled: "I will fill Hell with evil spirit-beings and people –all together."

With all that We relate to you from the stories of the messengers, We strengthen your heart. In them comes to you truth, advice, and a message to remember by those who believe.

Say to the disbelievers, "Go ahead and do as you will; we will do our mission. Just wait! We too will wait [to see God's plan unfold]."

—QUR'AN 11: 116-122

Daily living tip: When community members do evil things, they invite negative energies upon the whole community. Do good deeds so that you can invite positive energies that will benefit everyone. Even ugly words will invite evil upon you. Be careful of your speech.

Today's prayer: O my Lord, let my life so shine with grace and goodness so that I attract positive energies to myself and all around me.

Recognize All the Messengers, Who Were Only Inspired Men.

Before you [Prophet Muhammed], We also sent other messengers who were only men to whom We granted inspiration. If you don't realize this, ask those who possess the message [of the Bible]. We gave obvious signs and Scriptures. We have sent to you the message so that you may explain clearly to humanity what has been sent for them so they may ponder.

Do those who devise evil feel secure that Allah will not cause the earth to swallow them, or that the wrath will not seize them from directions that they cannot perceive? Or [do they think] that He may not seize them in the midst of their goings to and fro, without a chance of their escape. Or [do they think] that He may not seize them by a gradual decline? Indeed your Lord is Kindest, Most Merciful.

Do they not look at how Allah has created everything –how their shadows incline, to the right and to the left, humbly prostrating themselves to Allah?

Everything of Heaven and Earth obeys Allah –whether moving creatures or angels; none are arrogant. They all revere their Lord who is high above them, and they do all that they are commanded.

—QUR'AN 16: 43-50

Daily living tip: We are supposed to follow the examples of the prophets, so if you live in a way that is unkind and disrespectful, it's the same as telling a lie about the prophets. Live in a way that shows the kindness and grace of the prophets (peace upon them all). Don't be a sleaze ball.

Today's prayer: O my Lord, peace and blessings upon all the prophets. Help me to be a good representative for them.

The Qur'an is a Guide and a Mercy

If Allah were to punish people for their sins, He would not leave on the earth a single living creature, but He gives respite for an appointed term. When their term expires, they will not be able to delay the punishment for a single hour, just as they would not be able to advance it.

They attribute to Allah what they hate, and their tongues assert the lie that the best things are for themselves. Without doubt, for them is the fire, and they will be abandoned.

By Allah, We certainly sent Our prophets to people before (Prophet Muhammed), but Satan made their own acts seem alluring. He is also their buddy today, but they shall have a wretched penalty.

We bestowed the Book to you [Prophet Muhammed] only for the express purpose that you should clarify to them those things about which they differ, and that it should be a guide and a mercy to those who believe.

Allah bestows rain from the skies and gives with it life to the earth after its death. Truly, in this is a sign for those who listen.

—QUR'AN 16: 61-65

Daily living tip: Treat the Qur'an with respect because, on the Day of Resurrection, the Qur'an will be a witness for you. Consider the Qur'an like a best friend. It gives you good counsel, so regard it as a treasure.

Today's prayer: O my Lord, may the Qur'an be a light for my path so I may stay on the Straight Way.

Believe in All the Scriptures.

O Believers, firmly stand for justice as witnesses for Allah, even if it means blaming yourselves, your parents, or other relatives. Whether they are rich or poor, Allah is best to care for them. Do not follow your own desires, lest you waver. If you distort or prevent [justice], truly Allah is well aware of what you do.

O Believers, believe in Allah and His messenger [Prophet Muhammed] and in the Book sent to His messenger, and in the (Scriptures) sent previously. Anyone who denies Allah, His angels, His Books [of Scriptures], His messengers, and the Day of Judgment has surely lost the way, straying afar.

Certainly, those who believe, and then disbelieve, and then believe again, and then disbelieve, and then continually increase their doubts will not be forgiven by Allah. He will not guide them on the journey. To such hypocrites, give the good news that a dreadful penalty awaits them.

As for those who seek friendship from disbelievers rather than believers, do they seek honor among them? Indeed, all honor is with Allah.

He has already told you in the Book [what to do] whenever you hear the Scriptures of Allah being disrespected and ridiculed. You should not even sit with (the perpetrators) until they engage in a different conversation. They could negatively influence you. Allah will assemble all the hypocrites and the disbelievers into Hell.

—QUR'AN 4: 135-140

Daily living tip: If you hear people criticizing the holy books of any religion, avoid them. That kind of negativity does no good. Show respect for all religions and their holy books even if you disagree with their beliefs.

Today's prayer: O my Lord, may people of all religions learn to come together in a spirit of harmony.

Disbelievers Will Accept Neither the Bible Nor the Qur'an.

The disbelievers say, "We will neither believe in this Qur'an nor that [Bible] which came before it."

If only you could see when the offenders are made to stand before their Lord, trying to blame one another!

The weak ones will say to the arrogant ones, "If it weren't for you, we would have believed."

The arrogant ones will say to the weak ones, "Did we keep you from following guidance once it had been presented to you? No, you are the ones who transgressed."

The weak ones will say to the arrogant ones, "No, it was a conspiracy, day and night, when you instructed us in unbelief in Allah and to attribute equals to Him."

They will have concealed regrets when they see the penalty. We shall put yokes around the necks of the disbelievers. Won't that be fitting for their deeds?

We never sent a warner to a population without pampered ones among them saying, "We do not believe in that which you bring."

They said, "We excel in wealth and children and can suffer no punishment."

Say, "Truly, my Lord increases or diminishes provisions as He pleases, but most people simply do not understand."

—Qur'an 34: 31-36

Daily living tip: Some people will reject all the holy books and make fun of you for believing. They are the losers even though they do not realize it. Just live your faith and try to be a good influence on others. Maybe someone will believe just because he or she saw what a good person you are because of your religion.

Today's prayer: O my Lord, help me to be a good friend to all people, even to those who do not believe.

Many Bible-Believers Will Not Accept the Qur'an.

We gave Moses the Book [of the Torah]. We sent messengers after him. We gave Jesus, the son of Mary, evidence [miracles] and strengthened him with the Holy Spirit.

When a messenger comes to you with (a message) that you do not want, you become arrogant? You call some imposters, and you kill others.

(Some arrogant Jews) said, "Our hearts are wrapped."

Nonsense! Allah has condemned them because of their blasphemy. They believe only a little. A Book comes to them from Allah. It confirms [Scriptures] they already have. They had been asking for help against the disbelievers. When something familiar [in Scriptures] comes to them, they reject it. They should recognize this [Word of God]. Instead, they refuse to believe in it. The blame of Allah is on the disbelievers.

The price for which they have sold their souls is miserable. They deny what Allah has sent. They are jealous that Allah, out of His grace, would send it to anyone He wanted [instead of somebody they consider special. Because of their attitude, they have caused Allah to be mad at them. The punishment is shameful for those who reject faith.

—QUR'AN 2: 87-90

Daily living tip: Unbelievers will repeat horrible lies about Prophet Muhammed (peace upon him). It's hard not to get angry, but don't let such people get to you. Just tell them that those are all lies and that you are willing to share the truth whenever they're ready to hear it.

Today's prayer: O my Lord, peace and blessings upon Prophet Muhammed. May his name be cleared of all the lies they tell about him.

Most Jews Reject the Qur'an.

It is said to (some Jews), "Believe in what Allah has given." They say, "We do believe in (the Scriptures) that were given to us." They reject everything else, even though it is the truth confirming (the Scriptures) they have.

Say, "Why then have you [historically] killed the prophets of Allah in the old days if you did believe? Moses came to you with clear signs. You (worshiped) the calf afterward, and you behaved sinfully. Remember that We made a covenant with you and raised above you Mount [Sinai]. We said, 'Hold firmly to what We have given you and hearken to the law.'

"They said, 'We hear, and we disobey.' Their hearts became obsessed with the calf because of their unfaithfulness."

Say, "Your faith is commanded by evil, if you are believers."

Say, "If the last home with Allah is only for you and not for anyone else, then seek death if you are sincere."

They will never seek death, however, because of that which their hands have sent before them. Allah is well acquainted with the sinners.

You will find among them [ie, the unfaithful Jews], of all people, those most greedy for life –even more than the idolaters. Each one of them wishes that he/she could be given a thousand years to live. The grant of such life would not save him/her from punishment. Allah sees well all that they do.

—QUR'AN 2: 91-96

Daily living tip: Most of the Jews known to Prophet Muhammed (peace upon him) were Sadducees, a sect that no longer exists. Although Jews in general reject the Qur'an, be kind and loving to them, and perhaps they will be more accepting of the Qur'an's message. Try to visit a synagogue and make friends with the Jews there.

Today's prayer: O my Lord, bless the Jews, and help us all to realize we are all brothers and sisters in the family of the same Creator.

The Qur'an Has No Uncertainty in It.

Praise to Allah the One who has revealed to His servant the Book and has allowed no uncertainty in it. It is explicit to warn of a terrible punishment from Him and to give good news to the believers who perform righteous deeds. They shall have a handsome reward, which they shall enjoy forever.

In addition, He warns those who say that Allah has begotten a son. They have no knowledge of such a thing, and neither did their parents. It is nothing more than a scandal spewing from their mouths. It's simply a lie!

You would probably worry yourself to death, fretfully pursuing (the rejecters), because they do not accept this message.

We have caused what is on the earth as adornment for it so that We may test (people) and reveal who are best in conduct. Truly, We will make what is on (earth) to become barren dust.

—QUR'AN 18: 1-8

Daily living tip: You don't have to make someone else's holy book look bad in order to make the Qur'an look good. Let the Qur'an stand on its own without ridiculing other holy books. If you criticize other people's holy books, it just makes you look like a troublemaker. It doesn't help anything.

Today's prayer: O my Lord, make me able to share the message of the Qur'an in a kind and respectful manner.

Do Not Distort the Meanings of Scriptures.

Truly, those who distort Our Scriptures are not hidden from Us. Who is better –the one cast into the fire [of Hell] or the one who has safe passage on the Day of Judgment? Regardless of what you do, truly, He sees it all.

Truly, there are those who do not believe in the reminder [of the Qur'an] when it comes to them. Indeed (the Qur'an) is a glorious Book. No corruption approaches it from before or after it. It is a revelation bestowed by the Perfectly Wise, the Praised One.

Nothing is said to you [Prophet Muhammed] that was not said to messengers before you –truly, that the Lord possesses forgiveness as well as a horrific penalty.

Had We sent this Qur'an in a foreign language [other than Arabic], people would have wondered, "Why are the verses in a language foreign [to the Arabs] when the messenger is an Arab?"

Say, "It is a guide and a healing to those who believe, and for those who do not believe, there is unhearing in their ears and unseeing in their eyes. It is as if they were being called from a distant place."

—QUR'AN 41: 40-44

Daily living tip: How can you tell if a translation or interpretation of the Qur'an is wrong? It is not correct if it does not reflect the kindness and mercy of Allah. It must be logical and applicable to a decent society. It's a good idea to read different interpretations, and then you can consider more than one understanding. A verse can have more than one meaning.

Today's prayer: O my Lord, help me to find and follow the best interpretations of the Qur'an.

No One Can Change His Words.

Recite what has been revealed to you from the Book of the Lord. No one can change His words, and you will find no refuge other than Him. Let your soul be contented with those who call on their Lord morning and evening, seeking His face. Do not let your eyes stray from (the true worshipers) in order to seek the splendor of this life. Do not obey anyone whose heart We have permitted to neglect Our remembrance and who follows his/her own desires and who has strayed from all boundaries [of righteousness].

Say, "The truth is from your Lord. May he/she who will believe, do so; and may he/she who will not believe, do so."

Indeed, for the wicked, We have prepared a fire, which will surround them like walls. If they beg for relief, they will be granted water like molten brass that will scald their faces. How dreadful the drink! How prickly a bed on which to recline!

—QUR'AN 18: 27-29

Daily living tip: No one can force you to either follow the Straight Way or go down the path that leads to a wretched life. Make your own decision to live a righteous life so you may find success. You're the only one responsible for your life. Make a good run of it.

Today's prayer: O my Lord, light my path with Your guidance and help me to find the best future You have planned for me.

Those Who Misuse Verses
Out of Context Will Be Punished.

Tell My servants that I am indeed the Most Forgiving, the Most Merciful. My penalty will indeed be the most horrible punishment.

Do not strain your eyes at what We have given to certain groups of people, and do not worry over them. Lower your wing [of humility] to all believers.

Say, "I am certainly a lucid warner."

The same [punishment] as We deliver to those who carved [Biblical Scriptures] goes for those who hack the Qur'an.

Your Lord testifies that We will surely call them to account for all their deeds; therefore, expound openly what you are commanded and turn away from the idolaters. Sufficient are We for you against the scoffers –those who adopt another god with Allah. Soon they will understand.

Warn them of the approaching day, when the hearts will be in their throats, choking. For the sinners, no intimate friend or intercessor will be heard.

—QUR'AN 15: 49-50, 88-96 AND QUR'AN 40: 18

Daily living tip: Some people take verses from the Bible or the Qur'an and twist them to have meanings that were never intended. Be cautious of such people, and make sure not to become one that does that. Try to learn the context in which verses were revealed.

Today's prayer: O my Lord, help me to always find the true message of every verse and not to misuse any verse.

Avoid Those Who Make
a Mockery of Your Religion.

O Believers, do not take for guardians [of your personal interests] those who make a mockery and game of your religion. They could be among those who received (the Scriptures) before you or are among those who reject religion altogether. Fear Allah if you really have faith.

When you proclaim your call to prayer, they make a mockery and game of it. That's because they are a people without understanding.

Say, "O People of the Book, do you disapprove of us for no other reason than because we believe in Allah and what [revelation] has come to us, as well as that [Scriptures] that came before? Most of you are defiantly disobedient."

Say, "Shall I point out to you recompense from Allah that is much worse than this [disapproval by you]? Among those condemned by Allah and receiving of His wrath were some whom He transformed into apes and pigs. They worshiped false deities! Such as these are worse by rank and far more astray from the level path [than you think we are]."

—QUR'AN 5: 57-60

Daily living tip: Many among the non-Muslims are harsh and judgmental of Muslims and our beliefs. We all have to try to get along in this world, so be patient and kind even when people insult you. Trust that somehow Allah will make everything right.

Today's prayer: O my Lord, give me patience to endure in a world with people who have hatred and intolerance for one another.

People Are Always Going to Argue About Religion.

About what are they asking one another? [It is] about the good news concerning which they cannot agree. Absurd! But they will come to know [when it's too late]. Again: Absurd! They will come to know.

Have We not made the earth a wide expanse? [Haven't we made it] with mountains like anchors? We created you as pairs [male and female]. [We] made your sleep for rest. [We made] the night as a quilt. [We made] the day with resources for living. We established the seven layers [of Earth's sky]. [We] placed therein a splendid light [the sun]. We send from the clouds abundant water. [This is] so We may produce grain, other plants, and luxurious gardens.

Truly, the day of discernment has an appointed time. That day the trumpet will sound, and you will come forth in congregations. The skies will open as if there were doors. The mountains will vanish as if they had only been a mirage.

We have recorded everything in a book.

—Qur'an 78: 1-20, 29

Daily living tip: Different people have different beliefs, and each person is adamant that his or her belief is the true one. Don't stop searching for truth, but don't be easily swayed by people claiming to know everything. Use your own brain and decide what makes sense.

Today's prayer: O my Lord, keep me from vain arguments about religion.

Be Forgiving but Avoid the Ignorant.

Adhere to forgiveness. Command what is right, but distance yourself from the ignorant.

If a suggestion from Satan stalks you, seek refuge in Allah. He is the All-hearing, the All-knowing. Indeed, those who fear [Allah], when a thought of evil from Satan assaults them, bring [Allah] to remembrance, and then they realize.

Their alliance, however, tries to drag them into error and never lets up! If you do not bring them a verse [of Scripture], they ask, "Why don't you make one up?"

Say, "I only follow what is revealed to me from my Lord. Those [verses] are illumination from your Lord. They are guidance and mercy, for any who have faith.

When the Qur'an is read, listen to it attentively, so you may receive mercy. Bring your Lord to remembrance deep in your soul, with humility and reverence, without loud words, in the mornings and evenings. Do not be among those who are heedless.

Those near to your Lord are not haughty about worshiping Him. They glorify Him and prostrate before Him.

—QUR'AN 7: 199-206

Daily living tip: Be a friend to everyone, but also be wise enough to know when someone is not a friend to you. Avoid people who will drag you down. Always be alert to bad influences and don't get suckered in.

Today's prayer: O my Lord, bless me with good friends who help me to make wise decisions.

They Underestimate Allah.

Say, "Do you order me to worship someone other than Allah, O ignorant ones?"

It has already been revealed to you as it was to those before you, "If you were to idolize, your work would be a waste, and you will surely be among the losers."

Worship Allah and be among the grateful.

They have made no fair estimate of Allah –not such as is due to Him. On the Day of Resurrection, the whole of the earth will be but His handful. The skies will be rolled up in His right hand. Glory to Him! He is far above the associates they attribute [to Him].

The trumpet will have been sounded when all that is of Heaven and Earth will faint, except such as will please Allah. Then a second one will be sounded, when they will be standing and observing.

Earth will shine with the glory of its Lord.

The Record will be displayed. The prophets and the witnesses will be brought forward, and a just decision will be pronounced among them. They will not be wronged. Every soul will be paid in full for its deeds. He knows best all that they do.

—QUR'AN 39: 64-70

Daily living tip: Always be aware that Allah can do the most amazing things in your life. Do not underestimate His power, grace, and mercy.

Today's prayer: O my Lord, please be in my future and create for me amazing blessings to experience.

They Are Defiant.

Saad. Consider the Qur'an, filled with reminders. The disbelievers are egotistical and defiant. How many generations before them did We destroy? In the end, they called out, when there was no longer time for being saved.

They wonder that a warner has come to them from among themselves. The disbelievers say, "This is a deceitful sorcerer! He has made all the gods into one God! This is truly incredible."

The leaders among (the disbelievers) go away [saying], "Walk away and remain faithful to your gods, for this is certainly a contrived thing. We never heard of such a religion among the people of the latter days. This is nothing but conjecture. Has the message been sent to him –out of all among us?"

They are in doubt concerning My message. They have not yet tasted My punishment. Do they have the treasures of the mercy of your Lord, the Victorious, the Bountiful Provider? Do they have dominion of the skies and Earth and all among them? If so, let them ascend by whatever means. Even a team of warriors will be put to flight.

—QUR'AN 38: 1-11

Daily living tip: It's difficult for someone to walk away from a religion in which he or she was raised. Be gentle when witnessing to people about the truths of Islam. Christians, for example, may be in shock when they finally learn how Church doctrine evolved from human invention. Go easy on them.

Today's prayer: O my Lord, grant guidance to all those who are researching Islam and trying to decide if it is the right religion for them.

Say That Your Religion is Simply Worshiping Allah.

Say, "O Humanity, if you are in doubt as to my religion, [know that] I worship nothing of what you worship other than Allah. I worship Allah who causes you to die. I am commanded to be among the believers.

"Further, direct your face towards the honest religion, and never be among the polytheists. Do not call on anyone other than Allah; such [an idol] as that would neither profit you nor harm you. If you do such, you would certainly be among the sinners."

If Allah touches you with affliction, there is no one who can remove it except Him. If He designs some benefit for you, there is no one who can prevent His favor. He causes it to find whomsoever of His servants He pleases. He is the Most Forgiving, the Most Merciful.

Say, "O Humanity, truth has now arrived to you from your Lord. Whoever accepts guidance does so for the benefit of his/her own soul. Whoever strays does so at his/her own loss. It is not up to me to arrange your affairs."

—Qur'an 10: 104-108

Daily living tip: All true religion is the pure worship of the One God. Muslims call it the religion of Islam. Jews call it the religion of Noah. Try to find things in common with various religions and walk in peace and dignity.

Today's prayer: O my Lord, may all people find peace with one another by realizing we all worship the same God.

Say That You Do Not Associate
Any as Equal to Allah.

Say, "I only call upon my Lord, and I do not associate anyone with Him [as equal]."

Say, "It is certainly not within my power to cause you harm or to bring you into proper conduct."

Say, "No one could save me from [the wrath of] Allah, and I will find no refuge without Him. [That is] unless I convey what I receive from Allah and His messages. As for any who disobey Allah and His messenger, for them is Hell where they shall dwell eternally."

At length, when they see that [Hell] which they are promised, then they will know who is most helpless and counts for less.

Say, "I do not know if that which you are promised is near or whether my Lord will appoint it far into the future. He knows the unseen, and He does not acquaint anyone with His mysteries. The exception is a messenger whom He has chosen, and then He appoints a guard [ie, guardian angel] to march before him and behind him. [That is] so that (Allah) may ensure that they [the messenger and the angel] have indeed conveyed the messages of their Lord. He encompasses what is with them, and takes account of every single thing."

—QUR'AN 72: 20-28

Daily living tip: When Christians ask you why you do not accept Jesus (peace upon him) as God, simply tell them that Muslims believe that God is One and we do not believe in compromising that oneness. You could also mention that the word Trinity appears nowhere in the Bible.

Today's prayer: O my Lord, thank you for choosing me to be a Muslim who does not associate partners with Allah.

This Life is Filled with Struggles.

Do people think that, simply because they say, "We believe," they will not be tested? We tested others before them, and Allah recognizes those who are true, and He recognizes those who are false. Do those who practice evil think that they will defeat Us? How badly they judge!

Whoever hopes for the meeting with Allah, the time is surely coming. Allah is the All-hearing, the All-knowing.

Whoever strives does so for his/her own benefit, for Allah is independent from all creation.

From those who believe and perform deeds of righteousness, We shall blot away their sins. We shall reward them according to the best of their deeds.

O my believing servants, truly spacious is My Earth; therefore, worship Me.

Every soul will taste death, and then you will return to Us. To those who believe and perform righteous deeds, We will give a place in Paradise. [It will have] mansions and underground rivers. They will dwell there forever. It is an excellent reward for those servants who perform. [They are servants] who are patient and place their trust in their Lord!

—QUR'AN 29: 2-7, 56-59

Daily living tip: You will always have problems in your life. It's how you handle those problems that matter. Face every problem with faith and determination. Sometimes life is messy, and you have to clean it up. We were put into a world of struggle so we may rise above it. Some people make the struggle harder than it was originally intended. Take one day at a time and just do the best you can.

Today's prayer: O my Lord, help me to honor You in how I handle the struggles in my life.

The Faith Community Should Be United.

O Messengers, eat of the fine things, and live righteously. Truly, I [the Lord] am well aware of all that you do.

Truly, your faith community is one faith community, and I am your Lord and Cherisher; therefore, fear Me.

(People), however, have terminated their situation [of unity] and divided into sects. Each sect rejoices in its own (doctrine). Allow them their ignorance for the time being.

Do they really think that, just because We have blessed them with wealth and children, We would hasten upon them every good thing. Certainly not, but they do not understand.

Indeed, those who live in awe for fear of their Lord, who believe in the verses of their Lord, who do not assign partners with their Lord, and who dispense heart-felt charity out of reverence, knowing they will return to their Lord, are they who hasten to do every good deed and who are exemplary in doing so.

We do not burden a soul beyond its endurance. Before Us is a record speaking the truth. They will never be wronged.

—QUR'AN 23: 51-62

Daily living tip: Do not despise people because they belong to a different sect or religion than you do. We can't survive until we are united in faith and humanity. Walk with peace in your heart. Don't give people a reason to get mad. Life is hard, and we all have to help each other get along.

Today's prayer: O my Lord, teach my heart to love all people regardless of religious differences.

Believers Are One Faith Family.

Realize that Allah's messenger is among you. If he were to follow many of your desires, you would certainly fall into mishap. But Allah has endeared the faith to you. He has made it beautiful in your hearts. He has made hateful to you unbelief, wickedness, and rebellion. That is the way of those who walk in righteousness. [This is] a grace and favor from Allah. Allah is the All-knowing, the Perfectly Wise.

If two groups of believers enter into a dispute, establish peace between them. If one of (the two groups) trespasses against the other, strive against the trespassing group until it complies with the command of Allah. If it complies, make peace between them with justice. Be fair. Truly, Allah loves those who are fair.

The believers are one faith family. Make peace among the family members. Fear Allah so you may receive mercy.

O Humanity, We created you from one male and one female and made you into nations and tribes so that you may get to know one another. Truly the most honorable among you in the sight of Allah is the most righteous of you. Allah has full knowledge and is well aware.

—QUR'AN 49: 7-10, 13

Daily living tip: Try to be the kind of person that brings people together in friendship and not someone who engages in arguments. Division among people is not helpful. Everybody has struggles. We have to support and encourage one another.

Today's prayer: O my Lord, may all believers realize that we are all part of one faith family, and we must love, appreciate, and respect one another.

The Righteous Will Be Rewarded.

Truly, Allah will admit those who believe and do righteous deeds to gardens beneath which rivers flow. Those who reject Allah will frolic and consume as cattle consume [eating their fill with no higher interests]. The fire will be their home.

A parable of the Paradise promised to the righteous: There are rivers of unpolluted water, rivers of milk that never sours, rivers of [non-intoxicating] delicious wine for those who drink, and rivers of purified honey. For them are all types of fruits and grace from their Lord.

Compare that to the fate of those who will continuously dwell in the fire and be given boiling water to drink, which will pierce their bowels.

Among (the lost) are those who listen to you [O Prophet], but finally, when they depart from you, they say to those who have received knowledge, "About what was he talking just now?" Allah has sealed their hearts, and they follow their own desires.

To those who receive guidance, He increases guidance and bestows on them their righteousness.

—QUR'AN 47: 12, 15-17

Daily living tip: Don't proclaim righteousness with your words and then neglect righteousness with what you do. Let your actions show your faith. Don't just rap about what's right; do what's right.

Today's prayer: O my Lord, may my good deeds weigh greater than my errors.

The Charitable Will Be Rewarded.

Believe in Allah and His messenger. Donate from the resources of which He has made you heirs. For those who believe and donate is a great reward.

You must understand that the life of this world is only recreation and amusement, pageantry, and common bragging, and competition in increasing wealth and children. Consider this simile: Rain and the growth it causes delight the farmers, but soon (the growth) withers, and then you see it turning yellow until it crumbles.

In the hereafter is a severe penalty or forgiveness from Allah and wonderful bliss. What is the life of this world but enjoyment and deception?

Compete for forgiveness from your Lord and for Paradise, the width of which equates the skies and Earth and is prepared for those who believe in Allah and His messengers. Such is the bounty of Allah, bestowed on whom He pleases, and Allah is the Owner of Abundance, the Magnificent.

—QUR'AN 57: 7, 20-21

Daily living tip: Even if you only have a little money, try to find ways to be generous. Share your cookies with someone. Help someone with his or her schoolwork. Give someone a sweater you no longer wear. Be a friend to someone who is not popular. There are plenty of ways to be generous if you think about it.

Today's prayer: O my Lord, give me ideas for how I can be generous every day.

Your Charity Will Be Returned to You.

The parable of those who invest their belongings for the sake of Allah is that of a grain of corn. It grows into seven ears, and each ear has a hundred grains. Allah gives multiple increases to whom He pleases. Allah is All-embracing, the All-knowing.

Some people invest their belongings for the sake of Allah. They do not follow their donations with reminders of their generosity or with insults. They have a reward with their Lord. They will suffer no fear or grief.

Kind words and discretion about faults are better than charity followed by injury. Allah is Independent, Most Tolerant.

O Believers, do not void your acts of charity by reminders of your generosity or by injury. Don't be like those who donate in order to be seen by others and do not even believe in Allah or the last day. They are, in simile, a hard, barren rock on which is a little soil. Heavy rain falls on it, and nothing is left but a bare stone. They will not be able to do any good with their earnings. Allah does not guide those who reject faith.

—QUR'AN 2: 261-264

Daily living tip: When you help someone in any way, do not brag about it, and do not remind the person that he or she owes you a favor. Be generous out of the kindness of your heart, and trust that Allah will reward you for it.

Today's prayer: O my Lord, accept my acts of generosity and bless those who receive them.

Donate from the Blessings Allah Has Given You.

The simile of those who invest their resources, seeking to please Allah and to strengthen their souls, is a lush and fertile garden. Heavy rain falls on it and causes it to yield a double increase of harvest. If it does not receive sufficient rain, a sprinkle is good enough for it. Allah sees well whatever you do.

Does anyone want a garden with date palms and vines, underground streams, and a variety of fruit? Do you then want to become elderly with disabled children? Do you then want (your garden) to be caught up in a fiery whirlwind and burned up? Thus, Allah clarifies the signs so you may consider.

O Believers, donate from the good things you have earned and of the harvest of the earth, which We have produced for you. Do not select something inferior for donating that which you would not accept for yourself without complaint.

Know that Allah is Independent, the Praised One.

Satan threatens you with poverty and tempts you to act inappropriately. Allah, however, promises you His forgiveness and grace. Allah is All-embracing, the All-knowing.

—Qur'an 2: 265-268

Daily living tip: When you are generous with whatever Allah has given you, Allah will reward you. If you are stingy, He will leave you to struggle.

Today's prayer: O my Lord, bless me with enough that I can afford to be generous.

Your Charity Benefits Your Soul.

He grants wisdom to those He has chosen. The one who receives wisdom has received an abundant goodness. None remembers [God's graciousness] except those of pure minds.

Whatever you invest in charity or devotion, you can be sure that Allah knows it all.

The sinners, however, have no deliverer.

If you make known your acts of charity, it's okay; but, if you keep them to yourself, just making sure that they get to those in need, that is better for you. (Allah) will erase some of your sins. Allah is well aware of all that you do.

It is not required of you to save (sinners), but Allah saves whom He pleases. Whatever good you give benefits your own souls, and you will only do so if you are seeking the face of Allah. Whatever good you give will be returned to you, and you will not suffer injustice.

—QUR'AN 2: 269-272

Daily living tip: Whatever resources you have –whether it's money, food, time, etc.— budget some of it to help others. When you give to others, Allah will give to you.

Today's prayer: O my Lord, teach me how I can be generous with what I have though it may be little.

Charity Will Simplify Your Path.

Consider the night as it conceals! Consider the day as it appears in glory! Consider the creation of male and female!

Truly, that for which you all strive is diverse.

[Consider] the one who charitably gives in awe [of Allah] and testifies to the best. We will simplify for him/her the path to bliss.

[Consider] the one who is a greedy miser and [considers him-/herself] independent and denies the best. We will simplify for him/her the path to misery. His/her wealth will be of no use when he/she perishes.

Truly, We have taken the responsibility to guide. Truly, unto Us are the end and the beginning.

O Humanity, there has come to you undeniable evidence from your Lord, and We have sent unto you a guiding light [the revelations to and the ministry of Prophet Muhammed]. Those who believe in Allah and cling to Him will be shown His mercy and grace and be guided to Him along the Straight Way.

—QUR'AN 92: 1-13 AND QUR'AN 4: 174-175

Daily living tip: If you are generous with what you have and try to help people, Allah will brighten your path for you and bring more blessings into your life. If you're a tightwad, that negativity will come back on you.

Today's prayer: O my Lord, help me to cling to all Your guidance so that I may always benefit from Your mercy and grace.

You Can Recognize Those in Need

Those in need include those who are restricted in service to Allah because they are immobile and cannot work. The ignorant person thinks that, because of their meekness, they are free from need. You will recognize them by their handicaps. They do not beg annoyingly from everybody. Whatever goodness you give, you can be assured that Allah knows it well.

Those who charitably invest their resources, by night and by day, privately and publicly, have their reward with their Lord. They will know no fear or grief.

On no soul does Allah place a burden greater than it can bear. It gets every good that it earns, and it suffers every ill that it earns.

"Our Lord, do not condemn us if we forget or fall into error.

"Our Lord, do not put upon us a burden like that which You put upon those before us.

"Our Lord, do not put upon us a burden greater than we have strength to bear.

"Erase our sins and grant us forgiveness. Have mercy on us. You are our Protector. Help us against those who challenge our faith."

—QUR'AN 2: 273-274, 286

Daily living tip: Although we are called to be generous, be cautious of those who just want to take advantage of your good nature. Some people will abuse your kindness if you let them. Once you help someone out, he or she may keep asking for more and more. Don't let them wear you down. Sometimes you just have to say no.

Today's prayer: O my Lord, grant me the wisdom to know whom to help with money or other gifts and whom to help with merely advice so they don't take advantage of me.

Stop the Deeds of Those Who Steal for a Living.

As for the [unrepentant] thief, male or female, cut off his/her hands as recompense for the crime and as severe, exemplary punishment ordained by Allah. Allah is Almighty, Most Wise! If, however, the thief repents after his/her crime and amends his/her conduct, Allah will turn to him/her in forgiveness. Allah is Most Forgiving, Most Merciful.

Do you not realize that to Allah belongs the dominion of the skies and Earth? He punishes whom He pleases. He forgives whom He pleases. Allah is Most Capable over all things.

O Messenger, do not grieve over those who race each other in unbelief. [That includes] those who say, "We believe," with their mouths but whose hearts have no faith. [That includes certain] Jews who will listen to any lie and even to those who don't even know you. They take words out of context and say, "If you are given this [revelation], then you can have it! If not, beware!"

If anyone's test [of faith] is intended by Allah, you have no authority in the least for his/her sake against Allah. For such people, Allah's will is not to purify their hearts. For them there is disgrace in this world. In the hereafter is a profound punishment.

—QUR'AN 5: 38-41

Daily living tip: If you can, "cut off" someone's ability to steal, this is what the verse means. This could mean reporting the person to authorities who can take proper action. It does not mean a literal action of cutting off hands.

Today's prayer: O my Lord, help me to know what the right thing to do is when I see a wrong that needs to be addressed.

Obey Commandments.

Say, "Come, and I will cite what Allah has prohibited for you. Do not equate partners with Him. Honor your parents. Do not kill children because of your financial situation as We will provide for you and for (your babies). Do not even consider shameful deeds, whether publicly or privately. Do not destroy life that Allah has made sacred, unless it is necessary to maintain justice and order.

"Thus does He command you so you may learn good judgment.

"Do not advance toward the orphan's property, unless you intend to improve it, until he/she attains an age of competence.

"Measure and weigh fairly.

"No burden do We place on any soul except what it can bear.

"Whenever you speak, speak truthfully even if a relative is involved. Fulfill the Covenant of Allah.

"Thus does He command you so you may remember.

"This is My way leading straight. Follow it. Do not follow paths that mislead you from His path.

"Thus does He command you so you may be righteous."

—QUR'AN 6: 151-153

Daily living tip: Sometimes you will be faced with difficult decisions. Sometimes no decision will seem to be the best. That's why it is important to have Allah's commandments in your heart to guide you and give you peace with your choices.

Today's prayer: O my Lord, inscribe Your commandments on my heart and in my mind so that I will not depart from them and so they may guide me in all decisions.

Live Righteously.

Your Lord knows better than anyone what is in your hearts. If you live righteously, truly He is Most Forgiving to those who repeatedly repent to Him.

Render civil rights to your relatives, those in need, and those far from home. Do not, however, squander your resources. Truly, wasters are patrons of the evil spirits, and Satan is ungrateful to his Lord.

Even if you have to reject them in pursuit of your Lord's mercy, which you expect, speak to them words of tactful kindness.

Do not make yourself as if your hand were tied to your neck [unwilling to lend a helping hand], but also do not be so giving that you yourself become at fault and destitute. Truly, your Lord provides sustenance in abundance for whomever He pleases, and He reduces it. He does know and regard all His servants.

Do not destroy your children for financial reasons. We shall provide sustenance for them as well as for you. Truly, killing them is a tremendous sin.

—QUR'AN 17: 25-31

Daily living tip: Every morning, rededicate your life to serving the will of Allah and following His commands and guidance. Start every day with a prayer. You never know when the morning prayer saves you from a bad day.

Today's prayer: O my Lord, shower your blessings on all those of Your servants who are in need of Your grace and mercy today.

Live Morally.

Do not approach unlawful sexual activity. That is shameful! It is an evil, paving the road [to more sin].

Do not take life, which Allah has made sacred, except for reasons of justice. If anyone is wrongfully killed, We give his/her heirs authority [to demand equality or to forgive], but (an heir) should not exceed limitations in the matter of taking life, as the law already favors him/her.

Do not approach the orphan's property, except to improve it [ie, invest it], until he/she attains legal age of adulthood.

Fulfill every agreement, for each contract will be explored [on the Day of Judgment].

Give full measure when you measure, and weigh with a balanced scale. That is the most appropriate and the most advantageous in the final determination.

Do not pursue that of which you have no knowledge. Indeed, the hearing, the sight, and the heart will be questioned.

Do not walk upon the earth with impertinence, because you cannot split the earth asunder or climb the highest mountain.

Of all such things, sin is disgusting in the sight of your Lord.

These are among the wisdom your Lord has revealed to you.

Do not accept, along with Allah, another object of worship. If you do, you will be driven to Hell, guilty and scorned.

—Qur'an 17: 32-39

Daily living tip: Some people may try to tell you that sexual freedom is now part of our society and is no longer haram (forbidden). They are wrong. When Allah makes something haram, it stays haram. Sexual sins include any sexual activity outside marriage and sodomy for both men and women. (Of course, rape is a serious crime.)

Today's prayer: O my Lord, empower me to keep away from all sexual sins. If I know someone who is struggling with a sexual sin, empower me to help that person leave that lifestyle if he or she chooses.

Do Not Charge Exorbitant Interest.

You cannot attain perfection until you spend [charitably] from what you love. Allah is certainly well aware of whatever you give.

O Believers, do not consume usury, which is [interest or fees] doubled and multiplied, but fear Allah for your prosperity.

Fear the fire, which is prepared for the disbelievers. Obey Allah and the messenger so you may obtain mercy.

Hasten to forgiveness from your Lord. A garden whose expanse is that of the skies and Earth is prepared for the righteous. They invest, whether in times of prosperity or adversity. They restrain anger and forgive people. Allah loves those who perform goodwill. [He loves] those who, having committed a regretful deed or otherwise wronged their own souls, earnestly remember Allah and ask for forgiveness for their sins. And who can forgive sins except Allah? [The forgiven] do not intentionally persist in their sinful lifestyles. For such as those, their reward is forgiveness from their Lord and gardens, with underground rivers, for an eternal dwelling. How excellent a recompense for those who achieve!

—QUR'AN 3: 92, 130-136

Daily living tip: Usury (*riba* in Arabic, which means 'to exceed') is the addition of exorbitant interest on loans. In Islam, the proper fees added to a loan is called 'cost-plus financing' (*murabaha* in Arabic). If those murabaha fees are also exorbitant, that is another form of usury. If you make a loan, put the pay-back deal in writing, and charge a fair amount for paying it back. The written contract should be signed by the lender and the borrower.

Today's prayer: O my Lord, help me know how to be fair in all dealings with money and other resources.

Be Reasonable in Retribution.

The punishment for damages is equal to the damages. However, if a person forgives and reconciles, his/her reward is due from Allah. Allah does not love those who are unjust.

Certainly, as for whoever defends him-/herself after damages to him/her, there is no reason to blame him/her. The blame is only on those who oppress people and transgress throughout the land, in defiance of justice. For them will be a terrible punishment.

If any exhibit patience and forgiveness, that would truly be an exercise of courage in the conduct of affairs.

Follow the inspiration given to you. Be patient until Allah passes judgment. He is the best to decide.

If they argue with you, say, "I have submitted my whole self to Allah, and so have those with me."

To the people of the Book and to the people without any [religious] instruction, say, "Do you also submit?"

If they do, they are truly guided. If they regress, your duty is only to convey the message. In Allah's sight are all His servants.

—QUR'AN 42: 40-43 AND QUR'AN 10: 109 AND QUR'AN 3: 20

Daily living tip: It's not up to you to judge and punish people. Of course, justice must be done in cases of crimes, but do not retaliate out of anger. Do not try to make a judgment about the state of another person's soul. Leave that to Allah and be patient until He makes the final judgment.

Today's prayer: O my Lord, help me to control my anger when people wrong me. Teach me to respond with gentleness and kindness while also standing up for my rights.

Be Kind to Your Parents.

Your Lord has decreed that you worship none except Him and that you be kind to parents. Whether one or both of them live to attain old age, never say an unkind word to them. Do not reject them. Address them in terms of honor.

Out of kindness, lower to them the wing of humility. Say, "My Lord, have mercy on them as they cherished me in childhood.

We appointed each person to honor parents. In labor and agony did one's mother give birth and nursed him/her for two years. Show gratitude to Me and to your parents. To Me is your destiny.

If, however, parents try to make you associate partners with Me, [worshiping] things of which you get no instruction, do not obey them, but respectfully endure their company in this life. Follow the way of those who turn to Me. Finally, to Me is your return, and I will tell you about all that you did.

Whoever submits his/her whole self to Allah and lives righteously has secured the most trustworthy grasp. With Allah is the termination of all accounts.

—QUR'AN 17: 23-24 AND QUR'AN 31: 14-15, 22

Daily living tip: You are extremely blessed if you have loving, righteous parents. Some people have rotten parents. Some have no parents or only foster parents. If your parents or guardians are not the best, still honor them and be respectful to them. Remember that you do not have to grow up to be like them. Endure them until you are in a position to establish your life according to the will of Allah. Forgive your parents or guardians for any shortcomings. They are only human and may be doing the best they know how.

Today's prayer: O my Lord, bless my parents or guardians and give them proper guidance. Help me to honor them in the way that I live.

Allow Women the Same Dignity as Men.

Ensure that (the women) live in the same fashion as you [men] live, according to your means. Do not inconvenience them [with strict rules]. If they are pregnant, support them until they deliver what they carry; and then, if they breastfeed, give them money during that time too. Make decisions together [husband and wife] with kindness. If you have difficulties, get another woman to provide care [for the child] on your behalf.

The man of wealth should spend [on his wife] according to his means. The man with limited income should spend according to what Allah has given him. Allah does not burden anyone beyond what He has provided him. After any difficulty, Allah will soon grant relief.

If you avoid the worst actions forbidden to you, We shall acquit you of all sin and admit you to a gate of great honor.

Never covet the gifts that Allah has bestowed on some more freely than on others. Men are allotted what they earn, and women are allotted what they earn. Ask Allah of His bounty. Allah has full knowledge of all things.

—Qur'an 65: 6- 7 and Qur'an 4: 31-32

Daily living tip: Men and women have equal rights and responsibilities in Islam. Never deny anyone's right to fair and equal treatment. If you see someone being oppressed, try to help if you can. You can stick up for the person with words and with prayer.

Today's prayer: O my Lord, help me remember to always show respect and appreciation for everyone and to acknowledge their personal rights.

Do Not Defame the Character of Women.

Truly, those who slander virtuous women –even imprudent but believing women— are condemned in this life and in the hereafter. A grievous penalty awaits them. On that day, their tongues, hands, and feet will testify against them because of their actions. On that day, Allah will pay them their fair dues, and they will realize that Allah is the apparent truth.

Vile women are for vile men, and vile men are for vile women.

Women of purity are for men of purity, and men of purity are for women of purity. These are not affected by what people say. For them there is forgiveness and an honorable provision.

Allah offers an example for the disbelievers: the wife of Noah and the wife of Lot. They belonged to two of Our righteous servants, but they betrayed (their husbands), and they gained nothing before Allah because of their actions. They were told, "Enter the fire along with all those who enter."

Allah offers an example for the disbelievers: the wife of Pharaoh. She said, "My Lord, build for me, near to You, a home in Paradise. Save me from Pharaoh and his actions. Save me from the sinners.

[Another example is] Mary, a daughter of Imran, who guarded her chastity. We breathed into her of Our Spirit. She testified to the truth of the words of her Lord and of His revelations. She was one of the devout.

—QUR'AN 24: 23-26 AND QUR'AN 66: 10-12

Daily living tip: Do not listen to music that refers to women as "bitches" and "hoes." Do not use the offensive names "bitch" and "son of a bitch." These words demean all women and add to a culture of crimes against women. If you listen to music, let it rock you without using rocks that hurt your soul.

Today's prayer: O my Lord, help me avoid learning an offensive vocabulary. Instead, give me an effective vocabulary to express my feelings when necessary to do so.

Men and Women Should Not Be Provocative in Dress or Actions.

Say to the believing men that they should lower their gazes [ie, do not cast flirtatious glances] and maintain their modesty [ie, act and dress modestly].

Say to the believing women that they should lower their gazes [ie, do not cast flirtatious glances] and maintain their modesty [ie, act and dress modestly]. They should not [make a vain] display of their beauty except what is apparent [ie, what is appropriate for any given society]. They should cover their breasts with their outer garments and not [openly] display their beauty except to their husbands, their fathers, their husbands' fathers, their sons, their husbands' sons, their brothers or their brothers' sons, their sisters' sons and also their female servants, male servants free of sexual desires, and also small children who have no idea of sexual discretion. Also, they should not tap their feet in order to draw attention to their hidden attributes.

O Believers, turn all together towards Allah that you may succeed.

—QUR'AN 24: 30-31

Daily living tip: Some non-Muslims may make fun of your modest clothing because they don't think it's fashionable. That's okay. It's okay to be weird. You don't have to be like other people. You don't have to fit in with the in-crowd. Enjoy your weirdness as a Muslim. Make your own style and be happy to be you.

Today's prayer: O my Lord, if I see someone immodestly dressed, remind me that he or she may not know any better and let me not be judgmental.

Be Tactful in Speech.

Say to My servants that they should speak tactfully, because Satan instigates conflicts among them. Satan is an avowed enemy to Humanity.

Your Lord knows you best. If He pleases, He grants you mercy. If He pleases, He sends punishment. We have not sent you [Muhammed] as a guardian over them. Your Lord knows best all beings of the skies and Earth. We bestowed on some prophets more gifts than on others, and We gave to David the Psalms.

One day We shall call together all human beings with their [religious] leaders. Whoever is given his/her record in his/her right hand will [be among those who] read their records, and they will not be wronged even the width of a date seed fiber. Whoever would not see in this world will be blind in the hereafter and more astray from the path.

Their intention has been to tempt you away from that which We revealed to you [Muhammed], and to substitute, in Our name, something quite different. Certainly, they would have called you 'friend'. If We had not given you fortitude, you may have given-in to them just a little.

—QUR'AN 17: 53-55, 71-74

Daily living tip: You won't win anyone to Islam by being abrasive and condescending. Speak with respect and kindness to everyone. Even if someone insults you, respond in a way that takes him or her off guard. When you give a kind word in response to a mean word, it disarms the person.

Today's prayer: O my Lord, grant me the wisdom to select the best words in response to mean words. Help me to control my anger and represent Your grace and mercy.

Allah's True Servants Respond
with Words of "Peace!"

Blessed is He who made constellations in the skies and placed therein a lamp [the sun] and a moon reflecting light. He is the One who made the night and the day to follow each other, for the sake of whoever desires to remember [Him] and be grateful.

The servants of the Most Gracious are those who walk upon the earth in humility, and who, when the ignorant address them, say, "Peace!" [They are] those who spend the night in adoration of their Lord as they prostrate and stand. [They are] those who say, "Our Lord, avert from us the wrath of Hell, for its wrath is indeed inescapable. It is indeed a wretched residence and place for retirement." [They are] those who, in spending, are neither extravagant nor miserly, but maintain moderation.

[They are] those who call upon no god but Allah. They do not end life, which Allah has made sacred, except in matters of justice. They do not commit acts of sexual immorality. Anyone guilty [of any of these crimes] reaps punishment. The penalty on the Day of Resurrection will be doubled, and he/she will exist with shame continuously. [That is] unless he/she repents, believes, and lives righteously. Allah will exchange the evil of such a person for goodness. Allah is Most Forgiving, Most Merciful.

Whoever repents and lives righteously has truly turned to Allah with true conversion.

—QUR'AN 25: 61-71

Daily living tip: You will meet all kinds of rude and obnoxious people in this world. Be patient with yourself as you learn how to respond to them peacefully and with kindness without letting them walk all over you.

Today's prayer: O my Lord, may the words from my mouth be those of peace and goodwill regardless of how rude other people may be.

Observe Courtesy in Assembly and Consultation.

O Believers, when you are told to make room in assembly, make room [by moving closer together to allow others into the assembly]. Allah will provide space for you. When you are told to rise, rise [respectfully].

Allah will raise to prestigious levels those of you who believe and who have been granted knowledge. Allah is well acquainted with all that you do.

O Believers, when you consult the messenger, invest something in charity before your private consultation. That would be good for you and most appropriate. If you don't have [anything to donate], Allah is Most Forgiving, Most Merciful

Are you reluctant to give charitably before your private consultations? If you don't do so, and Allah forgives you, then establish routine prayer, practice standard charity, and obey Allah and His messenger. Allah is well acquainted with all that you do.

—QUR'AN 58: 11-13

Daily living tip: Learn the rules of courtesy for being in congregations, like in the mosques. Be respectful of those around you. Don't be loud or boisterous. Be polite.

Today's prayer: O my Lord, keep me reminded that good manners are a reflection of Your grace, and help me to do my best to portray You correctly.

Allow Allah to Consume Your Total Being.

Indeed, Allah commands justice, goodness, and generosity to neighbors and relatives. He forbids immorality, evil, and oppression. He admonishes you so that you may heed.

Fulfill the Covenant of Allah once you have entered into it [by submitting your whole self to Him]. Also, keep promises you have made because now you have made Allah your warranty. Allah knows all that you do.

What is of you must vanish; what is of Allah will endure. On those who patiently persevere, We will certainly grant their reward in response to the best of their deeds. To any man or woman who performs righteously and has faith, We will give New Life –a life that is good and pure. On such people, We will grant their reward in response to the best of their deeds.

When you read the Qur'an, seek Allah's protection from Satan, the rejected one. He has no authority over those who believe and put their trust in the Lord. His authority is only over those who ally with him and with those who assign partners [with Allah].

—QUR'AN 16: 90-91, 96-100

Daily living tip: Once you commit your whole self to Allah, everything you are and everything you have belongs to Him. When you realize this and accept it, you will be at peace with whatever happens to you because you know that your life belongs to Allah to do with as He wills.

Today's prayer: O my Lord, empty myself of all that is me and fill me with all that is You.

Live with Dignity.

[The servants of the Most Gracious are] those who do not witness falsely, and who, when encountering futility, pass it with dignity. [They are] those who, when they are admonished with the signs of their Lord, do not ignore them as if they couldn't hear or see.

[They are] those who pray, "Our Lord, grant us spouses and children who will bring pleasure to our eyes and allow us to be examples for the believers."

They are the ones who will be rewarded with the highest place [in Heaven] because of their patient perseverance. Therein, they will be met with greetings and peace. They will dwell therein forever. How beautiful an abode and place of retirement!

Say [to the scoffers], "My Lord will not bother with you if you do not pray. You have certainly scoffed! Soon the inevitable will come!

Consider time! Truly, humanity is at a loss. The exceptions are those who have faith, perform righteous deeds, and unite in teaching truth and perseverance.

—QUR'AN 25: 72-77 AND QUR'AN 103

Daily living tip: Become someone who lives with dignity and honor, always seeking to speak kindly and act righteously. Don't be rude and obnoxious. Don't be a smarty pants. Have good manners.

Today's prayer: O my Lord, bless my time and help me to use it wisely in striving to be a valuable contributor to society.

Do Not Engage in Gossip.

Beware, every slanderer and gossiper. He/she collects wealth and hoards it. He/she thinks that his/her wealth will make him/her immortal. Nonsense! He/she will surely be thrown into the crusher. What will explain to you the crusher? It is the fire kindled by Allah. It leaps to the hearts. Truly, it confines them. [It will be] in elongated columns.

O Believers, if a wicked person brings you any news, ascertain the truth. Otherwise, you may harm people unwittingly, and afterwards be sorry for what you have done.

O Believers, men among you should not laugh at others. It may be that (those ridiculed) are better than (such men). Women should not [laugh at others]. It may be that (those ridiculed) are better than (such women). Do not defame or be sarcastic to one another. Do not call each other ugly names. "Wretched" is the name of disobedience after having attained faith. Those who continue are in the wrong.

O Believers, avoid being overly suspicious because some suspicions are sinful. Do not spy on each other, and do not gossip. Would you eat the flesh of your dead brother? No, you would abhor it! Fear Allah who is the Most Forgiving, the Most Merciful.

—QUR'AN 104 AND QUR'AN 49: 6, 11-12

Daily living tip: Avoid bullying, gossip, name-calling, making fun of people, and any other activity that hurts people's feelings and damages their reputations. People that do those things are jerks. They're no good to anybody. They're losers.

Today's prayer: O my Lord, protect me from those who would tell lies about me. Give me courage to stick up for victims of gossip and bullying.

Do Not Be Insincere in Worship.

Do you know someone who denies the judgment? Such a person ignores the orphan. He/she does not encourage the feeding of the poor.

Woe to the worshipers insincere in their prayers. They want only to be seen. They deny simple aid.

Say, "O unbelievers! I do not worship what you worship. You do not worship what I worship. I will never worship that which you tend to worship. You may never worship what I worship. To you be your way, and to me be mine!"

Doomed are the hands of the Father of Flame! He will perish. He will not profit from all his wealth and belongings. He will burn in a fire of blazing flame. His wife will carry the wood for the fuel. [She will have] a rope of palm leaf fiber around her neck.

Truly, We have given you abundance. Therefore, pray to your Lord, and sacrifice. Truly, your enemy will be cut off.

—QUR'AN 107 AND QUR'AN 109 AND QUR'AN 111 AND QUR'AN 108

Daily living tip: Thousands of children and adults are homeless, hungry, and without medical care. Whatever you can do to help someone, do it for the love of Allah and humanity. Even a small act of kindness can make a big difference.

Today's prayer: O my Lord, provide me with opportunities to practice my faith by helping others.

Be Clean When You Approach Allah in Worship.

O Believers, when you prepare for prayer, wash your faces and your hands to the elbows. Rub your heads and your feet to the ankles. If you are in a state of ceremonial impurity, bathe your whole bodies. If you are sick, on a journey, coming from the toilet, or have been sexually involved, and you cannot find water, clean your faces and hands with clean sand. Allah does not want to place you in difficulty. He only wants to make you clean and to complete His favor to you so that you may be grateful.

Remember the favor of Allah unto you. [Remember] His covenant, with which He bound you when you said, "We hear and we obey." Fear Allah. Certainly, Allah knows well the secrets of your hearts.

O Believers, stand firmly for Allah as witnesses for justice. Do not let the hatred of others prevent you from bringing about justice. Be just; that is next to piety; and fear Allah. Indeed, Allah is well acquainted with all that you do.

To those who believe and do deeds of righteousness, Allah has promised forgiveness and a great reward.

—Qur'an 5: 6-9

Daily living tip: Use soap and water whenever possible to stay physically clean. Be prepared for when you don't have access to water by carrying a wudu stone. Choose a pretty stone, like a river rock, and keep it with you. If there is no water, simulate cleaning yourself by rubbing the stone between your hands and then symbolically wiping your face and head.

Today's prayer: O my Lord, when I cleanse myself physically, remind me that You are cleansing me spiritually. Help me to be deserving of Your grace.

Dress Nicely When You Go to Worship.

O Children of Adam, wear your beautiful clothes at every place of prayer. Eat and drink but do not waste by excesses [ie, gluttony]. Allah does not love wasteful people.

Say, "Who has forbidden the beautiful apparel of Allah that He has produced for His servants, and the pure things for sustenance?" Say, "They are, in the life of this world, for those who believe. They will be exclusively for them on the Day of Resurrection. Thus do We explain the signs for those who know."

Say, "My Lord has only forbidden shameful deeds, whether open or secret. [He has forbidden] sins and trespasses against truth. [He has forbidden] assigning partners, to Allah, for which He has given no authority. [He has forbidden] saying things about Allah that you don't know."

To every people is a term appointed. When their term is reached, they cannot cause an hour in delay or progress.

O Children of Adam, [listen] whenever there comes to you messengers from among you, reciting My Scriptures to you. Those who fear Allah and who reform shall have no fear or grief on them.

—QUR'AN 7: 31-35

Daily living tip: Before you leave your house, look in a full-length mirror and make sure you are presentable for being in public. Don't be among those who don't care how they look. If you are going to the mosque, make sure that you can prostrate without revealing your underwear or backside.

Today's prayer: O my Lord, make my physical appearance and my spiritual appearance both pleasing to You and good reflections of dignity and grace.

Success Comes from Obeying Allah's Commands.

Indeed, the believers succeed. [They are] those who are humble in prayers. [They] avoid frivolous talk. [They] are active in charity. [They] abstain from sex except with their spouses or whom their right hands possess [after the are freed and married], and then indeed they are free from blame. Whoever seeks beyond (those limits) are sinners. As for those who faithfully observe their trusts and covenants and who guard their prayers, they will be heirs who will inherit Paradise where they will dwell forever.

We originated humanity from a product of mud. Afterward, We placed him/her as a seed in safe lodging. Next, We fashioned the seed into a mass of blood, and then We fashioned the mass into a lump, [that looked like] something chewed [like chewing gum]. Next, We added bones and clothed the bones with flesh. We then developed all this as a new creation. Blessed is Allah, the Best of Creators!

Eventually, you will die. Again, on the Day of Resurrection, you will be raised.

We have made above you seven layers [of sky], and We never neglect creation.

—QUR'AN 23: 1-17

Daily living tip: In our society, you have to make a sincere commitment to do the right things. You can easily be misled if you don't remake that commitment every single day and be determined to keep it.

Today's prayer: O my Lord, make me strong in determination so that I will not be wrongly influenced by others and depart from Your ways.

Permission is Given to Fight in Self-Defense.

Permission is given to those against whom war is waged [to fight in self-defense] because they are wronged. Truly, Allah, for their victory, is Most Powerful. [They are] those expelled from their homes in defiance of right simply because they say, "Our Lord is Allah." If Allah had not curtailed one society by means of another, there would surely have been razed monasteries, churches, synagogues, and mosques in which the name of Allah is extensively celebrated. Allah will certainly aid those who help Him. Truly, Allah is the Strongest, the Victorious. [They are] those who, when We establish them in the land, institute ritual prayer, give the required charity, and promote the right and forbid the wrong. To Allah belongs the outcome of events.

If [the disbelievers] deny you [treating your ministry as false], truly, societies before them also denied –the people of Noah, the Ad and the Thamud, the people of Abraham and the people of Lot, and the inhabitants of Midian. Moses was also rejected. I granted a reprieve to the disbelievers, and later I seized them. How terrible was My punishment!

—QUR'AN 22: 39-44

Daily living tip: If you can, attend a martial arts school where practical and efficient self-defense techniques are practiced. Do not approach martial arts as a sport. Practice it as a life skill as well as an art form. Be prepared to defend yourself.

Today's prayer: O my Lord, grant me physical strength so that I can protect myself or others if confronted with a threat.

Even War Has Rules of Ethics.

You must fight, in the way of Allah, those who attack you. Do not break the rules [of fair fighting]. Allah does not love those who go too far.

You must execute them wherever you overtake them. Expel them from those places from where they have expelled you. Turmoil and oppression are worse than killing [in self-defense].

Do not fight them at the Sacred Mosque, unless they first attack you there. If they attack you, you must fight them. Such is the consequence of those who suppress faith.

If they cease, Allah is Most Forgiving, Most Merciful.

Fight them until there is no more oppression and until the religion is free for Allah. If they stop fighting, let there be no more trouble, except against those who continue being oppressive.

War [for national security] is ordained for you, even though you hate it. It is possible that something you hate is actually a good thing, and that something you like is bad for you. Allah knows, and you don't know.

—QUR'AN 2: 190-193, 216

Daily living tip: An old saying is, "All is fair in love and war." In Islam, this is not true. We have boundaries for all areas of living. Sometimes we must fight, but even then, we must have honor and integrity.

Today's prayer: O my Lord, make me smart enough to know when I need to act, brave enough to do the action, and wise enough to act within the boundaries of Islam.

Fight for Religious Freedom.

O Believers, fight [in self-defense] the disbelievers who surround you, and let them find fortitude in you. Know that Allah is with those who fear Him.

Whenever a chapter [of the Qur'an] descends, some of them say, "Who among you has had an increase in faith because of it?" Those who do believe experience an increase in faith, and they rejoice. But those in whose hearts is a disease experience doubt added to their doubt, and they will die as disbelievers. Do they not realize that they are tried [and called to faith] once or twice every year; yet, they do not repent, and they do not heed.

Whenever a chapter descends, they look at each other [and say], "Is anyone looking?" and then they turn aside. Allah has deflected their hearts because they are a people who [by their own choice] do not understand.

Now a messenger [Prophet Muhammed] from among yourselves [the common people] has come to you. It distresses him that you should perish [unsaved], so passionately concerned is he over you.

To the believers, he is most kind and merciful. If they regress, however, say, "Allah is sufficient for me. No god is there except Him. On Him I put my trust. He is the Lord of the Glorious Throne."

—QUR'AN 9: 123-129

Daily living tip: Freedom of religion is an important human right for everyone. You may never have to go to war to protect religious freedom, but you may find yourself in a position where you have to defend your personal freedom or the freedom of someone else. Stand up for what is right but try to do it in a way that is safe. Try to avoid a physical altercation.

Today's prayer: O my Lord, if someone or a group challenges the rights and freedoms of myself or others, help me to know what I should do. Grant me wisdom and safety.

Fight in the Defense of Others.

O Believers, take your precaution, and go forth either in units or as one army. Among you are certainly men who would lag behind. If a tragedy affects you, someone may say, "Truly, Allah did me a favor in my not being among them." If victory from Allah becomes yours, he would certainly say –as if there had never been ties of affection between you and him, "Oh, I wish I had been with them! I would have made a fine thing of it."

Those who fight in the cause of Allah should be those who trade the life of this world for the eternal life. To him/her who fights for the sake of Allah –whether he/she is killed or wins victory, We shall soon give him/her a great reward.

Why would you not fight, in the cause of Allah, for those who, being weak, are oppressed men, women, and children, who are crying, "Our Lord, rescue us from this society of oppressive people. Send, from You to us, someone who will protect. Send, from You to us, someone who will defend"?

Believers fight for the sake of Allah. Disbelievers fight for the sake of evil. Fight against Satan's advocates. Satan's cunning is indeed feeble.

—QUR'AN 4: 71-76

Daily living tip: Insh'Allah, you won't have to have a physical altercation to protect someone, but be wise enough to know when that is needed. The first thing to know about defense is to use physical force only as a last resort. Sometimes it takes more courage to just walk away. Avoid a fight when you can, but be brave enough to stick up for others when words and evasive actions fail. Learning a martial art is a life skill.

Today's prayer: O my Lord, grant me the wisdom to know when physical action is necessary and the courage to face what needs to be done.

Allied Forces Must Prevent Oppression.

Truly, those who believed and emigrated and struggled diligently, using their property and their lives, in the cause of Allah [are allies]. Those who gave refuge and assistance are also allies of one another.

As for those who believed but did not emigrate, you do not owe protection to them until they do emigrate. If they seek your aid in religion, however, it is your duty to help them. The exception is [not to help] against another people with whom you have a treaty of mutual alliance. Allah sees all that you do!

The disbelievers are allies of one another. Unless you do the same, there will be oppression over the earth, along with extensive corruption.

Those who believed and emigrated and struggled in the cause of Allah and those who provided refuge and assistance are truly believers. For them are forgiveness and a generous provision.

Those who believed subsequently and emigrated and struggled with you are part of you. Those who are connected by birth share birthrights in the Book of Allah [the universal plan].

Truly, Allah is the All-knowing of all things.

—QUR'AN 8: 72-75

Daily living tip: Show gratitude to veterans who served your country. Most of them enlisted for honorable reasons and were exploited and mistreated by the government. When you recognize a veteran (sometimes they wear hats), tell him or her, "Welcome home from your military service." Many of them never heard that.

Today's prayer: O my Lord, give comfort and peace to veterans plagued with memories of the horrors of wars –particularly unjust wars.

Don't Neglect Service.

[Sometimes] a chapter descends and beckons them to believe in Allah and to struggle along with His messenger. Those with influence among them ask you for exemption. They say, "Leave us to be among those who remain."

They prefer to be with those who remain behind. Their hearts are sealed, so they do not understand.

As for the messenger and those who believe with him and who strive, they use their financial resources and their physical beings. Good things are in store for them, and they will prosper. Allah has prepared for them Paradise, underneath which rivers flow, where they will dwell forever. That is the great victory!

O Believers, fear Allah and be among those who are true.

Those who believed, suffered exile, and fought in Allah's way have the hope of the mercy of Allah. Allah is Most Forgiving, Most Merciful.

Of those who died in the way of Allah, do not say, "They are dead." No, they are alive, although you do not perceive it.

—QUR'AN 9: 86-89, 119 AND QUR'AN 2: 218 AND QUR'AN 2: 154

Daily living tip: If you plan to join the military, be sure that you are strong in your morals, ethics, and values. Temptations and religious ridicule are difficulties you will face. You will need as much spiritual strength as physical strength to serve. Also, take some training in self-defense before enlisting because sexual assaults are rampant.

Today's prayer: O my Lord, protect all those serving with honor and integrity. May their service to my country not put them in spiritual danger from those who do not serve honorably.

Allah Can Use Even War to Strengthen Faith.

When the believers [engaged in combat] saw the opposing forces, they said, "Allah and His messenger warned us of this, and Allah and His messenger were right!" It added only to their faith and obedience.

Among the believers are people who have adhered faithfully to their covenant with Allah. Of them some have fulfilled their mission in life, and some are still in service and remain undaunted.

Allah will reward people of truth for their honesty. He will either punish the hypocrites or forgive them, in accordance with His will. Allah is Most Forgiving, Most Merciful.

Allah repelled the angry disbelievers. They gained no advantage. Allah spared the believers from having to fight. Allah is Strongest, Victorious.

As for those [specific] people of the Book who aided (the disbelievers), Allah cast them from their vantage points and wrought terror into their hearts. You killed some and took some as prisoners. He made you heirs of their acres, houses, resources, and a land with which you were not familiar. Allah is, concerning everything, the Most Capable.

—QUR'AN 33: 22-27

Daily living tip: If you do not plan to join the military, find other ways to serve. That can be as simple as donating pet food to an animal shelter or as time-consuming as volunteering to work in a food kitchen.

Today's prayer: O my Lord, help me find ways to be of service to my community and let this service make my faith stronger.

Believers Killed in Battle Are Alive with Allah.

(The disbelievers) say, about their brothers, while they themselves just sit, "If only (those soldiers) had listened to us, they would not have been killed."

Say, "Avert your own deaths if you are telling the truth."

Do not think of those killed in the way of Allah as dead. No, they live, finding their provisions in the presence of their Lord. They rejoice in the bounty provided by Allah. They receive good news about those who have not yet joined them and are left behind –that they will have no fear or grief. They glory in the grace and the bounty from Allah and in the fact that Allah does not allow the reward of the faithful to be lost.

Those who answered the call of Allah and the Messenger, even after being wounded, those who do right and refrain from wrong have a great reward.

People said to them, "A great army is gathering against you, so be afraid."

That increased their faith, however. They said, "Allah is enough for us, and He is the best Trustee."

They returned with grace and bounty from Allah. No harm ever touched them, for they followed the good pleasure of Allah. Allah is the owner of bounty.

—Qur'an 3: 168-174

Daily living tip: When someone's life is cut short, it seems so unfair. Certainly, the life of this world has its hardships. We take comfort in knowing that somehow, sometime Allah will make everything turn out alright. This life is not the end, and we have the hope of the hereafter.

Today's prayer: O my Lord, may Your servants find that death is only a beautiful and peaceful journey to our real home, which is Paradise.

Believers' Bodies and Possessions Belong to Allah.

Allah has purchased from the believers their selves and their possessions in exchange for Paradise. They fight in the way of Allah, and slay and are slain. There is a truthful promise upon Him in the Torah [spoken to Moses], the Gospel [of Jesus], and the Qur'an [delivered to Muhammed]. Who is more faithful to His covenant than Allah? So rejoice in the transaction you have contracted! It is the supreme accomplishment. [It is] for those who repent, who worship, who give praises, who go out [to do the will of Allah], who bow and prostrate [in prayer], who promote good and forbid evil, and who observe the limits set by Allah. So proclaim glad tidings to the believers.

Allah will not betray people after He has guided them in order to clarify to them what to beware. Allah is the All-knowing of such things. Truly, the dominion of Heaven and Earth belongs to Allah. He gives life, and He causes death. Except for Him, you have no guardian or assistant.

—QUR'AN 9: 111-112, 115-116

Daily living tip: When you realize that everything you are and everything you have all belong to Allah, you will feel more at ease. When you submit your whole self to Allah, you are in His care. Be assured that He has good plans for you.

Today's prayer: O my Lord, take my whole self and all that I have into Your loving care. Guide me safely into the future that You have prepared for me.

Fight to Win.

As for those who reject Allah and discourage people from the path of Allah, He will render their deeds astray. As for those who believe and perform deeds of righteousness and believe in what was revealed to Muhammed, as truth from their Lord, He will erase their sins, and He will heal their minds. This is because the disbelievers follow lies while believers follow truth from their Lord. Allah explains for people by such examples.

[When war is necessary for self-defense,] when you engage the disbelievers, smite them on their necks. Finally, when the enemies are subdued, firmly hold them to a bond [a fair POW agreement] until time for generous release or ransom after the burden of war has ended.

Thus you are commanded. If Allah had so willed, He could certainly have exacted retribution from them Himself, but [He allows war] in order to test you [for willingness to sacrifice] and others [in the event they might believe].

The deeds of those slain in the cause of Allah will never be for loss. Soon Allah will guide them and improve their conditions. [He will] admit them to the Paradise He has announced for them.

—QUR'AN 47: 1-6

Daily living tip: Go out every day, realizing that you are fighting a war. This is not a physical war, but it is a spiritual war to overcome all adversities in the path of peace, justice, and righteousness. You will be confronted with all kinds of vulgarity and ugliness in this world. You must stay strong and fight to win against all temptations and wickedness.

Today's prayer: O my Lord, help me to go out in the way of Your cause as I must battle the harmful influences of this world of evil and corruption.

Pray for Victory.

Muhammed is no more than a messenger. Certainly, many messengers passed before him. If he died or was killed, would you turn back on your heels? Whoever turns back on his/her heels will not harm Allah at all, but Allah will reward the grateful people.

A soul cannot die except by Allah's permission, at a determined time. To whoever desires a reward in this life, We shall give it to him/her. To whoever desires a reward in the hereafter, We shall give it to him/her. We will reward the grateful people.

How many of the prophets fought and with them large bands of devout people? They never lost heart from whatever [hardship] they met in Allah's way, and they did not weaken or give in. Allah loves the patient people.

Their only words were, "Our Lord, forgive us our sins and any excesses in our affairs. Establish our feet firmly and grant us victory over the disbelievers."

Allah gave them a reward in this world and the excellent reward of the hereafter. Allah loves the righteous people.

—QUR'AN 3: 144-148

Daily living tip: People may make fun of you for refusing to join them in such actions as drinking alcohol, smoking, using drugs, and engaging in sexual acts without marriage. Stand firm. When you get older, you will be glad that you abstained from sins that others are addicted to, and they will envy your good health.

Today's prayer: O my Lord, establish my feet firmly in obedience to Your will for my life. Let me not follow the ways of the misguided.

Struggle in the Purpose of Allah.

O Believers, shall I guide you to a bargain that will save you from a painful torment? Believe in Allah and His messenger and struggle in the purpose of Allah, risking your possessions as well as your lives. That would be to your advantage. If you could only imagine! He will forgive your sins and allow you to enter Paradise beneath which rivers flow and into elegant mansions in the gardens of eternity. That is the supreme achievement. You will get something else to cherish: help from Allah and a speedy victory [over your trials]. So give the good news to believers.

O Believers, be helpers for Allah in the manner that Jesus son of Mary invited his disciples, "Who will be my helpers for Allah?"

The disciples said, "We are Allah's helpers."

Some of the Children of Israel believed, and some disbelieved. We empowered the believers against their enemies, and they prevailed.

—QUR'AN 61: 10-14

Daily living tip: When you realize you are a soldier in the army of Allah, you are better prepared to face a world of enemies. These enemies may seem to be your friends and may even be members of your family. If anyone tempts you to leave the path of Allah, however, that person is not your friend. Stand for righteousness, and you will be successful.

Today's prayer: O my Lord, grant Your guidance to those who tend to go astray. Empower me to be able to be a positive influence in their lives so they may be guided to the Straight Way.

Be Firm in Matters of Conflict.

Like the behavior of the people of Pharaoh and of those preceding them, they rejected the signs of their Lord. We destroyed them for their crimes. We drowned the people of Pharaoh, for they were all sinful.

The worst of creatures, in the sight of Allah, are disbelievers who will never believe. They are among those with whom you made a treaty. Then they broke the treaty every time, with no fear [of God].

If you defeat them in battle, use them [ie, the harsh example of the defeat] to oust those behind them so that (those who follow them) may take heed.

If you fear treachery from any group, revert [from the treaty] on fair terms. Allah certainly does not love traitors.

Do not allow the disbelievers to think that they can overcome. Certainly, they will never overpower.

Prepare for them to the best of your ability with your strength and horsepower, in order to strike terror into the enemies of Allah and you. That includes any about whom you may be unaware, although Allah is aware.

Whatever you must spend in the cause of Allah shall be repaid to you. You will not be treated unfairly.

—QUR'AN 8: 54-60

Daily living tip: When people in your life confront you with ridicule for your beliefs, make sure they know you will not be swayed. Tell them and show them that your values, morals, and ethics are part of your lifestyle. Face the disbelievers with a happy face; that is your weapon.

Today's prayer: O my Lord, bless me with friends who share my lifestyle so that we may unite against those who would lead us away.

Settle Things Peacefully When Possible.

If (your enemy) inclines toward peace, you must also incline toward (peace), and trust in Allah. Truly, He is the All-hearing, the All=knowing.

If they intend to deceive you, then truly Allah is enough for you. He has strengthened you with His aid and with believers. Furthermore, He has placed affection among their hearts. If you had spent all that is contained in the earth, you could not have produced that affection, but Allah has done it! He truly is the Victorious, the Perfectly Wise.

O Prophet, Allah is sufficient for you and for those who follow you from among the believers.

O Prophet, rouse the believers to the fight! If there are twenty among you, who are persevering, they will vanquish two hundred. If there are a hundred, they will vanquish a thousand disbelievers, who are people with no understanding.

O Prophet, say to those who are captives in your care, "If Allah finds any goodness in your hearts, He will give you something better than what has been taken from you. He will forgive you, for Allah is Most Forgiving, Most Merciful."

—Qur'an 8: 61-65, 70

Daily living tip: Although you cannot hang out with those who don't share your morals, try to stay on good terms with them. Be friendly and helpful to them. Through you, they may see the glory of Allah and find the Straight Way.

Today's prayer: O my Lord, make me a light that reflects Your magnificent Light to show the way to the disbelievers.

Do Not Compromise on Your Values.

O Believers, obey Allah and obey the messenger and do not do vain deeds.

Truly, those who don't believe and who obstruct the path of Allah, and then die as disbelievers will not receive Allah's forgiveness.

Do not be feeble and settle for peace [on inequitable terms] when you are prevailing, for Allah is with you and will never allow your deeds to be for loss.

The life of this world is only frolic and entertainment. If you believe and guard against evil, He will grant you Your rewards and will not ask you for your possessions. If He were to ask you for all of them, asking persistently, you would covetously withhold, and He would bring out all your resentment.

You are invited to invest in the way of Allah, but among you are some who are stingy. Anyone who is stingy is so at his/her own expense. Allah has no needs, and it is you that are deprived. If you backslide, He will substitute in your stead another people, and then they would not be like you.

—QUR'AN 47: 33-38

Daily living tip: "Just try it," some of your buddies may say. They may tempt you to try an illegal drug or an unsafe act. Do not make such a compromise. Stick to your convictions no matter how much others make fun of you. It may be hard to do, but someday you will see the benefit.

Today's prayer: O my Lord, do not put me in difficult situations that I am not prepared to handle. Help me become stronger by giving me gentle struggles and faithful friends.

Respond Kindly to the Critics.

O Believers, do not be like the disbelievers who talk about their brothers when they are traveling through the earth or engaged in fighting. They say, "If they had stayed behind with us, they would not have died or been killed." Allah makes that a regret in their hearts. Allah gives life and causes death. Allah sees all that you do. If you are killed or die in the way of Allah, forgiveness and mercy from Allah are far better than all they could amass. Whether you die or are killed, you will be assembled before Allah.

Because of the mercy of Allah, you respond gently to them. If you were severe or condescending, they would break away from you. Pardon them and ask for forgiveness for them. Consult them in affairs; and then, when you have made a decision, put your trust in Allah. Truly, Allah loves those who trust Him.

If Allah helps you, none can overcome you. If He forsakes you, who is there, after Him, who can help you? In Allah, believers should put their trust.

—QUR'AN 3: 156-160

Daily living tip: When speaking with disbelievers, do not insult them like they insult you. Speak kindly to them and do not gossip about them. Pray for them so their hearts may be changed.

Today's prayer: O my Lord, forgive those who give me a hard time because of my beliefs. May their minds be open to learning about my faith so that their hearts will be changed.

Do Not Fear Satan's Allies.

It is only Satan that frightens you of his allies. Do not be afraid of them, but fear Me if you are believers.

Do not be grieved by those who rush into unbelief. Certainly, they can do no harm to Allah. Allah's plan is to give them no portion in the hereafter. Instead, a severe punishment awaits them.

Certainly, those who purchase disbelief at the price of faith can do no harm to Allah, but they will have a grievous punishment. Do not let the disbelievers think that Our respite to them is good for them. We grant them respite so they may grow in their iniquity, but they will have a shameful punishment.

Allah will not leave the believers in the state in which you are now until He separates what is evil from what is good. Allah will not disclose to you the secrets of the unseen, but Allah chooses of His messengers whom He pleases. So believe in Allah and His messenger. If you believe and have reverence, you will have a reward without measure.

Do not allow those who covetously withhold the gifts, which Allah has given them of His grace, think that it is good for them. No, it will be bad for them. Their necks will be encircled with what they withheld, on the Day of Resurrection. To Allah belongs the heritage of the skies and Earth. Allah is well aware of all that you do.

—QUR'AN 3: 175-180

Daily living tip: Prepare yourself as a warrior in the path of righteousness. When you go into the world, you are entering a spiritual warzone. Be strong in your faith and moral beliefs.

Today's prayer: O my Lord, give me strength and endurance to enter a world that puts up obstacles and distractions in the way of my struggle to do what is right.

Consider the Victory Over
the People of the Elephant.

Did you not see how your Lord handled the people of the elephant? Did He not make their treacherous plan go awry? He sent flights of birds against them. [The birds] struck them with stones of baked clay. He then made (the people of the elephant) like a ravaged field.

Many were the ways of life that have passed away before you. Travel throughout the earth and see what was the end of those who rejected truth.

Truly, We give life and death. We remain as inheritors. We recognize the achievers, and We certainly recognize those who delay. Certainly, your Lord will assemble them together. Truly, He is Perfectly Wise, the All-knowing.

So glorify Allah at twilight and when you rise in the morning. Yes, to Him be praise in Heaven and on Earth, in evening and noon. He brings the living from the dead and the dead from the living. He gives life to the earth after it appears dead; thus, you shall be brought.

—QUR'AN 105 AND QUR'AN 3: 137
AND QUR'AN 15: 23-25 AND QUR'AN 30: 17-19

Daily living tip: Don't worry when you are having a hard time staying true to your religion when everything seems against you. Allah will strengthen you in in amazing ways. Sure, you'll mess up sometimes, but you'll be okay.

Today's prayer: O my Lord, let me not lose hope in the power of being among Your righteous servants. Help me in all my struggles.

Allah Allows Adversity as Well as Blessings.

No hardship happens on earth or in your souls except that which is recorded in a Book before We bring it into existence. That is an easy thing for Allah. Therefore, you should not despair over missed (opportunities) or gloat over (blessings) bestowed upon you. Allah does not love arrogant boasters. Such people are covetous and encourage materialism. If any retreat [from holiness], truly, Allah is Independent, the Praised One.

Previously, We sent our messengers with obvious signs and descended to them the Book and the criterion [laws and commandments] that people may stand on justice. We bestowed iron wherein is mighty power and other benefits for humanity, so that Allah may reveal who secretly wants to help Him and His messenger. Truly, Allah is Strongest, the Victorious.

—QUR'AN 57: 22-25

Daily living tip: Sometimes life is hard, and sometimes it's wonderful. Rejoice in the blessings, and trust Allah to help you endure the hardships. Learn to take life one day at a time. Sometimes the best you can do is just get through the day and hope that tomorrow will be better.

Today's prayer: O my Lord, help me to remember that my life is already written in a Book, and I am just living the pages one page at a time.

For an Example, Consider Plant Life.

A parable of this present life is evident in the rain We send down from the sky. Absorbed by the earth, it beckons plants to emerge and provides food for people and animals. The earth becomes beautifully clad [with foliage and fruits]. Its people [the land's owners] think they have control of it, but Our command reaches the land at night or during the day. Suddenly the land is turned fallow [by frost, storm, or locusts], as if it had not flourished just the day before. Thus do We explain the signs in detail for those who ponder.

Allah calls you to the Home of Peace. He guides whom He pleases to the Straight Way. For those who do right is a good reward, and even more. No gloom or shame will veil their faces. They are companions of Paradise; they will live there forever.

—QUR'AN 10: 24-26

Daily living tip: The struggle affects all of creation. Plants can be healthy one day and then be heavily damaged the next. Allah is still in control, however, and He can restore those plants. In the same way, He can replace some lost source of happiness in your life. Never lose hope.

Today's prayer: O my Lord, bless me with a heart and mind that can find your messages in nature.

Humanity is to Blame for Most Struggles.

Whatever crisis afflicts you is because of what (humanity's) hands have earned [by introducing evil into God's perfect creation]. (Allah) grants forgiveness to many. However, you cannot escape [responsibility] anywhere on earth. And you have, besides Allah, no one to protect or help you.

Among His signs are the ships in the sea, looking like mountains. If it were His will, He could still the wind so that the ships would become stationary on the [water's] surface. Truly, in this are signs for everyone who is patient and grateful. Or He could destroy (people) for what they have earned, but He forgives much. Inform those who argue about Our signs that for them is no place of refuge.

Whatever you are given is a convenience of this life, but that which is with Allah is better and more durable for those who believe and put their trust in their Lord. [They] are those who avoid the most horrible sins and shameful deed. [They] forgive even when angered. [They] hearken to their Lord and maintain the traditional prayers. [They] conduct their affairs by mutual consultation. [They] spend [for charity] from the sustenance We bestow upon them. [They are] those who, when afflicted by an injustice, [properly] defend themselves.

—QUR'AN 42: 30-39

Daily living tip: We have been placed in a world of natural struggle, but people have made the struggle much harder that it was intended. For example, many diseases have been caused by chemicals formulated and haphazardly used by people. Take responsibility for being a responsible citizen of this planet.

Today's prayer: O my Lord, in my day to day living, help me find ways to contribute goodness and not harm to the planet.

This World is One of Struggle.

Oh, I attest by this city [of Meccah] to witness. You [Prophet Muhammed] are free from restriction in this city and a parent and child.

Truly, We have created humanity into struggle. Does he/she not think that there is a greater power above him/her? He/she may boast, "I have spent abundant wealth." Does he/she not think that someone sees?

Have We not made for each person a pair of eyes [in order to see the right way]. [Have we not made] a tongue [with which to ask for guidance], and two lips [with which to speak truth]? [Have we not] shown him/her the two roads? But (humanity) has made no haste on the road that is high. What will explain what is meant by "the road that is high"? It is giving freedom to the enslaved. It is giving food during a time of famine. [It is providing] for the orphaned relative or any poor person in dire need.

Then he/she is among the believers and endorses patience and compassion. Such people are the companions of the right hand.

—QUR'AN 90: 1-18

Daily living tip: You will have problems in your life. Some may make you feel like giving up. We are put here in a world of struggle. Remind yourself that these are opportunities to face obstacles with faith and courage in order to reap rewards in the life hereafter.

Today's prayer: O my Lord, do not give me problems that are too big for me to handle. Give me good friends and family members that can help me know what to do.

No Crisis Can Occur Without Allah's Permission.

No kind of crisis can occur without Allah's permission. Allah guides the heart of one who believes in Allah. Allah knows all. Obey Allah and His messenger. If you backslide, however, the duty of Our messenger is only to proclaim lucidly.

Allah! No god is there except Him. Upon Allah, may believers trust.

O Believers, certainly among your spouses and children there may be antagonists. Beware of those [family members who intentionally or inadvertently come between you and your duties to God]. If you forgive, ignore, and excuse, then certainly Allah is Most Forgiving, Most Merciful. Your wealth and children may pose a trial for you, but with Allah is the highest reward. So revere Allah to your fullest potential. Listen and obey, and expense [for charity] to benefit yourselves. Whoever is rescued [through his/her generous acts] from greed within his/her soul is among those who achieve prosperity.

Advance to Allah a beautiful loan, and He will multiply it for you and will forgive you. Allah is Most Appreciative, Most Tolerant. He knows what is secret and what is public. He is the Victorious, the Perfectly Wise.

—QUR'AN 64: 11-18

Daily living tip: One day, something so bad may happen to you that you may wonder if Allah is paying attention. Everything that is going to happen has already happened in Allah's time. He is certainly aware. It may seem hard to accept at the time, but Allah has a plan to make it okay, if not in this life, then in in the next. Don't lose faith.

Today's prayer: O my Lord, prepare me by making me wise and strong for whatever calamities await me in the future.

With Every Difficulty, There is Relief.

Consider the glorious morning light! Consider the still of the night! Your Lord has not forsaken you, and He is not displeased. Truly, the hereafter will be better for you than the present. Soon your Lord will give that which will please you.

Did He not find you as an orphan and give you shelter? He found you wandering, and He provided guidance. He found you destitute, and He made you independent. Therefore, do not treat the orphans harshly. Do not turn away the beggar. Proclaim the blessings of your Lord.

Have We not expanded your breast for you? We removed your burden from you. It was a weight upon your back. We elevated your reputation. Truly, with every difficulty, there is relief.

Truly, with every difficulty, there is relief. Whenever you are relieved [of difficulty], work diligently. Turn your attention to your Lord.

—QUR'AN 93 AND QUR'AN 94

Daily living tip: No matter how tough things get, keep faith and hope. Allah will provide relief in some form. This world is not for sissies. We all have to be tougher than the things life throws at us.

Today's prayer: O my Lord, help me to accept the problems of life in addition to the blessings. Keep my faith strong no matter what happens.

Humanity is Impatient.

Humanity tends to be impatient. [He/she is] fretful when adversity befalls him/her. [He/she] is stingy when fortune reaches him/her.

[Sarcastically:] What is wrong with the disbelievers that they are making a mad dash before you? [What is wrong that they come] in crowds, from the right and left? Does everyone long to enter the garden of bliss? No! Indeed, We have created them from what they know.

Now I do call to witness the Lord of All Risings and Settings that We can certainly substitute for them better than they. We are not to be defeated. Leave them to plunge into frivolous talk and silly frolic until they encounter their day promised to them. On that day, they will proceed from their graves in sudden haste, as if they were rushing to a goalpost. Their eyes will be downcast, and shame will cover them. Such is the day that they are promised!

—QUR'AN 70: 19-21, 36-44

Daily living tip: Most people are impatient whether slowed down in traffic, waiting on food in a restaurant, or wanting to get a homework assignment finished and over with. Learn to be calm and wait for things to happen in their time. Don't procrastinate though. Stay on task.

Today's prayer: O my Lord, if I get in a rush, remind me to be calm and patient.

Humanity's Lifestyle is a Prayer for Evil.

Humanity prays for evil just as he/she prays for good, and humanity is impatient. We made the night and the day as two signs. We made the sign of night to mean 'obscurity', and We made the sign of day to mean 'enlightenment'. Thus you may seek bounty from your Lord, as well as be knowledgeable of the number and calculation of the years. We have explained all things in detail.

We have fastened every person's fate around his/her own neck. On the Day of Judgment, We will bring him/her a scroll, and he/she will see it unrolled. "Read your record! This day your own soul is sufficient to make an account against you."

Whoever accepts guidance receives it for his/her own benefit. Whoever goes astray does so at his/her own loss. No tote-bearer may carry the burden of another. We will not, however, manifest Our wrath until We have sent a messenger [to each society].

—QUR'AN 17: 11-15

Daily living tip: When you use curse words or engage in vulgar activity, it is a prayer for evil. That is because you are sending negative energies into the universe, and that negativity will come back to you. Be polite and modest in your words and actions.

Today's prayer: O my Lord, cleanse my heart, mind, and soul so that my words and actions are pleasing to You and send out positive energies.

Humanity Abandons Hope
Every Time Something Bad Happens.

Humanity never tires of asking for blessings, but if a crisis occurs, he/she abandons hope, lost in despair.

When We give him/her a taste of mercy from Ourselves after some adversity has been endured, he/she is sure to say, "This [blessing] is my doing. I can't believe that the hour will ever come, but if I do return to my Lord, surely goodness awaits me with Him."

We will show the disbelievers all that they did, and We shall make them experience a severe penalty.

When We bestow blessings on humanity, he/she turns away and distances him-/herself; and, when evil grips him/her, he/she engages in elaborate prayer.

Say, "Do you understand that this [Qur'an] is from Allah, and then you still reject it? Who is more astray that one who is in extreme defiance?"

Soon We will show them Our signs in the horizons and within themselves until it becomes manifest to them that this is the truth. Is it not enough that your Lord witnesses all things?

Are they really in doubt about the meeting with their Lord? Does He not truly encompass all things.

—QUR'AN 41: 49-54

Daily living tip: Don't forget Allah when things are going well. Don't lose hope when something rotten happens. Always stay focused on Allah and His will. Remember to pray every day.

Today's prayer: O my Lord, inspire in me a heart and mind that never lose focus of You and Your amazing grace.

After Allah Delivers Them, They Waiver.

Do you not see that the ships sail across the ocean by the grace of Allah, so that He may show you His signs? Truly, in this are signs for all who persevere and give thanks.

When a wave covers (the idolaters) like a canopy, they call to Allah, offering Him sincere devotion. When He has delivered them safely to land, however, some of them waiver. No one rejects Our signs except treacherous ingrates.

O Humanity, do your duty to your Lord and fear a day [the Day of Judgment] when no parent can do anything for the benefit of his/her child, and no child can do anything for the benefit of his/her parent. Truly, the promise of Allah is true; do not therefore allow the present life to deceive you, and do not allow the chief deceiver to betray you about Allah.

Truly the knowledge of the hour [of the coming of the Day of Judgment] is with Allah alone. He sends the rain, and He knows [the future of] the life within the wombs. No person knows for certain what tomorrow will bring, and no one knows for certain exactly on what land he/she will die. Truly, with Allah is the All-knowing, the Fully Aware.

—QUR'AN 31: 31-34

Daily living tip: After Allah answers your prayers, do not neglect prayers of gratitude. Count your blessings. Have appreciation and don't neglect good deeds you perform for the sake of Allah. Don't be an ungrateful, little twerp.

Today's prayer: O my Lord, let me never forget to thank You for Your blessings, grace, mercy, and opportunities.

People Are Contrary.

Consider the dawn. Consider the [first] ten nights [of the formal pilgrimage]. Consider the even and the odd. Consider the passing night. In these, can evidence not be found by those with understanding?

As for the human, when his/her Lord tests him/her through generosity and favor, he/she (brags), "My Lord blesses me." But when He tests him/her by restricting provision, he/she (complains), "My Lord humiliates me."

Oh, when Earth is pounded to smithereens! [When] your Lord comes, along with angels, rank upon rank! [When] Hell, that day, is presented! That is the day that humanity will remember. How will that remembrance be of value then?

A person will say, "Oh, if only I had invested in my life!"

That day, (Allah's) punishment will be like no other affliction. His containment will be like no other imprisonment.

[To the righteous soul will be said,] "O Soul at peace! Return to Your Lord, well pleased and well pleasing to Him. Enter and be among My servants. Enter My Paradise!"

—QUR'AN 89: 1- 5, 15-16, 21-30

Daily living tip: Always be aware of Allah's presence in your life. This life is temporary. Set your goals for the life hereafter. Do your best to live up to the honor of being a servant of Allah. Take every opportunity to do a good deed.

Today's prayer: O my Lord, give me opportunities to do good works that reflect Your glory and honor.

People Are Distracted by This World's Hustle.

The competition of accumulating distracts you. Until you visit the graves! Indeed! You will soon know! Again! Indeed! You will soon know! Indeed! If you only knew with certainty! You will certainly see Hell. Again! You will see it with certainty of sight. You will then be questioned that day about pleasures.

The life of this world is only amusement and entertainment. Truly the home of the hereafter is [real] life, if they only knew.

If they embark on a boat, they call on Allah, making their devotion exclusively to Him. Then after He has delivered them safely to shore, they allocate praise to others. They are ungrateful for Our gifts and yield to leisurely pursuits. Soon they will realize.

Don't they know that We have made a safe sanctuary and that people are being snatched from their environments? They believe in what is vain and reject the grace of Allah.

—QUR'AN 102 AND QUR'AN 29: 64-67

Daily living tip: Nothing is wrong with working toward educational degrees, garnering meritorious awards, and earning a good income. When the hustle of life distracts you from the glory of Allah, however, these things become like false gods. Always put Allah's will first in your life.

Today's prayer: O my Lord, help me to achieve wonderful things with my life, but do not let those things distract me from my primary goal of serving You.

Do Not Accuse Another of Not Being a Believer.

One who participates in a good cause will share in its blessings. One who participates in an evil cause will be responsible for his/her part in it. Certainly, Allah is the custodian over everything.

When you are met with a greeting, respond with an even friendlier greeting or the same good wishes. Allah is an accountant over everything.

Allah! No god is there except Him. He will assemble you for the Day of Judgment, about which there is no doubt. And who can be more reliable than Allah in providing information?

O Believers, when you travel for the cause of Allah, investigate carefully. Do not say to anyone who offers you [a greeting of] peace, "You are not a believer." Do not seek perishable goods in this temporal life." Allah is in charge of abundant profits. You also were like that [materialistic] until Allah conferred His favor on you, so carefully investigate [a person's true heart while he/she is in the midst of his/her spiritual journey]. Truly, Allah is Fully Aware of all that you do.

—QUR'AN 4: 85-87, 94

Daily living tip: Whether it is someone in a different religion or in a different Muslim sect from you, it is not up to you to decide if another person is a believer. That is Allah's job, and He does not need your help. If someone claims to be a believer, do not judge him or her based on where he or she is on the spiritual journey.

Today's prayer: O my Lord, inspire me to know how to properly interact with those who believe differently from me.

Allah Does Not Ignore Sins.

Do not think that Allah ignores the deeds of the sinners. He only gives them reprieve until a day when eyes will stare [in horror]. Racing ahead, their heads will be raised, their stare will not yield, and their hearts will be void.

Warn humanity of the day when punishment will come to them. Then the offenders will say, "Our Lord, reprieve us for a short time, and then we will answer Your call and follow the messengers."

Didn't you previously swear that you would never suffer such defeat?

You lived in the dwellings of those [communities of old; eg, Sodom and Gomorrah] who wronged themselves. You were clearly shown how We handled them, and We offered parables for you. They devised their schemes, but their plots were known to Allah, even if their plans could have moved mountains.

Never think that Allah would fail His messengers in His promise, for Allah is Victorious, Owner of Retribution.

—Qur'an 14: 42-47

Daily living tip: Take responsibility for any wrongs you have done. If possible, make amends if you have wronged a person. Be humble enough to apologize and vow to do better.

Today's prayer: O my Lord, forgive me for any sins I have committed. Wash my soul and make me pure. If I have hurt anyone in any way, help me find a way to make it right.

Disbelievers Hinder Others from the Truth.

Who is more sinful than the one who invents a lie about Allah or rejects His signs? Truly, the sinners will never prosper. One day, We will assemble them. We will say to those who committed idolatry, "Where are those false gods you used to claim?"

No plea will they have except to claim, "By Allah, our Lord, we were not idolaters."

Look how they have deceived themselves and how their inventions have forsaken them.

Of such people, some listen to you, but We have covered their hearts with veils. In this way, they do not understand because of the [spiritual] deafness in their ears. If they saw every one of Our signs, they would not believe in them. [They would disbelieve] to such extent that, when they approach you, they just want to argue.

The disbelievers claim, "These [signs] are nothing but tales of the ancients."

They hinder others from (the message) as they keep away from it themselves. They only destroy their own souls, and they don't even realize it.

—QUR'AN 6: 21-26

Daily living tip: A disbeliever is someone who deliberately rejects belief in God and His messengers. Be a friend to everyone but be cautious of those who disbelieve. They will misguide you if you give them a chance.

Today's prayer: O my Lord, help me know how to tread the line between being a friend and being influenced by those I befriend, especially when they are disbelievers.

Those Who Lie About Allah Are in Danger.

Who is worse than those who invent a lie about Allah? They will return to the presence of their Lord. Witnesses will say, "These are they who lied about their Lord." Undoubtedly, the condemnation of Allah is on those who sin. Those who create a hindrance from the path of Allah and look for something faulty in it are the same ones who deny life after death. They cannot interfere [with Allah's will] on Earth, and they have no protectors besides Allah. Their penalty will be doubled. They lost the power to understand, and they did not see. They lost their own souls, and what they invented did them no good. Without a doubt, they will lose the most in the afterlife.

Those who believe, perform righteousness, and humble themselves before their Lord, however, will be companions of the Garden, where they will live forever.

Those who are blessed will be in Paradise. They will dwell there for as long as the skies and Earth endure, except as the Lord wills. It is a gift without end.

—QUR'AN 11: 18-23, 108

Daily living tip: A lie about Allah is not always with words. If you claim to be a believer and then live as a disbeliever, that also is a lie about Allah. Tell the truth about Allah by being a kind and merciful Muslim.

Today's prayer: O my Lord, help me not live a lie but help me to live a life that truly reflects Your glory, honor, and grace.

Disbelievers Are the Ones Deluded and Confused.

The hour advances, the moon splitting asunder. But when [the disbelievers] see a sign, they turn away and claim, "[This is nothing but] recurring illusion." They reject [the warning] and follow their own inclinations, but every matter is already settled [in cosmic time]. There has already come to (the disbelievers) information with ample warning and profound wisdom, but (such advice) has no effect.

Truly, those lost in sin are the ones deluded and confused. One day, they will be dragged through the fire, face down. "Taste the touch of Hell!"

We have created everything according to plan. Our command is only one [action], like the twinkling of an eye.

[In the past] We destroyed mobs like you [disbelievers], so are there any willing to take heed? All that they do is recorded in books; every matter, small or great, is a matter of record.

As for the righteous, they will be in the midst of gardens and rivers and in an assembly for truth, in the presence of a Sovereign King.

—QUR'AN 54: 1-5, 47-55

Daily living tip: People think they're so cool, and they walk with that swag. If they are out of touch with the Creator, however, they're just a hot mess. Don't be impressed with them. They may think you're a freak. So what! Better to be a freak for Allah than a freak for Satan.

Today's prayer: O my Lord, may Your guidance come to those lost in the appeal of this world.

Disbelievers Think They Will Not Be Resurrected.

The disbelievers think that they will not be resurrected. Say, "Yes, by my Lord, you shall surely be resurrected, and then you will be told all that you ever did. That is an easy task for Allah."

Believe, therefore, in Allah and His messenger and in the light We have descended. Allah is Fully Aware of all that you do.

The day that He assembles you on the Day of Congregation will be a day of mutual loss and gain. For those who believed in Allah and achieved righteous deeds, He will conceal any sins. He will admit them to gardens, beneath which rivers flow, wherein they will live forever. That will be the supreme achievement.

But those who reject faith and treat Our signs as fiction will be companions of flames in which they will dwell forever. That fate is an evil goal indeed.

One day, every soul will be struggling for itself. Every soul will be repaid for all its actions. No one will be treated unjustly.

—Qur'an 64: 7-10 and Qur'an 16: 111

Daily living tip: It is a fact of science that energy cannot be destroyed. Your life is energy from the Creator. Be assured that death is only the beginning of your true life. You will grieve because you miss loved ones who have passed. Find comfort in knowing their lives continue as they enter the Day of Resurrection.

Today's prayer: O my Lord, grant me comfort anytime a loved one leaves this life. May his/her journey to the afterlife be beautiful and peaceful.

Don't They Realize Allah Created Them in the First Place?

People say [with doubt], "After I am dead, I will be raised back to life?"

Does humanity not recall that We created him/her before, when he/she was nothing? As Allah is your Lord, We shall assemble them together, along with the demons, and then We will bring them to their knees, all around Hell. We will then most certainly pull from each sect all those who were the worst in rebellion against the Most Gracious. Certainly, We know best who are the most worthy to be set ablaze therein. There is not a single (unrepentant sinner) who will not advance to it. This is the Lord's inevitable decree. We will deliver those who feared, and We will leave the sinners therein, on bent knees.

Allah advances in guidance those who seek guidance. Everlasting, righteous acts are best in the sight of your Lord, in respect to rewards and eventual returns.

We shall drive the sinners to Hell, thirsty. No one will have the power of intercession except someone who has received permission from the Most Gracious.

—Qur'an 19: 66-72, 76, 86-87

Daily living tip: Salvation is by Allah's grace. Do not be too proud in your religion because you could well be among the unrepentant sinners if not for the guidance of Allah. Now it is your job to live an admirable life so that you inspire others to believe.

Today's prayer: O my Lord, thank you for choosing me to be among the believers. Help me to live a life worthy of Your grace and mercy.

Disbelievers Depend Upon Gods Besides Allah.

Who responds to the distressed one when he/she calls upon Him? Who relieves his/her suffering and makes you inheritors of Earth? A god besides God? Little you heed [if you think that].

Who guides you through depths of darkness on land and sea? Who sends the winds as [heralds of] glad tidings ahead of His mercy [of rain]? A god besides Allah? Allah is far above whatever may be associated [with Him].

Who originates creation and then continues it? Who provides for you from the skies and Earth? A god besides Allah? Say, "Produce your evidence if you are telling the truth."

Say, "No one of Heaven or Earth, other than Allah, knows what is hidden, and neither can anyone else perceive when all shall be resurrected."

No, [the disbelievers] cannot comprehend the hereafter. In fact, they are in doubt and confusion and are unseeing.

They say, "When will this promise [of the end times] happen, if it's the truth?"

Say, "Perhaps some of (the events) you [want to] hasten may already be in close pursuit of you."

Truly, your Lord is full of grace for humanity, although most people are ungrateful. Truly, your Lord knows all that their hearts conceal as well as all that they reveal.

—QUR'AN 27: 62-66, 71-74

Daily living tip: In some religions, idols are used for worship in order to focus on specific attributes of God. We don't need those because we can experience the attributes of Allah in His creation, in His answers to our prayers, in His guidance, and in His grace and mercy. Always be conscious of the evidence of Allah in your daily life.

Today's prayer: O my Lord, may I wake up every morning with an attitude of seeking You in every sunbeam, every raindrop, and every soft breeze.

Consider the Example of Your Own Associates.

He offers you an example from your own life: Do you have partners from among your servants with whom you would share equally from the wealth We given you? Do you fear them as you fear others [in your position]? [How then can people equate things of creation with the Creator?] Thus do We explain the verses in detail to people using reasoning skills.

The sinners, however, follow their own desires, being void of knowledge. Who can guide those whom Allah leaves astray? For them there are no aids.

So lift your face sincerely to the faith, which is natural according to how Allah made humanity. No change [should be] in the design of Allah. That is the correct religion, but most people do not understand.

Repent to Him, fear Him, establish routine prayers, and do not be among the polytheists. [Do not be among] those who fragment their religion so that each sect rejoices with its own doctrine.

—Qur'an 30: 28-32

Daily living tip: Islam is the religion created by Allah. The various sects are created by people. If you belong to a specific sect, do not let that sect become a partner with Allah. You do that if you preach your doctrine instead of Islam. You do that if you ridicule the sectarian beliefs of other Muslims. You do that if you claim someone is "not a real Muslim" because he or she belongs to a sect you disapprove of.

Today's prayer: O my Lord, give me beauty of speech so I may discuss beliefs respectfully with all those calling themselves Muslims.

Disbelievers Place Their Faith in the Wrong Places.

Allah takes souls at the time of death, and [He keeps] the souls of those who do not die in their sleep. He retains the souls of those for whom death has been decreed. He returns the others, each for an appointed time. Truly, in this are signs for people who ponder.

Do [the idolaters] acknowledge intercessors other than Allah? Say, "Even though they have no power at all and no intelligence?"

Say, "Exclusively to Allah belongs intercession. To Him belongs the dominion of Heaven and Earth. Finally, to Him you will return."

When only Allah is mentioned, the hearts of those who do not believe in the hereafter are filled with disgust. When others are mentioned instead of Him, however, look; they are filled with joy.

Even if the transgressors had all there is on Earth, and as much more, they would offer it for ransom from the pain of penalty on the Day of Judgment. Something, on which they could never have figured, will confront them from Allah. Appearing to them will be the sins they acquired, and they will be encircled by that which they once scorned.

—QUR'AN 39: 42-45, 47-48

Daily living tip: The worldview of the disbelievers is so different from that of the believers that being around them may make you feel like a misfit. Truly, they are the misfits. The faith of the believers is what is natural. When you feel like you don't belong to this world, connect with nature to remind you of your place in Allah's plan.

Today's prayer: O my Lord, help me to realize my purpose in this life while I keep my hopes in the life hereafter.

The False Gods Have No Share in Anything.

Say, "Call upon that which you adore above Allah. They have no possession –even to equal the weight of an atom— in the skies or on Earth. They possess no share thereof, and none of them assists Allah.

"No intercession can avail in His presence except for those to whom He has granted permission. When terror [of His presence] is removed from their hearts, they will be asked, 'What did your Lord command?' and they will answer, 'Truth, and He is the Highest, the Almighty.'"

Say, "Who provides for you from the skies and the earth?" Say, "Allah! Truly, you [disbelievers] or we [believers] are on right guidance or in obvious error."

Say, "You shall not be questioned about our sins, and we shall not be questioned about yours."

Say, "Our Lord will assemble us together, and then He will judge between us [two groups] with truth. He is the Judge, the All-knowing."

—QUR'AN 34: 22-26

Daily living tip: Some people let TV shows, movies, the government, friends, or celebrities decide their morals for them. This is a form of idolatry. Do not let anyone convince you that such things as sex outside marriage and using drugs and alcohol are no longer haram because they are part of our culture. When Allah declares something haram, it stays haram.

Today's prayer: O my Lord, do not let me be misled by those who follow the ways of immorality. Help me enjoy only the parts of my culture that meet Your approval.

Day
244

Praise Allah Alone and Put Your Trust in Him.

Say, "Praise to Allah! Peace on His servants whom He has chosen. Which is better: Allah or the false gods they attribute?"

It is Allah who sends the winds to beckon the clouds, and We herd them to a land [that seems] dead and revive the earth after its decay. Thus will be the resurrection.

He merges night into day and day into night. He has subjected the sun and the moon each to its own laws [of physics] for an appointed time. Such is Allah your Lord. To Him belongs all dominion. Those whom you may invoke besides Him have no power in the least –not even the measure of the membrane of a date seed. If you call them, they will not hear your call; and, if they were to hear, they cannot answer your petition. On the Day of Judgment, they will reject your association. No one can inform you like the Fully Aware.

O Humanity, you need Allah! Allah, however, is Independent, the Praised One.

—Qur'an 27: 59 and Qur'an 35: 9, 13-15

Daily living tip: Do you think that the Creator of all that exists is not capable of handling all your problems? When Allah is the Lord of your life, even your problems belong to Him. Don't neglect to talk to Him about whatever is on your mind.

Today's prayer: O my Lord, I give my whole self to you, including all my imperfections and my problems. I realize I need You in every aspect of my life.

Allah Will Forgive You.

Say, "O my servants who have sinned against your own souls, do not despair concerning Allah's mercy, for Allah forgives all sins. Truly, He is the Most Forgiving, the Most Merciful. Repent to your Lord and submit to Him before the penalty is upon you. After that, you cannot be helped.

"Follow the best of what has been revealed from your Lord before the penalty comes upon you suddenly before you know what's happening. Otherwise, the soul will say, 'Oh, how miserable I am! I neglected to acknowledge Allah and was among those who mocked.' Or perhaps it will say, 'If only Allah had guided me, I would have been among the righteous.' Or perhaps, when the penalty is seen, it will say, 'If only I had another chance, I would be among the righteous.'

"[The reply to that:] 'Truly, My signs did appear to you, and you rejected them. You were haughty and among the disbelievers.'"

On the Day of Judgment, you will see those who told lies against Allah. Their faces will be darkened. Is there not a place in Hell for the haughty?

—Qur'an 39: 53-60

Daily living tip: When you commit a wrong deed, sometimes it's hard to forgive yourself. Repent to Allah and do your best to live righteously. Allah's forgiveness is greater than your guilt.

Today's prayer: O my Lord, forgive me of my sins and save me and my family from the fire of Hell.

Ignore the Disbelievers' Contempt.

If it had been Our will, We could have sent a warner to the center of every population. Do not listen to the disbelievers, but, with great determination, strive against them with (guidance from the Qur'an).

The hypocrites and those with diseased hearts say, "These people are misled by their religion." But, for any who trust in Allah, Allah is Victorious, Perfectly Wise.

If you could see, when the angels take the souls of the disbelievers, they smite their faces and their backs. "Taste the burning torture. That is because of what your hands have forwarded."

Allah is not unjust to His servants.

Like the behavior of the people of Pharaoh and of those preceding them, they rejected the signs of Allah. Allah punished them for their crimes. Allah is Strongest and severe in punishment.

Allah will never change the grace that He has bestowed upon a people until they themselves change what is in their souls. Truly, Allah is All-hearing, the All=knowing.

—QUR'AN 25: 51-52 AND QUR'AN 8: 49-53

Daily living tip: Muslims are often like strangers in this world. In this case, it is good to be strange. The hypocrites ridiculing us are the ones who should worry. Do not let them cause you grief. Be happy to be a weirdo. It's okay if you hit differently.

Today's prayer: O my Lord, empower me to endure the ridicule of the hypocrites. Give me the best words and actions with which to respond to them.

Allah is a Sufficient Witness for You.

We certainly sent messengers before you [Prophet Muhammed], and We made wives and children for them. It was never the intention of a messenger to deliver any sign except as Allah commanded. For everything is a season declared. Allah cancels what He pleases and confirms what He pleases. With Him is the Mother [Origin] of the Book.

Whether We allow you [Muhammed] to experience a segment of what We have promised [portending the Day of Judgment] or cause you to die [beforehand], your duty is to communicate [the message]. Our responsibility is to call them to account.

Did they not see that We visited upon the land and reduced the size of their domain? Allah commands, and no one can subvert His command. He is swift in declaring accountability.

Those before them devised schemes, but in all things the ultimate planning is Allah's. He knows what every soul acquires, and soon the disbelievers will know who finally make it home.

The disbelievers claim, "You [Muhammed] are not a messenger."

Say, "Sufficient is Allah as a witness between me and you, as well as anyone who has knowledge of the Book."

—QUR'AN 13: 38-43

Daily living tip: When people give you a hard time over your religion, remember that Allah is on your side. It may be tough sometimes to put up with hateful people but remind yourself that their hatefulness is their struggle –not yours. Just be cool and be happy with who you are.

Today's prayer: O my Lord, give me the strength to leave hateful people to their own struggles and not make them my struggles.

Disregard the Disbelievers.

O Believers, celebrate the praises of Allah often. Glorify Him morning and evening. It is He who sends blessings upon you and His angels, so that He may bring you from the depths of darkness into light. He is, for the believers, Most Merciful. Their greeting on the day they meet Him will be "Peace!" He has prepared for them a generous reward.

O Prophet, we have truly sent you as a witness, a bearer of glad tidings, a warner. [We have sent you as] a summon to Allah, by His will, and a lamp spreading light. Announce good news to the believers –that they shall have from Allah a grand reward.

Disregard the disbelievers and hypocrites and pay no attention to their taunts. Put your trust in Allah, and Allah is sufficient as a Trustee.

Allah most certainly recognizes those who believe just as certainly as those who are hypocrites.

—QUR'AN 33: 41-48 AND —QUR'AN 29: 11

Daily living tip: An old African proverb says, "It takes a village to raise a child." In today's societies, however, the village is broken. Modern and popular influences are often harmful. Do not follow the examples presented to you by celebrities and others who have no morals, ethics, and values no matter how popular those people are.

Today's prayer: O my Lord, give me courage and wisdom to not be misled by the enemies of my soul.

The Faith of Some Believers is Shaky.

There are among people such as one who serves Allah, but just on the edge [of faith]. If good befalls him/her, he/she is content; but, if a trial comes to him/her, he/she turns impetuously. He/she is lost both to this world and the hercafter. That is a loss for all to see.

Instead of on Allah, he/she calls on (false idols) that can neither harm nor profit him/her. That is wandering too far indeed! He/she may call on one who can give more harm than profit. Evil indeed is the patron, and evil indeed is the client.

Truly, Allah will admit those who believe and perform righteous deeds to Paradise beneath which rivers flow. Truly, Allah implements all His plans.

If anyone thinks that Allah will not help (His servant) in this world and in the hereafter, he/she should stretch a rope [to climb] to the sky in order to sever [Allah's grace]. After that, he/she will see whether his/her plan will remove that which enrages. Thus We sent clear signs, and, truly, Allah guides whom He will.

—QUR'AN 22: 11-16

Daily living tip: You may have a friend who is weak in faith. Help that person to avoid temptations and encourage him or her to stay away from those who would easily misguide. Through your friendship, that person's faith may become stronger. Be a superhero in spiritual warfare.

Today's prayer: O my Lord, make me an instrument through which someone else may strengthen his or her faith.

Hypocrites Should Take Warning.

The hypocrites, both men and women, are in cahoots with each other. They compel evil and forbid what is right, and they close their hands [from doing good deeds]. They have forgotten Allah, so He has forgotten them. Truly, the hypocrites are defiantly disobedient.

Allah has promised the hypocrites, both men and women –along with the disbelievers— the fire of Hell. They shall dwell therein continuously; it is sufficient for them. They have the condemnation of Allah and an enduring punishment.

Concerning those previous (hypocrites), they were mightier than you [hypocrites] in power. They exceeded more in wealth and children. They had their enjoyment of their term, and you have yours just as they did. You indulge in idle talk just as they did. Their accomplishments are futile in this world and in the hereafter. They are losers!

Haven't they heard all the stories of those before them –the people of Noah, Ad, and Thamud, the people of Abraham and the people of Midian, and the destroyed cities [of Sodom and Gomorrah]? Messengers came to them with evidence. Allah was not unjust to them; they were unjust to themselves.

—Qur'an 9: 67-70

Daily living tip: Don't be among those who are always pointing out others' faults while neglecting their own. Don't be among those who promote hate and use religion as an excuse for it. Don't be among those who judge others without realizing they will be judged for their feelings of superiority.

Today's prayer: O my Lord, if I criticize someone else without seeing my own faults, lift the veil from my eyes and let me not be among the hypocrites.

Don't Let the Hypocrites Deceive You.

O Prophet, strive your best against the disbelievers and the hypocrites, and be firm against them. Their abode is Hell. What a terrible destination! They swear by Allah that they said nothing. Actually, they uttered blasphemy, and they did so after accepting Islam. And they conceived a plot, which they were unable to enact. They were only resentful because of the bounty with which Allah had enriched them and His messenger.

If they repent, that would be best for them. If they regress, however, Allah will punish them with a grievous penalty in this life and in the hereafter. There will be no one on earth to protect or help them.

Among (the so-called Muslims) are people who made a covenant with Allah [saying], "If He blesses us from His bounty, we would certainly be generous in charity and be among the righteous." But after He did bless them from His bounty, they became covetous and regressed while being averse. Therefore, He has given them the consequence of hypocrisy in their hearts until the day in which they shall meet Him. This is because they broke their covenant with Allah and because they repeatedly lied.

—Qur'an 9: 73-77

Daily living tip: Sometimes people will disappoint you, including people you thought you could trust. It's okay to be sad or angry sometimes. You don't have to be strong all the time. It's okay to feel like you need a hug and a candy bar.

Today's prayer: O my Lord, give me strength to endure, but when I feel weak, embrace me with Your grace and mercy.

The Hypocrites Are Delusional.

When the hypocrites come to you, they say, "We bear witness that you [Prophet Muhammed] are indeed the messenger of Allah."

Allah knows that you are indeed His messenger, but Allah bears witness that the hypocrites are indeed liars. They have made their oaths a veil [for their true feelings]. In this way, they are obstructions to the path of Allah. Truly evil are their deeds. The reason is that they believed, and then they rejected their faith, so a seal was set on their hearts; therefore, they do not understand.

When you look at them, you are pleased with their outer appearances; when they speak, you listen to their words; but they are like wooden studs propped up [without any permanent supports]. They think every critical comment is about them. They are the enemies, so beware of them. Allah's condemnation is upon them! They are delusional!

When they are invited, "Come; the messenger of Allah will pray for your forgiveness," they turn their heads away. You would see them turning away in arrogance. It makes no difference whether you pray for their forgiveness or not; Allah will not forgive them [unless they repent]. Allah does not guide sinners!

—Qur'an 63: 1-6

Daily living tip: Someone may pretend to be your friend, and then you find out he or she has been gossiping about you or betrays you in some other way. The Prophet (peace upon him) had to put up with such people too. They are messing up their own lives. Don't let them mess up yours by worrying over them.

Today's prayer: O my Lord, bless me with good and faithful friends.

The Hypocrites Are Unable to See.

The parable of (the hypocrites) is that of a man who kindled a fire. After it had shed light all around him, Allah took away the light. He left them all in utter darkness, unable to see. Unhearing, unspeaking, and unseeing, they will never return.

Another [parable] is that of a rainstorm in the sky. Inside it are values of darkness, thunder, and lightning. They press their fingers into their ears to block out the awesome thunder. They are terrified of death, but Allah is always around the disbelievers.

The lightning nearly blinds them! Every time the light helps, they take a step, but when it gets dark again, they stand still. If Allah so willed, He could get rid of their senses of hearing and seeing, for Allah has power over all things.

O Humanity, adore your Lord who created you and those who came before you so you may become righteous. He has made the earth your resting place and the sky your canopy. He sent down rain from the sky and used it to make fruits as your food. Do not establish rivals against Allah now that you know better.

—Qur'an 2: 17-22

Daily living tip: Hypocrites are cool with Allah as long as things are going their way. As soon as things go awry, however, they are ready to give up on Allah. Keep your faith no matter what happens. Bad things are going to happen; that's just life. Don't let life do you in.

Today's prayer: O my Lord, make my faith strong enough to endure whatever life throws at me.

Hypocrites Can Be Saved if They Repent.

O Believers, do not trust as allies disbelievers instead of believers. Do you want to offer Allah testimony against yourselves?

Hypocrites will be in the lowest depths of the fire. No helper can be found for them, except for those who repent, make amends, become faithful to Allah, and purify their faith in Allah's sight. If so, they will be among the believers. Allah will grant the believers a valuable reward.

What would Allah have to gain by your punishment if you are grateful and believe? Allah is Most Appreciative, the All-knowing.

Allah does not tolerate public scandal, unless an injustice has been done [which must, for the sake of justice, be exposed]. Allah is All-hearing, the All-knowing.

Whether a good deed is made public or is anonymous, or a bad deed is forgiven, truly Allah is the Forgiver, the Most Capable.

Some people believe in Allah and [all] His messengers. They do not distinguish one above another. We shall give their rewards. Allah is Most Forgiving, Most Merciful.

—QUR'AN 4: 144-149, 152

Daily living tip: Don't give up on people. Sometimes the worst people become the most faithful servants of Allah. As long as a person is alive, he or she has a chance to repent and live righteously.

Today's prayer: O my Lord, have mercy on those who are astray. Make them aware of their sins and make them repentant and ready to change their ways.

Don't Expect Non-Muslims to Protect Islam.

O Believers, do not expect Jews and Christians to be your guardians [in pursuit of Islamic interests]. Some of them are guardians of one another. Anyone among you who depends on them is truly one of them.

Truly, Allah does not guide sinful people. Look at those in whose hearts is a disease. You see how eagerly they [the hypocrites] dart to them [Muslim-haters within the Judeo-Christian community] and say, "We are afraid that disaster may strike us."

It may be that Allah will grant victory or a command, in accordance with His will, and then they will repent of the secret thoughts contained in their hearts. The believers will then say [to the hypocrites], "Are these [Muslim-haters within the Judeo-Christian community] the same people who swore their strongest oaths, in witness of Allah, that they were with you?" (The hypocrites') deeds will be worthless, and (the hypocrites) will be the losers.

—Qur'an 5: 51-53

Daily living tip: You can be friends with anyone, but you cannot expect non-Muslims to protect Islamic interests. They won't know enough about Islamic values and laws to be able to ensure they are followed. For example, if you are invited to a party at a non-Muslim's house, ask questions to make sure nothing wrong will be going on there.

Today's prayer: O my Lord, help me to choose friends wisely and to know whom to trust where my values are concerned.

Be Wary of Disbelievers
as Guardians of Your Interests.

Say, "O Allah, Master of Sovereignty, You give power to whom You please, and You strip power from whom You please. You honor whom You please, and You debase whom You please. In Your hand is all goodness. Truly, You have power over all things.

"You cause the night to overcome the day, and You cause the day to fade into the night. You bring the living from the dead, and You bring the dead from the living. You give sustenance to whom You please, without measure."

The believers should not accept disbelievers for guardians in preference to believers. If any do that, no help from Allah will come, except in the form of caution so you may seek protection. Allah Himself cautions you. The final goal is to Allah."

Say, "Whether you hide what is in your hearts or reveal it, Allah knows it. He knows what is of the skies and on Earth. Allah has power over all things.

"On the day when every soul will be confronted with all the good it has done and all the evil it has done, it will wish that there was a great distance between it and its evil. Allah Himself cautions you, and Allah is full of kindness to those who serve Him.

—QUR'AN 3: 26-30

Daily living tip: Non-Muslims may have morals and ethics of their own, but they do not share enough knowledge of Islamic morals, ethics, and laws to be able to advise or help you with issues of daily living. Seek advice from good, knowledgeable Muslims.

Today's prayer: O my Lord, bless me with Muslim friends that are knowledgeable and wise enough to advise and help me.

You Should Not Admire Disbelievers.

Certainly, those who oppose Allah and His messenger will be disgraced, as were those before them. Certainly We have already bestowed evident signs. For the disbelievers is a humiliating penalty on the day that Allah will raise them all and make their past conduct apparent. Allah has evaluated it, though they may have forgotten it. Allah is Witness of all.

Those who oppose Allah and His messenger will be among those most humiliated. Allah has decreed, "I and My messengers must prevail!" Allah is Strongest, Victorious.

You will not find any people who believe in Allah and the last day in a state of admiring those who resist Allah and His messenger, even though they are their fathers or their sons or their brothers or other relatives. For (the believers), He has written faith into their hearts and strengthened them with a Spirit from Himself. He will admit them to gardens beneath which rivers flow, wherein they will dwell forever. Allah will be well pleased with them, and they, with Him. They are the assembly of Allah. Isn't it truly the assembly of Allah that will achieve [life in all its fullness]?

—QUR'AN 58: 5-6, 20-22

Daily living tip: Sometimes it does not seem fair when people who have no regard for Allah have better successes that some of the believers. Your success lies in Paradise, so do not feel defeated when you don't achieve what you think you should. You may get depressed sometimes; that's normal. You have to just keep going and keep trying.

Today's prayer: O my Lord, grant me success when that is Your will. If I must fail, help me to accept that failure gracefully and set new goals.

Enemies of Islam Cannot Be Your Trustees.

O Believers, do not accept My enemies and yours as trustees. [Don't] offer them devotion even though they have rejected the truth that has come to you. [Don't offer them devotion] after they have driven out the messenger and yourselves because you believe in Allah your Lord. Do not come to struggle in My way and to seek My good pleasure while harboring secret admiration for them. I know full well all that you conceal and all that you reveal. Any of you who do this has strayed from the Straight Way. If they were to overcome you, they would behave to you as enemies. [They would] and use their hands and tongues against you for evil. They want you to disbelieve.

It may be that Allah will grant love between you and those whom you consider enemies. Allah has such power. Allah is Most Forgiving, Most Merciful. Allah does not forbid you [from being kind] to those who do not fight you because of your faith. [As for those] who do not drive you from your homes. [Allah does not forbit you] from interacting kindly and justly with them. Allah loves people with integrity. Allah only forbids you from trusting those who do fight you because of your faith and do drive you from your homes. Those who partner with them are in the wrong.

—QUR'AN 60: 1-2, 7-9

Daily living tip: Be kind to everyone, regardless of his or her religious views. Be extremely cautious, however, of anyone who is decidedly against Islam. Such a person will always devalue your worth as a human being. You are valuable in the sight of Allah, and that's what's important.

Today's prayer: O my Lord, grant me the wisdom to know when to be cautious of a person. Help me know how to keep myself safe from my enemies.

Satan Has Guided the Apostates.

Those who regress as apostates after guidance was clearly shown to them are those whom Satan has prompted and sustained with false aspirations. To those who hate what Allah has revealed, they say, "We will agree with you in certain matters." Allah, however, knows their secrets.

What about when angels will take their souls at death and smite their faces and their backs. This will be because they followed that which inflicted the wrath of Allah. They despised Allah's good pleasure, so He made their deeds worthless.

Do those in whose hearts is a disease think that Allah will not expose their malice? If We had willed, We would already have exposed them to you, and you would have known them by their marks. Surely, however, you will recognize them by the character of their speech! Allah knows your deeds.

We shall test you until We make evident those among you who strive and persevere in patience, and We shall test your reputation.

Those who do not believe, hinder others from following Allah, and reject the messenger after guidance has been made evident to them will not injure Allah in the least, but He will nullify their deeds.

—QUR'AN 47: 25-32

Daily living tip: An apostate is someone who has left the religion and stopped believing. Save yourself from ever being an apostate by making a firm commitment to stick with Islam no matter what happens or what anybody tells you.

Today's prayer: O my Lord, I commit my whole self to You. Take my mind, soul, and body and keep me safe from doubt and disbelief.

Truly Spiritual People Will See
the Beauty of the Qur'an.

You will find that the people most hostile to the [Muslim] believers are [among] the [unfaithful] Jews and idolaters. Those nearest in friendship to the [Muslim] believers are [among] those who say, "We are Christians," because some of these [Christians] are (scholarly leaders and devout parishioners) who are not arrogant.

When they listen to the (revelation) received by the Messenger, you will see their eyes overflowing with tears, for they recognize the truth. They pray, "Our Lord, we believe, so record that we are among the witnesses. What reason do we have not to believe in Allah and the truth that has come to us? We long for our Lord to include us in the company of the righteous."

Because of their prayer, Allah has rewarded them with Paradise, underneath which rivers flow, for their eternal home. Such is the incentive for those who live righteously.

Those who reject faith and contradict Our Scriptures, however, will be companions of Hell.

—QUR'AN 5: 82-86

Daily living tip: Many people come to Islam because of the beauty of the Qur'an. Be someone who reflects the Qur'an in such a way that people can see the beauty of Islam in you. When you act like a despicable, little creep, you're telling a lie about Islam. You're a terrific person. Act like it.

Today's prayer: O my Lord, make me a beautiful reflection of the Qur'an so that non-Muslims will be attracted to Islam because of my living testimony.

Those Who Truly Surrender to Allah
Are the Best People.

Those who disbelieved among the People of the Book and among the polytheists would not change until they had received clear evidence. [They wanted] a messenger from Allah, reciting Scriptures, kept pure and holy. In them are valuable commandments.

The people of the Book did not divide into sects until after they had received clear evidence. They had been commanded no more than this: Worship Allah, offer Him sincere devotion in submission to Him, be faithful in establishing routine prayer, and contribute regularly to charity. That is the religion, plain and simple!

Those who [continue to] disbelieve among the people of the Book and among the polytheists will be in Hell's fire wherein they will dwell continuously. They are the worst part of creation!

Those who have faith and perform righteous deeds are the best of creation.

You [who are truly surrendered to God's will] are the best people evolved from humanity. You promote what is righteous and prohibit what is evil and believe in Allah. If only [all] the people of the Book had faith, it would be better for them. Among (the people of the Book) are some who [truly] have faith, but most of them are wretched sinners.

—QUR'AN 98: 1-7 AND QUR'AN 3: 110

Daily living tip: Discerning is different from judging. Only Allah can judge someone, but you have to be discerning so you can figure whom to hang with. To discern means that you can detect people's spiritual condition simply by how they act and speak. Don't hang with people who can drag you down.

Today's prayer: O my Lord, make become wise in figuring out whom I can trust to be a friend who will help me in my walk on the Straight Way.

Forsake Your Business Long Enough to Worship.

Say, "O you of Judaism, if you think that you, and no others, are Allah's exclusive friends, then express your desire for death [in order to be closer to Allah], if you are truthful."

They [who think such a thing] would not express such a desire because of (the deeds) their hands have forwarded [for the eternal record]. Allah is the All-knowing of the ones who sin.

Say, "Truly, the death you avoid will certainly overcome you, and then you will return to the All-knowing of private and public affairs. He will announce your deeds."

O [Muslim] Believers, when the call is proclaimed to pray on Friday [the Day of Assembly], hasten to the remembrance of Allah, leaving business behind. That is best for you, if you only knew. Then, when prayer is finished, you may disperse across the land and seek the gifts of Allah. Glorify Allah often so you may prosper.

[Some], however, when they see some bargain or entertainment, they rush off to it and leave you [the Prophet] standing [alone].

Say, "What is in the presence of Allah is better than any amusement or sale! Allah is the Best Provider."

—QUR'AN 62: 6-11

Daily living tip: You may be in a situation where you cannot leave school or work to attend Jummah. If that is the case, try to find a few minutes in your day, where you can say salat privately. If you are in a place where you do not feel comfortable doing the movements, then sit and pray quietly. If you cannot even do that, then do some good deed and ask Allah to accept that as your worship.

Today's prayer: O my Lord, let me not make excuses for not being able to worship. Help me to always find a way no matter the situation.

Worship During Part of the Night.

O you shrouded in garments, stand by night [in prayer], except a little. [Stand] half of it or a little less or a little more. Recite the Qur'an in slow, measured, rhythmic tones. Indeed, We shall bestow to you a profound message. Truly, the rising by night is very studious and most effective and most suitable for the Word.

True, there is for you by day prolonged occupation. But remember the name of your Lord and devote yourself wholeheartedly to Him. [He is] Lord of the East and the West. No god is there except Him. Accept Him, therefore, as your defender. Also, have patience with what (the disbelievers) say, and abandon them in a dignified manner. Leave to Me those who deny while possessing blessings. Tolerate them a while longer. With Us are restraints and a fire and a food that chokes and a painful torture. One day the earth and the mountains will quake and heave. The mountains will become like piles of sand sliding down.

—QUR'AN 73: 1-14

Daily living tip: Most people are busy with school and work during the day. Take advantage of the night or whenever you have time off to spend some time in sincere worship and prayer.

Today's prayer: O my Lord, help me to never fail to find time to spend precious time with You.

Allah is Aware of Your Worship.

Your Lord certainly knows that you stand praying nearly two-thirds of the night or half the night or a third of the night, and so does a party of those with you. But Allah appoints night and day in due measure. He knows that you are unable to keep count thereof. So He has responded to you. Read, therefore, as much of the Qur'an as may be easy for you. He knows that there may be among you some sick ones. [He knows there may be] others traveling through the land, seeking Allah's bounty, and others fighting in Allah's cause. Read, therefore, as much of the Qur'an as may be easy for you. Establish routine prayer and give consistently to charity. Loan to Allah a beautiful loan, and whatever good you invest for your souls, you shall find it in Allah's presence.   [It will be] even better and greater in reward. And seek the grace of Allah, for Allah is the Most Forgiving, the Most Merciful.

—QUR'AN 73: 20

Daily living tip: Allah never intended for the religion to be too hard. If someone tries to make the religion too difficult for you to follow, know that rigid rules are not from Allah. Don't make the religion hard on others by demanding they obey rules made up by people and not in the Qur'an.

Today's prayer: O my Lord, do no burden me with religious demands that are too hard for me to stick with. Let me know whether a rule is really from you or just made up by men.

False Scribes Are Like a Donkey Carrying Books.

Everything of Heaven and Earth glorifies Allah –the Sovereign, Holy One, the Victorious, the Perfectly Wise. He sent to the uneducated people a messenger from among them to recite to them His verses, to sanctify them, and to instruct them in the Book and wisdom. [He did this] although they had been in obvious error. [They had been in error] along with others [throughout the world] who have not yet joined them [in pursuit of Islam]. He is the Victorious, the Perfectly Wise. Such is the grace of Allah, which He bestows on whomever He will. Allah is the Lord of the most wonderful blessings.

Here is a simile of those responsible for keeping the Torah but who have failed to uphold it: They are like a donkey carrying books [but unable to read them and apply their teachings]. Evil is the simile of people who falsify the verses of Allah [by professing Judaism (or any other religion) but failing to apply its true teachings]. Allah does not guide people in the wrong.

—QUR'AN 62: 1-5

Daily living tip: This passage is given as an example of what we should not do. We should not memorize the Qur'an while having no understanding of its message. Memorize the Qur'an but also memorize the meanings and then apply them to your daily life.

Today's prayer: O my Lord, help me to not only know the words of the Qur'an but to also live the message.

The Bible Was Exploited.

[Remember that] Allah took a covenant from the people of the Book to make (the Word) obvious to humanity and not to hide it. They tossed it aside and exchanged it for a miserable gain. Vile was the bargain they made!

Do not concentrate on those who exult in what they have brought about and love to be praised for what they have not done. Do not think that they can escape the penalty. For them is a dreadful penalty.

To Allah belongs the dominion of Heaven and Earth. Allah has power over all things.

Certainly, some People of the Book believe in Allah, in what was revealed to (Prophet Muhammed), and in what was revealed to them. They bow in humility to Allah. They do not exchange the signs of Allah for a miserable gain. For them is a reward with their Lord. Certainly, Allah is swift in account.

O Believers, persevere in patience and faithfulness. Be resolute and fear Allah so you may prosper.

—QUR'AN 3: 187-189, 199-200

Daily living tip: Some preachers have exploited the Bible in order to gain money and power for themselves. Some even use the Bible for political gains. The followers of such preachers are misguided by twisted interpretations of the Bible. Be patient with them and pray that they discover the truth.

Today's prayer: O my Lord, may Your will be done in the lives of people who are misguided by the wrong intentions of preachers who are exploiting the Bible.

Some People of the Book Are Upstanding.

They are not all alike! Some of the people of the Book are upstanding! They recite the Scriptures of Allah all night, and they prostrate [in adoration]. They believe in Allah and the Day of Resurrection. They endorse what is right and forbid what is wrong, and they rush to do good deeds. They are among the righteous.

Of the good done by (the people of the Book), nothing will be rejected. Allah well knows those who live righteously.

For the disbelievers, neither their possessions nor their descendants will avail them anything against Allah. They will be companions of the fire, dwelling therein.

What they expense in the life of this world is comparable to a cold front bringing a biting frost. Stricken are the harvests of people who have deceived themselves. Allah has not betrayed them; they betrayed themselves.

O Believers, do not intimately trust those outside (your value system). They will succeed in corrupting you. They only want to ruin you. Despicable hatred has already appeared from their mouths; what their hearts conceal is far worse. We have made the signs clear, if you have wisdom.

—QUR'AN 3: 113-118

Daily living tip: Do not let anybody teach you to hate people of other religions. Leave judgment to Allah alone. You only have to be careful about entrusting them with issues that require understanding of Islamic values. Respect and appreciate people of all religions.

Today's prayer: O my Lord, bless me with friends of all religions.

They Study the Book as It Should Be Studied.

Those for whom We have sent the Book study it as it should be studied. They believe in it. Those who reject it are the losers.

If you have doubts about what We have revealed to Our servant [Prophet Muhammed], produce a chapter like it. Call your witnesses besides Allah if you are on the level. If you cannot –and you cannot— then fear the fire whose fuel is people and stones. It is prepared for the disbelievers.

Give good news to those who believe and work righteousness. Their portion is gardens beneath which rivers flow. Every time they are fed with fruits thereof, they will say, "This is like what we used to have." They will be given similar things. They will have decent companions with whom they will abide eternally.

Truly, the believers [in the Qur'an], those who are [practicing] Jews, the Christians, the Sabeans, and any others who believe in Allah and the last day and do what is right [are all okay]. They will find their reward with their Lord. They won't have fear or grief [in the next life].

—QUR'AN 2: 121, 23-25, 62

Daily living tip: Instead of ridiculing what other people believe, try to learn from them. Even if you don't agree, it will broaden your understanding of other people. We can't get along with each other if we have no understanding of one another's beliefs.

Today's prayer: O my Lord, give me opportunities to learn about others' beliefs and cultures.

Your Reward May Be Doubled.

Indeed, We have conveyed to them the Word so that they may be mindful. Those to whom We previously gave the (Scriptures) believe in it. When it is recited to them, they say, "We believe in it; it is certainly the truth from our Lord. Indeed, even before it came, we had already devoted ourselves to Him."

They will be given their reward doubled because they are patient, they repel evil with goodness, and they give to others from what We have provided for them. Whenever they hear vain talk, they turn aside, saying, "We have our lifestyle, and you have yours. Peace to you! We do not seek the company of ignorant people."

Indeed, you cannot guide everyone you love [to the truth]; Allah guides whomever He will. He knows best those who follow guidance.

Whatever material things you have been given are only for enjoyment of this life and its glamour, but that which is with Allah is better and more enduring. Will you not be wise?

—QUR'AN 28: 51-56, 60

Daily living tip: Nothing is achieved by arguing with rude, judgmental people. Just leave them with a few kind words. You never know if your courtesy may influence someone to see the Straight Way.

Today's prayer: O my Lord, when someone is rude to me, give me the wisdom to respond with the most appropriate words for a person with a Muslim heart.

Believe in All Allah's Word.

Remember that We set a covenant with the Children of Israel: Worship no one but Allah. Show kindness to your parents, relatives, orphans, and the poor. Speak nicely to people. Be faithful in prayer, and practice routine charity. Then you failed, except the few among you, and you still backslide.

Remember that We set your covenant: Shed no blood among you, and do not cast your own people from your homes. You solemnly agreed to this. You know you did.

Afterward, you killed your own people and kicked some out of their homes. Now you give aid against them. You are guilty and sinful. If they come to you as captives, you ransom them but it was not lawful for you to kick them out [in the first place].

Do you believe only part of the Book and then reject the rest? What is the reward for those among you who behave like this, other than disgrace in this life? On the Day of Resurrection, they will get the worst punishment. Allah does not ignore what you do.

—QUR'AN 2: 83-86

Daily living tip: The Qur'an is given for guidance and a reminder for everybody. It is not given so you may use it to judge others. Let people learn from the Qur'an without shoving it down their throats.

Today's prayer: O my Lord, help me to represent Islam in the most beautiful ways without any spite or hate in my heart.

Consider the Qur'an as Scripture.

Alif. Lam. Ra. This Book of Scriptures is perfected and clarified. It is from the One who is Perfectly Wise and Fully Aware. You should worship none but Allah. I [Muhammed] am sent from Him for your benefit, to warn and to announce good news.

Seek the forgiveness of your Lord and turn to Him in repentance. He may award you a satisfactory life for an appointed time and bestow His abundant grace on all who are meritorious.

But if you reject Him, I fear for you the penalty of an awesome day.

To Allah you will return, and His power extends over all.

Observe how they twist their hearts so they may be concealed from Him. Even when they shroud themselves, He knows what they conceal as well as what they reveal. He well knows the secrets of hearts.

To those who desire the worldly life and its glitter, We will pay them for their deeds, without any deductions.

—QUR'AN 11: 1-5, 15

Daily living tip: Someone may ask you, "We already had the Bible, so why did we need the Qur'an?" Say, "The Qur'an ties everything together, and it explains and clarifies things that confused people." They may still challenge you. It's okay. It's their struggle. Just do the best you can talking to them.

Today's prayer: O my Lord, thank you for giving me a religion that gives more –more prophets and more Scriptures.

Day
272

Those Who Recite the Qur'an
and Act Charitably Will Be Rewarded.

Do you not see that Allah descends rain from the sky? With it We produce fruits of various colors. In mountains are tracts of hues varying from white to red to very black. Among people, wildlife, and domestic animals are also a variety of colors. Only His servants who have knowledge fear Allah. Indeed, Allah is the Victorious, the Most Forgiving.

Truly, those who recite the Book of Allah do pray routinely and invest [in charity], privately and publicly. [They do this] from what We have provided for them, hoping for an exchange that will never perish. He will give them their rewards in full and give them extra from His bounty. Truly, He is Most Forgiving, Most Appreciative.

They will enter an eternal Paradise, wherein they will be adorned with bracelets of gold and pearls, and their garments will be of silk. They will say, "Praise Allah, who has removed all our sorrow! Truly, Our Lord is Most Forgiving, Most Appreciative. Out of His bounty, He has settled us into a home that will prevail. No strife or sense of weariness shall affect us here."

—QUR'AN 35: 27-30, 33-35

Daily living tip: Always be conscientious of doing good deeds and performing the traditions of Islam. You should do these just because that's the right way to live. Being rewarded by Allah is a bonus.

Today's prayer: O my Lord, do not reward me if my performance is only for Your reward. Give me a sincere desire to live righteously just because it's the right thing to do.

The Qur'an Offers Healing.

O Humanity, direction from your Lord has come, along with healing for your diseased hearts and, for believers, guidance and mercy.

Say, "For the bounty of Allah and His mercy, rejoice! These are better than your savings account."

Say, "Do you see what Allah has bestowed upon you for provisions? Yet you decide what is forbidden and what is lawful." Say, "Has Allah indeed given permission, or did you attribute your own fabrications to Allah?"

What is the mindset of those inventors of lies about Allah when it comes to the Day of Resurrection? Truly Allah is most bountiful for humanity, but most people are not grateful.

Regardless in what business one may be involved, what portion one may be reciting from the Qur'an, or what deed one may be doing, We are witnesses of that on which you are focused. Hidden from your Lord is not even the weight of an atom, neither on the earth nor in the sky. The least and the greatest of things are recorded in a concise record.

—QUR'AN 10: 57-61

Daily living tip: Someone may ask you, "What does the Qur'an offer that is not already in the Bible?" Say, "The Qur'an offers healing for those who are lost. For those already on the Straight Way, it provides additional guidance and mercy." You don't have to criticize the Bible to make the Qur'an look good.

Today's prayer: O my Lord, if I have any defect in my spiritual connection to You, please grant me healing through Your beautiful words and Your grace and mercy.

The Qur'an is from Allah.

Alif. Lam. Ra. These are the verses of the Book and Qur'an, which clarify.

Perhaps the disbelievers will [eventually] wish that they had submitted [to Allah]. Allow them to eat and frolic. Allow them to be preoccupied with their ambitions. [Someday] they will understand.

We never destroyed a population that did not have a set time. People cannot anticipate their term or delay it.

They say, "O recipient of the message, you really are crazy! Why do you not bring angels to us if you really have the truth?"

We do not dispatch angels without a good reason. [If angels did come,] (the sinners) would not have a respite at all!

We have undoubtedly bestowed the message, and We will most certainly preserve it.

Will they not ponder the Qur'an? If it had been from anyone other than Allah, they would have found contradictions in it.

Truly, this Qur'an guides to what is most righteous. It gives good news to the believers who perform deeds of righteousness. They will have a wonderful reward. As for those who do not believe in the hereafter, We have prepared for them a horrible punishment.

—QUR'AN 15: 1-9 AND QUR'AN 4: 82 AND QUR'AN 17: 9-10

Daily living tip: Some people believe in the Qur'an simply from reading it. Others need the evidence of a life well lived. Live the Qur'an in addition to speaking beautiful words about it.

Today's prayer: O my Lord, let my words and my actions be a lovely reflection of the Qur'an.

Prophet Muhammed's Ministry is from Allah.

Consider the setting star. Your companion [Prophet Muhammed] is neither astray nor being misled. He does not speak from self-desire. No less than inspiration is sent to him. He was taught by one [angel] mighty in power, endued with wisdom. [The angel] appeared while in the highest part of the horizon. He then approached and came closer until he was closer than two bow-shots. [Through the angel Gabriel,] (Allah) conveyed inspiration to His servant [the Prophet] what He intended. The [Prophet's] mind did not falsify what he saw [in the vision of Gabriel standing on the horizon].

Are you going to argue with him about what he saw? He saw (Gabriel) a second time [during the Prophet's ascension in his visit to Heaven]. [He saw him] near the lote tree [guarding the Garden of Eden] beyond which no one may pass. Near it is the Garden of Eden. The lote tree is shrouded [in mystery] with what encircles it. (The Prophet's) sight never swerved or failed. Truly, he did see one of the greatest signs of his Lord!

—QUR'AN 53: 1-18

Daily living tip: Some people will say horrible things about Prophet Muhammed (peace upon him). Sometimes it is hard to keep from losing your temper. If they persist, tell them, "Those are all lies. If you're ever interested in hearing the truth, I'll be glad to talk to you," and then just walk away. Don't waste your time "throwing pearls to pigs" as taught by Jesus (peace upon him).

Today's prayer: O my Lord, give me wisdom to know when to engage in conversation and when it is better to just walk away.

Inspiration Was Given to Prophet Muhammed.

To no person does Allah speak unless by inspiration, or from behind a veil, or by the sending of a messenger to reveal, with Allah's permission, whatever Allah wills. He is the Highest and Wisest! Thus, We have, by Our command, sent inspiration to you [Prophet Muhammed]. You did not know what revelation was or what faith was, but We made (the Qur'an) a light by which We may guide those among Our servants as We will. Truly, you guide to the Straight Way. [That is] the way of Allah, to whom belong everything in the skies and everything on earth. See how everything tends toward Allah.

For every people was a messenger. Now that their messenger has come, the matter will be judged among them with justice. They will not be wronged.

They say, "When will this promise come to pass, if you're telling the truth?"

Say, "I have no power over any harm or profit to myself except as Allah wills. To every people is an appointed term. When their term has ended, they can neither delay nor advance an hour."

—QUR'AN 42: 51-53 AND QUR'AN 10: 47-49

Daily living tip: Sometimes you may get an inspiration or idea that pops in your head, and it's not your own thoughts. This may be Allah communicating with you. Be open to that and don't be hasty to dismiss it.

Today's prayer: O my Lord, let me hear Your still, quiet voice as You guide me in miraculous ways.

Truth Has Arrived.

[Prophet Muhammed,] say, "I advise you on one point –that you appear before Allah in couples or individually and reflect. Your companion [Prophet Muhammed] is not possessed; he is no less than a warner to you in the face of a terrible penalty."

Say, "No reward do I ask of you. It is within your interest. My reward is due only from Allah, and He is witness to all things."

Say, "Truly, my Lord casts truth –He who has full knowledge of the unseen." Say, "Truth has arrived, and deceit neither creates nor restores."

Say, "If I go astray, I only stray to my own loss. If I receive guidance, it is because of the inspiration of my Lord to me. He hears all things and is near."

If you could only see when they will quake with terror! But then there will be no escape, and they will be seized from a near position. They will say, "Now we believe in it," but how could they receive [truth] from a place distant [from the Prophet's ministry]? [How could they believe then,] seeing that they rejected faith from (that time) and that they cast slander about the unseen from a place distant [from the eternal life]?

—QUR'AN 34: 46-53

Daily living tip: Don't delay in submitting your whole life to Allah. Start living righteously now while you are young. If you don't, when you are old, you will realize you wasted too many years apart from Allah's grace.

Today's prayer: O my Lord, I dedicate my life to You. Take me and make me into one of Your faithful servants.

Allah Taught the Qur'an.

The Most Gracious! He taught the Qur'an. He created humanity. He taught him/her articulate speech.

The sun and the moon follow calculations (of bio-mathematical physics).

Stars and trees bow [in adoration]. He lifted the sky, and He formed the balance [using gravity] so that you may not fault in measure. You must, therefore, establish weight with justice and not fall short in the balance.

He has spread the earth for His creatures. Therein are fruits and date palms producing clusters. There is also corn, with husks, and other sweet-smelling plants.

So, which of the Lord's favors will you both [humans and spirit-beings] deny?

He created humanity from sounding clay, similar to pottery.

He created spirit-beings from fire free of smoke.

So, which of the Lord's favors will you both deny?

He is the Lord of the two Easts and Lord of the two Wests.

So, which of the Lord's favors will you both deny?

—QUR'AN 55: 1-18

Daily living tip: If you keep your heart and mind open, Allah will teach you the message of the Qur'an and how to apply it to your daily life. Life is much easier to handle when a person has set rules of ethics, values, and morals. Anything else is like trying to wade through quicksand.

Today's prayer: O my Lord, let me not be stubborn and hardheaded. Grant me understanding and help me make the Qur'an relevant to my life.

The Qur'an Even Chastises the Prophet.

He [the Prophet] frowned and turned away because the blind man approached him. How do you [O Prophet] know whether he may have corrected himself? Or whether he may have been reminded [of God] and have benefited from the reminder? To one who regarded himself as independent, you attended. There would have been no blame on you, however, if he did not correct himself. As for one who approached you earnestly and reverently, you were too preoccupied. That's not right! It is indeed a reminder [that you have been given]. Therefore, whosoever will may remember it. [It is] from pages of honor. [It is] exalted and kept pure by the hands of scribes who are honorable and righteous.

Destruction to humanity! How ungrateful he/she is! From what did (Allah) create him/her? He created him/her from sperm, and then He molded him/her in appropriate stages. He makes his/her path simple [by giving rules by which to live]. He causes him/her to die and be cast into the grave. In accordance with His will, He will resurrect him/her. Certainly, (humanity) has not fulfilled what Allah has commanded!

—QUR'AN 80: 1-23

Daily living tip: Even Prophet Muhammed (peace upon him) was not perfect. He made a mistake, but Allah used his mistake to teach you something. Do not be rude to someone just because he or she has a disability. Treat everyone with respect.

Today's prayer: O my Lord, make me a faithful friend with whom everyone feels safe.

The Prophet Suffered Ridicule.

"Our Lord, remove the penalty from us, for now we really do believe!"

How shall the message solidify for them, seeing that a message clearly explaining had come to them? Yet they turned away from him and said, "He's been coached! He's possessed!"

We shall indeed withdraw the penalty for a while, but truly you [sinners] will lapse [back to your wicked ways]. One day We will seize you with a mighty onslaught. We will indeed exact retribution.

Before them, We tried the people of Pharaoh. An honorable messenger came to them. [He was] saying, "Restore to me the servants of Allah. I am for you a trustworthy messenger. Do not be arrogant against Allah. I come to you with evident authority. Indeed, I have sought refuge, with my Lord and your Lord, so you will not stone me. If you do not believe in me, separate yourselves from me."

[After their aggression], he cried to his Lord, "These people are lost sinners."

[God's orders:] "March forth with My servants by night, for you will certainly be pursued. Leave the sea as a furrow, for they [Pharaoh's army] are a host to be drowned."

—Qur'an 44: 12-24

Daily living tip: If you ridicule someone, you make him or her a partner with the Prophet (peace upon him) while you make yourself a partner with the wrongdoers. Don't make fun of others' beliefs. Share truth in a respectful manner.

Today's prayer: O my Lord, may Prophet Muhammed (peace upon him) be vindicated because of the lies told about him.

Allah Could Have Forced Everyone to Believe.

The disbelievers say, "Why isn't a sign sent to him from his Lord?"

Say, "Truly, Allah leaves astray whom He will, but He guides to Himself those who repent, those who believe, and those whose hearts find joy in the remembrance of Allah. Without a doubt, in the remembrance of Allah, hearts do find joy! For those who believe and perform righteous deeds, there is a blessing and a beautiful place to return."

We have sent you [O Prophet] among people, before whom other peoples have passed, so that you may recite to them what We send to you through inspiration. Yet, they reject the Most Gracious!

Say, "He is my Lord. No god is there except Him! On Him I place my trust, and to Him I turn."

[Consider] if there was a revelation with which mountains were moved, the earth split apart, or the dead made to speak! No! With Allah is every command. Don't the believers know that, if Allah had willed, He could have guided all humanity?

As for the disbelievers, disaster will never cease to strike them for their deeds or cease to strike near their homes until the promise of Allah comes to pass. Truly, Allah will not fail in His promise.

—QUR'AN 13: 27-31

Daily living tip: If Allah did not feel the need to force everyone to believe, certainly you should not. It's none of your business what religion others choose. Share what you believe and trust Allah to do His will as He pleases.

Today's prayer: O my Lord, On You I place my trust. To You I turn. Let me not forget that Your plans will unfold according to Your will.

Believers Protect One Another from Evil Influences.

The believers, both men and women, are protectors of one another. They enforce what is just and forbid what is evil. They observe routine prayers, practice the required charity, and obey Allah and His messenger. On them Allah will pour His mercy. Indeed, Allah is Victorious, Perfectly Wise.

Allah has promised to believers, both men and women, gardens, underneath which rivers flow, for their dwelling, plus beautiful mansions in gardens of everlasting bliss. The greatest blessing of all is the approval of Allah. That is the best achievement.

Those who believe, suffer exile, and struggle for the cause of Allah, using their possessions and their selves, have the highest rank in the sight of Allah. They are the achievers! Their Lord gives them good news of a mercy from Himself, of His approval, and of Paradise where there are gifts that endure. They will dwell there forever. Truly, in Allah's presence is the ultimate reward.

—QUR'AN 9: 71-72, 20-22

Daily living tip: Protection is not all about physical defense. It is also about spiritual defense. You protect others by using polite speech (not vulgar words), dressing modestly (so as not to incite bad thoughts), offering good counsel, giving words of encouragement when people face temptations and challenges, and giving words of praise for whatever good someone achieves.

Today's prayer: O my Lord, make me a protector and bless me with those who protect me.

Allah Grants Tranquility.

Truly, We granted you [Muhammed and comrades] a manifest victory. Allah may forgive you for the sins of your past and future. [He may] fulfill His favor to you, and guide you on the Straight Way. Allah makes you victorious with prevailing support. Allah sent tranquility into the hearts of the believers so they may layer faith onto their faith.

To Allah belong the physics of the skies and Earth. Allah is the All-knowing, the Perfectly Wise. [He will] admit believing men and women to Paradise, where underground rivers flow, wherein they will live forever. He will blot any sins from them. In the sight of Allah is the highest goal. He will punish the hypocritical men and women, the polytheistic men and women who imagine an evil opinion of Allah. Evil surrounds them, and the wrath of Allah is upon them. He has condemned them and prepared Hell for them. Their destination is dreadful!

To Allah belong the physics of the skies and Earth, and Allah is Victorious, Perfectly Wise.

—QUR'AN 48: 1-7

Daily living tip: Tranquility means calmness. When you allow Allah to be in control of your life, your heart and mind will feel calm and serene. That doesn't mean you never get upset, but when you do get upset, you will be able to remind yourself that Allah is always in control.

Today's prayer: O my Lord, when my life is a mess, remind me that You will make everything turn out okay. Give me peace of mind and help me persevere.

There Are Always People
Who Ridicule True Religion.

Praise Allah who created the skies and the earth. He made the darkness and the light. Yet the disbelievers consider equals to their Lord. It is He who created you from clay, and then decreed an intended term [of life in this world] –a term known only by Him. Yet, you have doubts.

He is God of Heaven and Earth. He knows what you conceal and what you reveal. He knows what you earn [in the hereafter].

Not one of the signs of their Lord came to people without their opposition. Now they reject the truth when it comes to them [in this Qur'an]. Soon, however, they shall learn the reality of that which they ridicule.

Do they not see how many generations before them We destroyed? We established them on the earth more securely than We strengthened you. We blessed them with abundant rain from the sky, and We provided streams flowing beneath them. Yet, because of their sins, We destroyed them and succeeded them with new generations.

—QUR'AN 6: 1-6

Daily living tip: It's okay to spend some time playing computer games, watching movies, and enjoying other leisurely activities. Don't spend so much time on those things that you don't learn to socialize, however. Make time for face-to-face conversations with people. This will help you know how to talk to people when you are confronted with ridicule. Socializing helps you learn poise and grace. You will need that someday.

Today's prayer: O my Lord, make me one who can easily discuss controversial topics in a graceful manner.

Forgive Them.

It is Allah who has subjected the sea to you so that ships may sail across it by His command. That is so you may seek His bounty and be grateful. He has subjected to you, from Him, all that is in the skies and on the earth. Truly, in that are signs for people who ponder.

Tell those who believe to forgive those who do not anticipate the days of Allah when He compensates people according to what they have earned. Whoever does a righteous deed benefits his/her own soul. Whoever does evil works against (his/her own soul). In the finale, you will return to your Lord.

We put you on the ordained way of (religion), so follow it, and do not follow the desires of the ignorant. They will be of no benefit to you in the sight of Allah. Sinners protect one another, but Allah is the Guardian of the righteous. The evidence is clear for all people, and a guidance and mercy to those of true faith.

Do those who seek evil ways think that We will consider them equal with those who believe and live righteously –that their life after death will be equal? They use poor judgment [if they think that]!

—QUR'AN 45: 12-15, 18-21

Daily living tip: Sometimes forgiveness is a process. Sometimes you have a right to be mad for a little while. After that, start preparing your mind to forgive. First, come to a point where you neither forgive nor not forgive; you just leave it to Allah. Eventually, you will be able to forgive and move on.

Today's prayer: O my Lord, when I get mad, grant tranquility to my soul and help me prepare my heart to forgive the person who made me mad.

Do Not Ridicule Their False Gods.

We explain the signs in various ways so they may say, "You are knowledgeable," and so We may clarify matters for those who discern. Follow what has been revealed to you from your Lord. No god is there except Him. Avoid those who enlist other gods.

If Allah had so planned, they would not have enlisted false gods. We do not require that you be their guardian or manager.

Do not condemn what [gods] they enlist besides Allah, because, out of spite, they may condemn Allah in their ignorance. We have allowed each society to be enamored by its own activities. To their Lord they will return, and then We will account to them about all they did.

They swear their strongest oaths by Allah that, if a sign came to them, they would certainly believe in it. Say, "Signs are only within Allah's power." What will make you realize that they would not believe even if (a sign) came?

We shall confound their hearts and eyes. They refused to believe in this in the first place, We will leave them to their sins, to wander in distraction.

—QUR'AN 6: 105-110

Daily living tip: When you make fun of someone else's religion, that opens a door so that others will make fun of Islam. That's not smart. You have to show respect in order to get respect. Of course, that doesn't always work, but at least it won't be your fault.

Today's prayer: O my Lord, don't let my big mouth be the cause of someone else's sin.

Invite Others to Come to Allah.

Who is better in speech than one who invites others to Allah, performs righteousness, and says, "I am among those who submit to Allah"?

Righteousness and evil cannot be equal. Repel [evil] with what is better, and then you may make an intimate friend of one with whom there was hatred. Such [harmony] will be granted to no one except those who exercise patience. No one finds such [harmony] except the truly blessed.

If a provocation to discord is made to you by Satan, seek refuge in Allah. Indeed, He is the All-hearing, the All-knowing.

Among His signs are the night and the day, the sun and the moon. Do not worship the sun or the moon, but worship Allah who created them if you wish to serve Him alone. Even though (the disbelievers) are arrogant, in the presence of your Lord are those who glorify Him night and day, and they never tire.

Among His signs is that you see the barren, desolate earth, but, when We bestow rain upon it, it is aroused [back to life] and yields [harvest]. Truly, He who revives (the dead earth) can surely revive the deceased [people]. He has power over all things.

—QUR'AN 41: 33-39

Daily living tip: The best way to invite others to Islam is to be kind and respectful to everyone. We are all part of the family of humanity regardless of religion, culture, race, gender, or any other aspect of pluralism. Speak out against what is wrong without targeting people.

Today's prayer: O my Lord, help me to remember that everybody has a struggle. Do not let me judge others for having struggles different from mine.

Warn Your Relatives.

Do not call on any other god with Allah, or you will be among the convicted. Warn your nearest relatives. Lower your wing [of kindness] to the believers who follow you. If they disobey you, say, "I am not responsible for what you do." Put your trust in the Victorious, the Most Merciful. He sees you standing [in prayer]. [He sees] your movements among those who prostate. He is All-hearing, the All-knowing.

Shall I tell you on whom the demons descend? They descend on every liar and sinner. They repeat what [gossip] is heard, and most of them are liars. Those who follow the poets [who chant senselessly] are misguided. Do you not see that they wander distractedly into every dip, and that they preach what they don't practice? The exceptions are those who believe, live righteously, engage much in the remembrance of Allah, and defend themselves only after they are unjustly attacked. Those who cause oppression will know to where [Heaven or Hell] they will return.

—QUR'AN 26: 213-227

Daily living tip: Your parents (or guardians) are humans who are struggling to do the best job they know how to do. If they make a mistake, you can remind them in a kind and loving way. Don't be disrespectful. If a family member says hateful things out of anger, for example, you can say something like, "I understand that you're upset, but maybe you should take a few minutes to breathe before you react." If your mama then smacks you, go to your room to pout.

Today's prayer: O my Lord, help me to treat my family members with the same respect and consideration as I give people outside the family.

Praise Allah
When You See People Entering Islam.

(This concerns) the pacts made with the Quraysh for their protection. [These are] during winter and summer journeys [on the trade routes]. May (the Quraysh) worship the Lord of this House [the Ka'bah]. He nourished them against hunger and safeguarded them from fear.

When will the help of Allah come? [When will] you see the people enter Allah's religion in multitudes? Celebrate the praises of your Lord. Pray for His forgiveness. Truly, He is Most Responsive.

Say, "He is Allah the One! Allah! The Absolute! He does not beget, and He is not begotten. Nothing is like Him!"

We have sent to you a messenger to witness to you, just as We sent a messenger to Pharaoh. Pharaoh, however, did not believe the messenger, so We seized him with a heavy punishment. How then can you, if you disbelieve, protect yourselves against a day that will cause children to become old? The sky will rip apart! His promise will be realized! Truly, this is a reminder; therefore, whosoever will come may come on the path to his/her Lord.

—QUR'AN 106 AND QUR'AN 110 AND QUR'AN 112 AND QUR'AN 73: 15-19

Daily living tip: When people come to Islam, do not make the mistake of bombarding them with rules that make the religion hard. The religion is easy; people make it hard. Allah spent twenty-three years revealing the Qur'an. He does not expect a new Muslim to be perfect overnight. Let Allah take whatever time He will to guide a person along the new path of Islam. Don't make someone sorry he or she ever met you.

Today's prayer: O my Lord, guide the new Muslims along a path that is not rocky but is gentle and easy.

You Can Recognize True Believers by Their Deeds.

If Allah were to hasten trouble for people as quickly as they want to be blessed, their respite would be over immediately. For those who do not expect a meeting with Us, We abandon them in their sin to wander haphazardly.

Is one who recognizes the truth bestowed to you from your Lord, the same as one who is unseeing? Only those with understanding pay any attention.

They fulfill the Covenant of Allah and do not fail in their promise. They endorse what Allah has commanded to be sanctioned. They revere their Lord and fear the terrible reckoning. They patiently persevere, seeking the countenance of their Lord. They establish a prayer routine. They expense, secretly and publicly, from what We have provided them. They repel evil with goodness.

For such people, there awaits the final glory of the home. There will be Gardens of Eden. They will enter them, along with their righteous parents, spouses, and children. Angels will come to them from every gate: "Peace to you because you patiently persevered! Excellent is the final home!"

—QUR'AN 10: 11 AND QUR'AN 13: 19-24

Daily living tip: Be cautious of whom you hang with. Your parent(s) or guardian(s) give good advice concerning friends. They have more experience in spotting losers. If your parent tells you that someone is rotten, believe it. Be friendly to everyone but be cautious of whom you choose as your friends.

Today's prayer: O my Lord, grant me the humility to listen to the adults in my life and to accept the wisdom they offer.

The Spirit is Commanded by Allah.

They ask you [Prophet Muhammed] about the Spirit. Tell them, "The Spirit is commanded by my Lord. Only a little knowledge is communicated to you.

"If We wanted, We could take back that which We have sent you by inspiration, and then you would find no one to plead your case against Us. The exception is from the mercy from your Lord, for His bounty to you is tremendous."

Say, "If all humanity and all spirit-beings were to collaborate on a production like this Qur'an, they could not produce anything like it, even if they coordinated all efforts."

We have explained to humanity, in this Qur'an, with every kind of example, but most people are indifferent except with an attitude of spite. They say, "We will not believe in you [Prophet Muhammed] until you cause a spring to gush forth for us from the earth. Or until you have a garden of date trees and grapevines and cause rivers to gush forth in their midst, carrying abundant water. Or until you cause the sky to fall in pieces, as you predict, against us, or until you bring Allah and the angels to face us. Or until you have a house adorned with gold, or until you ascend into the skies. Even then, we won't believe in your ascension until you bring us a Book ready to read!"

Say, "Glory to my Lord! Am I anything more than just a man –a messenger?"

—QUR'AN 17: 85-93

Daily living tip: What is "the Spirit" of the Qur'an? Depending on your research, you may find different explanations. It is enough to know that the Spirit is real and active. Allah uses the Spirit to convey messages and inspire guidance. You don't have to be a prophet or messenger to experience guidance in your life.

Today's prayer: O my Lord, may the Spirit inspire the world to understand the best meanings of Your beautiful Words.

Do Not Reject the Truth.

O Believers, obey Allah and His messenger. Do not turn away from him when you hear. Do not be like those who say, "We hear," but do not listen. The worst of creatures, in the sight of Allah, are the unhearing and the silent –those without understanding. If Allah had found any goodness in them, He certainly would have caused them to listen. If He had made them listen, however, they would have responded with rejection.

O Believers, respond to Allah and His messenger when he calls you to that which will give you life. You must realize that Allah comes between a person and his/her heart and that it is to Him that you will be assembled.

Fear a trial, which does not affect only those of you who sin, and realize that Allah is firm in punishment.

Remember when you were few and considered weak throughout the land and afraid that people would do away with you. He provided a safe refuge for you, strengthened you with His aid, and supplied you good things, so that you may be grateful.

—QUR'AN 8: 20-26

Daily living tip: If He so willed, Allah could have forced everyone to listen to the message. As the verse says, however, some people would have responded with rejection of the message. Perhaps Allah's mercy is in that He did not give certain people the opportunity to reject the message. He would then have to judge them for that rejection. Don't be haughty with your belief then. It is by Allah's grace that you have believed. Just be happy you're not among the losers.

Today's prayer: O my Lord, make me among those who never reject Your truth. Keep me in Your grace and mercy.

You Should Already be Acquainted
with the Scriptures.

Is (the one who shuns) not acquainted with what is in the Scriptures of Moses? [Is he/she not acquainted with that] of Abraham who fulfilled [his duty]? [They witnessed] that no carrier can bear the burden of another. [They witnessed] that a person can have nothing but that for which he/she strives. [They witnessed] that his/her striving will be realized. [They witnessed] that he/she will be rewarded with a complete reward. [They witnessed] that to your Lord is the final goal. [They witnessed] that He grants laughter and crying. [They witnessed] that He grants death and life. [They witnessed] that He created in pairs –male and female—from a single cell lodged [in the uterine wall]. [They witnessed] that He promises a second creation. [They witnessed] that He gives wealth and satisfaction. [They witnessed] that He is the Lord of [the phenomenal star] Sirius. [They witnessed] that it is He who destroyed the ancient 'Ad and Thamud and spared no one. [They witnessed] that before them [He destroyed] the people of Noah who were even more oppressive and arrogant. [They witnessed] that He destroyed the decadent cities [of Sodom and Gomorrah] so that they have been consumed.

About which of the gifts of your Lord will you dispute?

—QUR'AN 53: 36-55

Daily living tip: Religious books exist all over the world. Only a few remote villages do not have written Scriptures, but they still have the scriptures of nature. There is no reason for anyone to not know of the awesome deeds of Allah. Do not dismiss any of His amazing works. His gifts are even within you. Remember that when you feel like a dummy.

Today's prayer: O my Lord, help me to get the most benefit from all your holy works and gifts.

Disbelievers Will be Questioned About the Scriptures.

To Allah belongs the dominion of the skies and Earth. When the day of the [last] hour begins, that will be a day of loss for the falsifiers. You will see every nation kneeling. Every nation will be summoned to its Record [of Deeds]: "This day you shall be recompensed for whatever you did. This, Our Record, tells the truth about you. Truly, We have recorded everything you did."

Those who believed and performed righteous deeds will be admitted by their Lord to His mercy. That will be the achievement for all to see.

To those who disbelieved: "Were Our verses not recited for you? You were arrogant and became sinful people. When it was said that the promise of Allah was true and that there was no doubt about the coming hour, you said, 'We don't know anything about this hour; it's just a theory with no evidence to support it.'"

Their sins will appear to them, and they will be surrounded by everything they used to ridicule. It will be said to them, "Today We will forget you just as you forgot your meeting for this day. You will dwell in the fire; no one can help you now."

—QUR'AN 45: 27-34

Daily living tip: The Qur'an is a warning for all people. It's not up to you to nag people about what they believe. You have enough to worry about trying to live your own life. You should share the truths of the Qur'an every opportunity you get. Other than that, it's none of your business what other people believe.

Today's prayer: O my Lord, help me be a person who speaks well of the religion without making other people feel uncomfortable with their own beliefs.

Which of the Lord's Favors
Will Humans and Spirit-beings Deny?

He has given freedom to the two bodies of flowing water, meeting together. A barrier keeps them apart.

So, which of the Lord's favors will you both [humans and spirit-beings] deny?

Out of (the waters) come pearls and coral.

So, which of the Lord's favors will you both deny?

He owns the ship sailing smoothly across the sea, [with sails] as lofty as mountains.

So, which of the Lord's favors will you both deny?

All that is of (Earth) will perish, but the face of your Lord will abide forever, full of glory and splendor.

So, which of the Lord's favors will you both deny?

Every creature of the skies and the earth seeks from Him. Every day He appears in splendor.

So, which of the Lord's favors will you both deny?

Soon shall We settle your affairs, O both worlds [of humans and spirit-beings].

So, which of the Lord's favors will you both deny?

O assembly of spirit-beings and humans, if you can pass beyond the zones of skies and earth, pass, but you will not be able to pass without [Our] authorization.

So, which of the Lord's favors will you both deny?

—QUR'AN 55: 19-34

Daily living tip: Three kinds of pride are (1) being conscious of one's own dignity as a human being, (2) a feeling of satisfaction for one's achievement, and (3) a feeling of superiority or overrated importance. It is good to have a healthy type of pride as in (1) and (2), but a superior pride as in (3) without giving glory to Allah is a wrong kind of pride. Everything you are and all that you have accomplished are by Allah's grace. Do not forget to give Him due honor.

Today's prayer: O my Lord, erase any false pride in me and let me never deny Your favor to me.

Many Spirit-beings Love the Qur'an.

Say, "It has been revealed to me that a company of spirit-beings listened [as the Qur'an was being recited]. They said, 'Truly, we have heard a wonderful Qur'an! It gives guidance to the righteous, and we have believed in it. We will not attribute any others with our Lord. Exalted is the majesty of our Lord. He has not taken a wife and has no son.

"'Some foolish ones among us made huge lies against Allah. We had thought that humans and spirit-beings would never state lies concerning Allah. It is true that some people among humanity took refuge with individuals among the spirit-beings, but they [the spirit-beings] caused them [the misguided humans] to increase their foolishness. They began to think, as you [misguided people] think –that Allah will not raise anyone [to face the judgment]. We sought to reach Heaven, but we found it surrounded with unyielding guards and flaming fires.

"'We used to sit in hidden realms to hear, but anyone who tries to listen now will find flaming fire waiting in ambush. We do not understand whether disaster is intended for those on earth, or whether their Lord intends to guide them to proper conduct.'"

—QUR'AN 72: 1-10

Daily living tip: If you try to contact the spirit world with a séance, Ouija board, witchcraft, or some other method, that can be very dangerous. You can cause an evil spirit to cross into your world and create problems for you. The spirit world is real. Don't invite trouble.

Today's prayer: O my Lord, protect me from evil spirits and any influences of Satan.

Some Spirit-beings Are Contrary.

"Among us [spirit-beings] are some who are righteous and some who are contrary. We follow divergent paths. But we think that we can by no means frustrate Allah throughout the earth, nor can we frustrate Him by flight. As for us, since we have listened to guidance, we have accepted it. Any who believes in his/her Lord fears neither injustice nor oppression. Among us are some who submit their wills and some who deviate. Those who submit their wills have sought correct conduct. But those who deviate are only fuel for Hell fire."

If (the idolaters) had remained on the [divine] path, We should certainly have given them plenty to drink. [eg, good rain].]That would be] so We could test them by that [blessing]. As for any who turns from the remembrance of his/her Lord, He will cause him/her to endure a severe penalty.

The places of worship are only for Allah, so do not invoke anyone else along with Allah. Yet, when a devotee of Allah approaches in order to invoke Him, (the idolaters) crowd around him/her to intimidate him/her.

—QUR'AN 72: 11-19

Daily living tip: A spirit has free will, so it can be good or evil. If you live a righteous life, you will attract the good spirits, and their energy will support you.

Today's prayer: O my Lord, give me an aura of goodness so that only positive energies are attracted to me.

Some Spirit-beings Witness to Their Community.

We previously destroyed populations around you, and We showed signs in various ways so they would repent. Why did those that they accepted as gods besides Allah, as a means of access to Allah, not help them? (The gods) abandoned them, but that was their deceit and fabrication.

We turned towards you a company of spirit-beings listening to the Qur'an. When they stood in the presence thereof, they said, "Listen in silence!" When it was finished, they returned to their community to warn. They said, "O our community, we have heard a Book revealed after Moses, confirming what came before it. It guides to the truth and to the Straight Way. O our community, listen to the one who invites to Allah and believe in Him. He will forgive you of your sins and deliver you from a tragic penalty. If any does not listen to the one who invites to Allah, he/she cannot frustrate Allah's plan on the earth. No protectors can he/she have besides (Allah). Such beings are in evident error."

—QUR'AN 46: 27-32

Daily living tip: Don't be outdone by the spirit-beings. They are witnessing to their community. You should do the same but learn how to do it in a non-abrasive manner. Don't ridicule someone else's religion in order to try to make yours look good. That doesn't work. All that does is make you look like a jerk.

Today's prayer: O my Lord, give me wisdom to know how to witness for you in beautiful and attractive ways.

Why Do the Disbelievers Not Learn Humility?

Before you [Prophet Muhammed], We sent [messengers] to many nations. We afflicted the nations with suffering and adversity in order that they may learn humility. When they received affliction from Us, why did they not learn humility? On the contrary, their hearts became hard, and Satan made their deeds appealing to them.

When they forgot the warning they had received, We opened to them the bounty of blessings. In the midst of their enjoyment of their gifts, We suddenly called them to account. They were plunged into despair. Of the sinners, the last remnant was cut off. Praise Allah, the Lord of the Worlds!

Say, "Do you think that, if Allah removed your hearing and sight and sealed your hearts, a god other than Allah could restore them?" See the various ways We explain the signs; yet they turn aside.

Say, "Do you think that, if the punishment of Allah came to you suddenly or by announcement, would any be destroyed besides the sinners?"

We send messengers only to proclaim the good news and to warn. Those who believe and change shall have no fear or grief upon them. Those who reject Our signs shall be punished because they wouldn't stop sinning.

—QUR'AN 6: 42-49

Daily living tip: Someone can be a believer in one religion and an unbeliever in Islam. Some of those unbelievers in Islam are arrogant. They think their religion is the only way to God. Do not be like them. You can believe your religion is the best without being a freaky little jerk about it.

Today's prayer: O my Lord, may my words and actions reflect a person of good character and proper humility.

You Are Not Accountable
for Those Who Refuse to See.

[Prophet Muhammed,] say, "I do not say that the treasures of Allah are with me, or that I know what is hidden. I do not say that I am an angel. I only follow what is revealed to me."

Say, "Can the unseeing be considered equal to the seeing? Will you then not consider?"

Give this warning to those who fear that they will be assembled before their Lord: Except for Him, they will have no protector or intercessor. Perhaps they may become righteous.

Do not reject those who call on their Lord morning and evening, seeking His face. You are not accountable for them, and they are not accountable for you. If you reject them, you are unjust.

We tested some of them by [the conditions of] others, so they might say, "Among us, are these favored by Allah?" Doesn't Allah know best who are grateful?

When believers in Our signs come to you, say, "Peace to you! Your Lord has inscribed His mercy. If any of you committed evil in ignorance, and then repented and made amends, He is Most Forgiving, Most Merciful.

Thus do We explain the signs in detail, so that the way of sinners is exposed.

—QUR'AN 6: 50-55

Daily living tip: Dressing and acting modestly is an act of rebellion. Be a rebel! Be outrageous! How other people dress and act is none of your business, however. You are not accountable for them. Do your best to set forth a good example and, insh'Allah, that will influence someone else to do better with his or her own life.

Today's prayer: O my Lord, let me not be judgmental of others' lives but help me to be a good influence on them as I do my best to reflect Your goodness.

Allah Will Allow the Sinner
the Path He/She Has Chosen.

Someone might argue with the messenger after ample guidance has been conveyed to him/her and follow a path other than the believers' path. We shall leave him/her in what he/she has chosen and will allow him/her to suffer in Hell. What a dreadful destination!

Allah does not forgive joining other gods with Him. He forgives whom He pleases of any other sins. One who joins other gods with Allah has strayed too far [to be forgiven, unless he/she repents and amends].

(The idolaters) abandon Him and call upon goddesses. They even call upon Satan, the relentless rebel.

Allah condemned him, and (Satan) said, "I will take a certain portion of Your servants. I will mislead them, and I will stir in them desires. [In their superstitious folly,] I will order them to slit the ears of cattle. I will order them to (ruin) Allah's creation."

Whoever forsakes Allah and trusts Satan for a friend certainly suffers a true loss.

—QUR'AN 4: 115-119

Daily living tip: When a person consciously abandons Allah's guidance, the subconscious mind follows. That person is truly lost. Allah leaves him or her lost unless that person makes a wise decision to return to Allah's guidance. That is why it is dangerous for you to experiment with something you know is wrong. Stay away from all sinful behavior so you don't get dragged down into a pit you can't get out of.

Today's prayer: O my Lord, may my conscious and subconscious mind be devoted to You. Keep me from sin and sinful lifestyles.

Consider the Sign of Trees.

The parable of those who reject their Lord is that of their deeds being as ashes furiously blown by the wind on a stormy day. They have no power over their fate because of how far they strayed.

Those who believe and live righteously will be admitted to gardens beneath which rivers flow, where they will live forever, by permission of their Lord. Their greeting will be, "Peace!"

Do you understand how Allah explains by way of a parable? A good word is like a good tree whose roots are firmly planted and whose branches extend to Heaven. It always brings forth its fruit, by permission of its Lord.

Allah presents such parables for people so they may reflect.

The parable of an evil word is that of an evil tree. Its roots are ripped from the earth's embrace. It has no stability.

Allah will strengthen the believers with the Word that stands firmly in this world and in the hereafter. Allah will leave the sinners astray. Allah does what He will.

—QUR'AN 14: 18, 23-27

Daily living tip: Do not be like a tree with shallow roots. It will get blown over in a fierce storm. Nourish your spiritual roots with the Living Water of Allah's Word and His grace and guidance. When life gets tough, you will stand tall and strong. Be a spiritual superhero!

Today's prayer: O my Lord, make my roots strong in faith so that I can face life with grace and dignity no matter what happens.

Belief Elevates a Person.

Is the person who believes no better than the person who is rebellious? They are not equal. For those who believe and live righteously are gardens as hospitable homes in exchange for their deeds.

As for those who are rebellious, their abode will be the fire. Every time they want to get away from it, they will be forced into it, and it will be said to them, "Taste the penalty of the fire that you rejected as false."

We will indeed make them taste the penalty of this worldly life prior to the supreme penalty so that they may repent.

Who is more wrong than one to whom are recited the verses from his/her Lord and then rejects them? Truly, We shall exact retribution from the sinners.

They ask, "When will this decision be, if you are telling the truth?"

Say, "On the Day of Decision, no profit will belief be to the disbelievers, and they will not be granted a respite."

Turn away from them and wait. They too are waiting [whether or not they realize it].

—Qur'an 32: 18-22, 28-30

Daily living tip: If you are a sincere and dedicated believer, you certainly are a superhero. Don't let the disbelievers get you down. They are the losers whether they realize it or not.

Today's prayer: O my Lord, may those who are lost and far from the Straight Way have a longing to repent of their sinful lifestyles. May they turn in sincere repentance and live righteously.

A Record Details Every Sinner's Actions.

Certainly, We created humanity, and We know what suggestions his/her soul makes to him/her. We are nearer to him/her than his/her jugular vein. The two receivers [angelic correspondents] on the right and on the left are seated [to record his/her deeds]. Not even a word does he/she utter without an observer [angel] ready [to note it].

With the stupor of death, the truth is flashed: "Here is what you sought to escape!"

The trumpet will sound to announce the day of which you had been warned. Every soul will come, each with an usher and a witness. "Certainly, you were heedless of this event, so We have lifted the veil [of ignorance] and made your sight keen for this day."

And his/her companion [the witness] will say, "Here is that [record] which I have prepared."

—QUR'AN 50: 16-23

Daily living tip: Take this seriously: your deeds are being recorded. Don't do anything that you would be ashamed for people to know. Certainly, Allah's knowing it is much worse. If you repent, however, Allah has a big eraser. He can erase those bad deeds if your repentance is sincere, and you make amends.

Today's prayer: O my Lord, keep me from all major sins and erase any mistakes I make. Be gracious to me and cover me with Your mercy.

What is the Prison Record?

Woe to the frauds. [They are[those who, when receiving for themselves, exact full measure from others. But when giving to others by measure or weight, they slight the measure. Do they really think that they will not be made accountable on a profound day? [That will be] on the day that humanity will stand before the Lord of the Worlds.

No [they don't believe]! Truly, the account of the wicked is in the Prison Record. What will explain to you what the Prison Record is? It is a penned document.

Woe that day to those that deny [the reality of] the Day of Judgment. No one is able to deny it except one who transgresses beyond all bounds –the sinner! When Our signs are recited to him/her, he/she simply says, "Myths of old!"

Truly, the account of the righteous is in the Honor Roll. What will explain to you what the Honor Roll is? It is a penned document listing those near [to Allah].

There is nothing hidden of Heaven or Earth that is not neatly recorded.
—QUR'AN 83: 1-13, 18-21 AND QUR'AN 27: 75

Daily living tip: Today is the day for you to decide if you want your name on the Prison Record or the Honor Roll. Make a commitment to Allah and to yourself to do your best to make it onto Heaven's Honor Roll.

Today's prayer: O my Lord, today I make a sincere commitment to strive to be among those listed on the Honor Roll for admittance into Paradise.

The Disbelievers Will Come
to Their Senses Too Late.

Those who do not expect the meeting with Us say, "Why do angels not descend to us?" or, "Why can't we see our Lord?"

They certainly are obnoxious! What audacity! The day they do see angels will not be a day of joy for sinners. (The angels) will say, "A barrier [of sin] blocks your way [to Heaven]." We will review their past deeds and make their deeds as [worthless as] scattered dust.

The Companions of Paradise will be well that day, in their homes, with the nicest places for midday relaxation.

The day the sky is rent asunder, with clouds, and angels descending, is the day that the dominion of truth is held by the Most Merciful. It will be a day of dire straits for the disbelievers.

That day, the sinner will gnaw at his/her fists and will say, "Oh, how I wish I had taken the path along with the messenger! How miserable I am! I wish I had never made friends with old so-and-so. He led me away from the message after I heard it! Satan is nothing but a traitor to humanity!"

—QUR'AN 25: 21-29

Daily living tip: Be a friend to everyone, but do not accept everyone as your friend. The wrong kind of friends will drag you down. You can lose your superhero status quickly if you follow the disbelievers down into the darkness of wicked lifestyles.

Today's prayer: O my Lord, teach me how to choose friends wisely. Keep me on the straight Way no matter what those around me do.

They Will Face the Great Catastrophe.

Have you heard the story of the great catastrophe?

Some faces that day will be humiliated. {They will be] sullen and tired. [That will be] while they enter the blazing fire. [That will be] while they are given to drink from a boiling spring. The only food will be a bitter, thorny fruit. It will neither nourish nor satisfy hunger.

Some faces that day will be joyful. {They will be] pleased with their striving. {They will be] in a garden on high. They will hear no foolish talk. In it will be a bubbling spring. In it will be thrones raised high. [There will be] placed goblets. {There will be] cushions set in rows. Rich carpets will be laid.

Do they not observe the camels and how they are made? [Do they not observe] the sky and how it is raised high? [Do they not observe] the mountains and how they are firmly fixed? [Do they not observe] the earth and how it is spread?

Give advisement, for you are one to advise. You can't control them. If anyone turns away and rejects faith, Allah will punish him/her with the greatest punishment. Truly, to Us will be their return. It will be up to Us to make them accountable.

—Qur'an 88

Daily living tip: We can do our best to guide others to the Straight Way, but it is their own decision. Each person has within him or her the knowledge of Allah, but it is by choice that one denies or accepts Him. Denying Allah's role in one's life is like a person making shark bait of him- or herself. Stay out of the shark's house.

Today's prayer: O my Lord, help me to live in such a way that others will see the Light of Your love and grace and want to be within it.

Souls Will Be Either Ripped Out or Gently Lifted.

Consider (the angels) who violently rip out [the souls of the wicked]. Consider (the angels) who gently lift [the souls of the blessed]. Consider (the angels) who glide on errands [of mercy]. They press forward as in a race. [Their mission is] to make arrangements on command [of their Lord].

Are you any more difficult to create than the skies that Allah has constructed? He raised its canopy, and He perfected it. He covered the night with darkness and lit the day with splendor. Afterward He expounded Earth. He enticed from it its water and pastures. He firmly anchored the mountains as a provision for you and your cattle.

Therefore, there will come the awesome and overwhelming event. [It will be] the day when every person shall regard that for which he/she has struggled. Hell fire shall be presented in full view for all to see. For those who transgressed the boundaries and showed preference for the life of this world, the abode will be Hell.

As for those who feared to stand before their Lord and restrained their souls from lustful desires, their abode will be Paradise.

—QUR'AN 79: 1- 5, 27-41

Daily living tip: Like a shark rips its prey, angels will rip out the souls of the wicked. It's up to you to go out that way or to go out gently. Don't wait to think about your day of dying. Everyone has to face that day. Make it a good day for you.

Today's prayer: O my Lord, may my day of dying be one of peace and gentle release. Save me from a death of pain and agony.

The Sinners Will Whine in Vain.

When angels take the souls of those who die in sin against their souls, (the angels) ask, "How did you fare?"

(The sinners) reply, "We were deprived while on the earth."

(The angels) ask, "Was Allah's earth not spacious enough for you to migrate?"

Such people will find their abode in Hell. What an evil refuge!

Exempted are disadvantaged men, women, and children who have no means within their power or anything to direct their way. For these, there is hope that Allah will forgive. Allah is the Forgiver, the Most Forgiving.

He/she who leaves his/her home in the cause of Allah will find in the earth many a refuge, wide and spacious. If he/she dies as a refugee away from home, for the sake of Allah and His messenger, his/her reward is certain with Allah. Allah is Most Forgiving, Most Merciful.

—QUR'AN 4: 97-100

Daily living tip: It's interesting that the matter of the earth being spacious enough is put in the form of a question. In the time of the Prophet (peace upon him) those oppressed could find safe havens. In today's world, however, it is extremely difficult to immigrate to a place where Muslims will not be oppressed or ridiculed. Even in so-called Muslim countries, freedoms are often limited. We just have to do the best we can living with jerks in this world and know that Allah is the Forgiver, the Most Forgiving.

Today's prayer: O my Lord, relieve me from ridicule and oppression when that is Your will, and give me strength to endure ridicule and oppression when that is Your will.

They Will Try to Blame Someone Else.

Do you not see that Allah created the skies and Earth in truth? If He wanted, He could remove you and replace you with a new creation. That would not be a big deal for Allah!

They will all be assembled before Allah.

The weak will say to the arrogant, "We only followed you. Can you then help us at all against the wrath of Allah?"

They will reply, "If Allah had guided us, we would have guided you. It doesn't make a bit of difference for us whether we panic or endure with patience. For us, there is no escape."

When the matter has been decided, Satan will say, "Truly, Allah gave you a true promise. I also promised, but I deceived you. I had no authority over you except to invite you, and you responded to me. Do not blame me but blame your own selves! I cannot help you, and you cannot help me. Indeed, I reject your previous association of me. Indeed, a horrible punishment awaits the sinners!"

—QUR'AN 14: 19-22

Daily living tip: One problem many people have is trying to blame others for their own actions and bad decisions. Take responsibility for what you do. If you mess up, admit it and try to make it right. Don't go around being a knucklehead.

Today's prayer: O my Lord, help me realize my own mistakes, forgive me, and help me to do better.

Finally, the Sinners Will Acknowledge Their Own Fault.

"O assembly of spirit-beings and people, were there not messengers among you to present My signs and to warn you of the meeting of your day [to be judged]?"

They will say [on that day], "We testify against ourselves."

The life of this world deceived them, so they themselves will testify that they would not believe. So it is, because your Lord would not destroy, due to sin, inhabited territories while the populations had not been advised.

To all are ranks according to their deeds, for your Lord is not unaware of a single thing that they do. Your Lord is the independent owner of mercy. If it were His will, He could destroy you. In your place, He could appoint His choice as your successors, just as He raised you from the lineage of another generation. Certainly, all He has promised you will come to pass, and you cannot foil it.

Say, "O my people, do whatever you can. I surely will also. You will soon know who will have a home in the finale! Certainly, the wicked will not succeed!"

—QUR'AN 6: 130-135

Daily living tip: The life of this world is ready to deceive you. People will tell you that wrong things are okay in our society. Don't believe them. Such things as sex outside marriage, using vulgar language, and viewing pornography have become normal, but Allah did not make it normal or acceptable. Don't be suckered in by foolish people doing foolish things.

Today's prayer: O my Lord, grant me strength to resist all the temptations this world offers. Let me not be afraid to be different when everyone else is going along with the crowd.

No Protector Will Come to the Aid of the Sinners.

For any whom Allah leaves astray, no protector will come thereafter.

You will see the sinners viewing the punishment. [They will] say, "Is there any way to return?" You will see them brought forward to (the punishment) in a state of humbleness. [They] will look with a stealthy glance.

The believers will say, "Those are truly in loss who committed themselves and their followers to damnation on the Day of Judgment."

They have no protectors to help them, other than Allah. For any whom Allah leaves astray, there is no way.

Respond to your Lord before the day comes from Allah that you cannot avoid. That day, no place of refuge will be there for you. There will be no chance for your denial.

If they turn away, We have not sent you [Prophet Muhammed] as a guard over them. Your duty is only to preach. Truly, when We give a person a taste of mercy from Us, he/she takes joy in it. When something bad happens as a result of what he/she has done, truly then the person is ungrateful.

—QUR'AN 42: 44-48

Daily living tip: The problem with pride is that when something good happens, people take credit for it; but when something bad happens, people blame Allah. You can be proud of your accomplishments, but don't forget to acknowledge Allah's help.

Today's prayer: O my Lord, help me to accomplish good things in my life, but let me never forget to give you the honor and glory.

No Associates Are Empowered.

Say, "Are there any of your associates [with Allah] who initiates creation and then repeats it?"

Say, "Allah initiates creation, and then repeats it. How can you be so contrary?"

Say, "Are there any of your associates [with Allah] who guides to the truth?"

Say, "Allah guides to the truth. Who is more worthy to be followed –the One who guides to truth, or the one who must first be guided before he/she can guide others? What is wrong with you and your way of figuring?"

Most of them follow nothing but conjecture. Surely conjecture can never be a substitute for truth. Truly, Allah is the All-knowing of all that they do.

Consider the fig and the olive. Consider Mount Sinai. Consider this secure city [of Meccah].

We created humanity in the best design. Then We abased him/her the lowest of the low. The exceptions are those who believe and perform righteous deeds. They will have an unfailing reward. After this, what causes you to deny the judgment? Is Allah not the wisest among judges?

—QUR'AN 10: 34-36 AND QUR'AN 95

Daily living tip: It's okay to have favorite singers, actors, musicians, authors, etc. It's a problem, however, when you let them set the standard for your own morals and ethics. When you do that, they become false gods. Don't let anybody control your life except Allah.

Today's prayer: O my Lord, remind me to keep the people I love in proper perspective. Do not let me follow them when they are in the wrong.

Day
314

Your God is One God.

Those whom (the idolaters) invoke besides Allah create nothing; they themselves are created! Dead and lifeless, they do not know when they will be resurrected.

Your God is One God. As for those who do not believe in the hereafter, their hearts refuse [to know], and they are arrogant. Undoubtedly, Allah knows what they conceal and what they publicize. Truly, He does not love the arrogant.

When it is said to them, "What has your Lord revealed?" they say, "Tales of the ancients!"

Let them bear, on the Day of Judgment, their own burdens in full and also some of the burdens of those without knowledge, whom they misled. How painful the burdens they will bear!

Those before them also plotted, but Allah ripped their structures from their foundations. The roof fell down on them from above. The wrath seized them from directions they did not perceive.

—QUR'AN 16: 20-26

Daily living tip: Ignore those who argue about "which God" is the true God. Say, "There is One God for everyone, and we glorify Him best when we glorify Him together." Leave it at that. Don't continue arguing with them. Be cool.

Today's prayer: O my Lord, may the whole world know Your awesome deeds and know that You are One.

To Allah is the Final Goal.

Ha Meem. The revelation of this Book is from Allah, the Victorious, the All-knowing. He forgives sin, accepts repentance, is strict in punishment, and is bountiful. No god is there except Him. To Him is the final goal.

No one can dispute about the signs of Allah, except the disbelievers. Do not let their influence throughout the land deceive you. Before them, the people of Noah and groups after them rejected [the message]. Every community plotted against its prophet to seize him and to dispute with deception to condemn the truth, but I [the Lord] seized them. How was My punishment?

Thus was the decree of your Lord proven true against the disbelievers. They are companions of the fire.

Truly, the disbelievers will be addressed, "Greater was the aversion of Allah to you than your aversion to yourselves, seeing that you were called to the faith and you refused."

They will say, "Our Lord, twice You have made us die, and twice You have given us life. We now recognize our sins. Is there any way out?"

This [punishment] is because, when Allah was invoked as the only One, you rejected faith, but when associates were joined with Him, you believed. The command is with Allah, the Highest, the Almighty.

—QUR'AN 40: 1-6, 10-12

Daily living tip: How can you prove to someone that God is real? Every person has that knowledge within his or her own soul. Scientists have discovered a "God part" of the brain. It is up to the individual whether to let that God part wither and starve or whether to nourish it with prayer and devotion. You can't prove it to someone who insists on denying it.

Today's prayer: O my Lord, may my life reflect the glory of Your splendor so that others can see proof of Your existence in the way I conduct myself.

All Matters Will Be Referred to Him.

It was Allah who created the skies and the earth and all among them in six days, and then He established Himself on the throne [of ultimate power]. Besides Him, you have no one who can protect or intercede. Won't you remember? He rules matters from Heaven to Earth. Ultimately, all matters will be referred to Him on a day consisting of a thousand years by your perspective. Such is He, the All-knowing of all things, secret and exposed, the Victorious, the Most Merciful.

He has made everything created in excellence. He began the creation of humanity with clay. He made the descendants from an extract of a repulsive liquid. He fashioned him/her, and then breathed into him/her from His Spirit.

He gave you your sense of hearing, sight, and feeling. Little thanks you give!

They say, "What? When we are lost to the ground, are we to be a new creation?"

No, they do not believe in the meeting with their Lord.

Say, "The Angel of Death, in charge of you, will take your souls. You will then return to your Lord."

If only you could see how the guilty ones will hang their heads down before their Lord! "Our Lord," [they will plead], "We have seen, and we have heard. Now return us [to the earthly dwelling], and we will live righteously, for now we do believe."

—QUR'AN 32: 4-12

Daily living tip: We are put here in a world of struggle to have opportunities to take steps toward Paradise. Every day is your big chance to get it right. Don't blow it.

Today's prayer: O my Lord, make my path lit for me so that I can easily tell which choices I should make.

Disbelievers Think That the Religion is a Cult.

There is not a mobile creature on the earth that does not depend on Allah for its sustenance. (Allah) knows (each creature's) residence and its final destiny. Everything is perfectly recorded.

He created the skies and the earth in six days. His throne was over the waters, so that He may test which among you are best in conduct.

If you were to say, "You will be resurrected after death," the disbelievers would certainly say, "Obviously, this is a cult."

If We delayed the penalty for them for a definite term, they would certainly say, "What is preventing it?" On the day it finally comes to them, nothing can divert it from them. They will be completely encircled by that which they used to mock.

If We give humanity a taste of mercy from Us and then retrieve it, he/she surely falls into despair and loses faith. But then, if We give him/her a taste of grace after adversity has affected him/her, he/she is certain to say, "Misfortune has left me" [without acknowledging God's involvement]. See how he/she falls into ecstasy and pride.

—QUR'AN 11: 6-10

Daily living tip: A cult is defined as 'a religious group whose beliefs are commonly regarded as strange or extreme'. Some people think Islam is a cult. You don't have to prove yourself to anybody. You have religious freedom, insh'Allah. Get your freak on and be a freak in the way of Allah.

Today's prayer: O my Lord, if I am strange, may my strangeness be for Your glory. I don't need to fit in if it means neglecting Your ways and Your guidance.

They Don't Believe in the Day of Atonement.

Praise to Allah to whom belongs what is of Heaven and Earth! To Him be praise in the hereafter. He is the Perfectly Wise, the Fully Aware. He knows all that enters the earth and all that comes from it, all that descends from the sky and all that ascends to it. He is the Most Merciful, the Most Forgiving.

The disbelievers claim, "Never will the hour [of doom] come upon us."

Say, "Nonsense! Most surely, by my Lord, it will come upon you. Consider He who knows the unseen, from whom is not hidden the smallest particle in Heaven or Earth. There is nothing less than that or greater that isn't in an obvious record. [This is] for the purpose of rewarding those who believe and work deeds of righteousness; for such is forgiveness and a most generous sustenance.

For those who strive against Our signs, to frustrate them, will be a penalty of painful wrath.

Those blessed with knowledge can see that what has been bestowed to you [Prophet Muhammed] from your Lord is the truth. [They can see] that it guides to the way of the Victorious, the Praised One.

—QUR'AN 34: 1-6

Daily living tip: Be humble enough to admit there are things you don't know and don't understand. Allah has not told us everything. We just have to remember that He has it all figured out, and everything is going according to plan.

Today's prayer: O my Lord, I don't know all the secrets of the unseen, but I trust in Your plan. May my life be on the right side of that plan.

They Flounder in Confusion.

Consider those scattering, dispersing. [Consider] those carrying burdens. [Consider] those that flow with ease. [Consider] those that assign command. Truly, all that you are promised is true. Truly, judgment must come to pass.

Consider the sky with its numerous orbits. Truly, you are in doctrinal discord. Those who would be deluded will be deluded [regardless of what message they hear].

Condemned are the liars –those who flounder in a flood of confusion!

They ask, "When is the Day of Judgment?"

That day they will be tested over the fire. "Taste your trial! This is what you wanted hastened."

For the sinners, their portion is like the portion of their ancestors. They should not ask Me to hasten it.

Woe to the disbelievers because of that day of theirs, which has been promised to them.

—QUR'AN 51: 1-14, 59-60

Daily living tip: The disbelievers are confused and floundering in their confusion. Do not let them drag you down. It's their struggle. Don't make it yours. If they ridicule your religion, just say, "It works for me, and I'm cool with it."

Today's prayer: O my Lord, may the disbelievers have a wakeup call before it's too late for their souls.

Consider Allah's Rejection of Them.

One day He will assemble them and say to the angels, "Did these people used to worship you?"

They will answer, "Glory to You! You are our Guardian –not them. No, but they worshiped the spirit-beings; most (people) believed in them."

On that day, you will have no power over each other, to help or to harm. We will say to the sinners, "Taste the penalty of the fire, which you denied."

When Our signs are recited to them, they say, "This (prophet) is only a man who wishes to hinder you from the worship practices of your fathers." They also say, "This is only an invented tale!" The disbelievers say of the truth when they hear it, "This is nothing but obvious magic."

We never gave (the Arabs contemporary to Muhammed) books to study or messengers before (Prophet Muhammed) as warners. Their ancestors, who were in denial, did not receive even a tenth of what We granted to (the contemporary Arabs). Yet, when they rejected my messenger, consider My rejection of them!

—Qur'an 34: 40-45

Daily living tip: Imagine what it would be like to be rejected by Allah. Don't worry about fitting in with the in-crowd. You can survive being rejected by them. Fit in with Allah's plan for your life and be among His in-crowd.

Today's prayer: O my Lord, bless me with friends who are in sync with Your plan for how people should live.

The Disbelievers' Faces
Will Be Dismal on That Fateful Day.

Bunk! (People) love this fleeting life and ignore the hereafter. Some faces that day [of resurrection] will beam, looking towards their Lord. Some faces that day will be dismal in the thought of some calamity about to be inflicted.

Undoubtedly, when (the final breath) reaches the throat, there will be a cry: "Who can save?"

(The dying person) will conclude that it is his/her turn to go. One leg is joined with the other leg [as death pulls the soul from the body]. On that day, compulsion will be to your Lord!

He/she gave nothing in charity and never prayed. On the contrary, he/she rejected truth and ignored it. He/she arrogantly returned to his/her family [with its poor family values]. Woe to you! Yes, woe! Again, woe to you! Yes, woe!

Does humanity think that he/she will be left disregarded? Was he/she not a single cell of sperm emitted? He/she then became a clot clinging [to the uterine wall]. (Allah) designed (humanity) in due proportion. Of him He made two genders –male and female. Does He not then have the power to give life to the dead?

—QUR'AN 75: 20-40

Daily living tip: It's nice to have an attractive face in this life, but it's more important to have a beaming face on the Day of Resurrection. If your light shines in this world, it will shine in the life hereafter. Don't be a grump. Toxic Islam in not Islam. Be kind, generous, and loving.

Today's prayer: O my Lord, may my face be among those who are beaming on the Day of Resurrection and not among those who are dismal.

The Disbelievers Will Not Be Able to Prostrate.

On the day that the shin will be exposed, they [the unforgiven sinners] will be summoned to prostrate [before the Lord], but they will not be able to do so. Their eyes will be downcast. Humiliation will overwhelm them [as they recall] that they were indeed summoned to prostrate when they were healthy.

Leave Me [the Lord] with those who reject this message. We will punish them by degrees from directions they cannot even imagine. I grant them respite, and My plan is truly powerful.

[What is their excuse?:] Did you [Prophet] ask them for some kind of reward so that they are burdened with a load of debt? Or is the unseen [Word] in their own hands, so that they can write it themselves?

The disbelievers would like to knock you down with their stares when they hear the message. They say, "He must be crazy!"

This message, however, is nothing less than a message for all the worlds.

—QUR'AN 68: 42-47, 51-52

Daily living tip: Every deceased body returns to Allah as a Muslim. That is because the person no longer has free will. The body and soul are compelled to do whatever is the will of Allah. Live a beautiful life in this world, and you will have a beautiful life in the hereafter.

Today's prayer: O my Lord, may my living and dying be for you so that I may not be disgraced in the life hereafter.

The Disbelievers' Prayers Will Be Worthless.

Those in the fire will say to the keepers of Hell, "Pray to your Lord to lighten the punishment for just one day."

(The keepers of Hell) will say, "Did messengers not come to you with clear signs?"

They will say, "Yes."

They will reply, "You may pray, but the disbelievers' prayers are worthless."

Those who reject the Book and that with which We sent Our messengers will soon know, with yokes around their necks, and with chains with which they will be dragged into boiling water. In the fire, they will burn.

To them, it will be said, "Where are your false idols now, which you adored instead of Allah?"

They will answer, "They have forsaken us. No, we invoked nothing."

Thus, Allah leaves the disbelievers astray.

"That was because you rejoiced [concerning our sins] on the earth without honesty, and you were insolent. Enter the gates of Hell to dwell therein. Wretched is the abode of the arrogant."

—QUR'AN 40: 49-50, 75-76

Daily living tip: How do people rejoice in their sins? It happens all the time. "I got laid last night." "I got so drunk I can't remember what happened." "I cheated on my test and passed without getting caught." Don't be among those who do wrong and then brag about it.

Today's prayer: O my Lord, let me not sit among those who openly brag about their sins.

Doom Will Come.

Consider the mountain! Consider a Book inscribed on unfurled parchment! Consider the frequented house [of worship]! Consider the roof raised high! Consider the ocean swelled!

Truly, the doom of your Lord will come to pass. No one can avert it. [It will be] the day when the sky will be in dreadful commotion and the mountains will violently shift.

Woe that day to those who reject [God's truth] and wallow in shallow discourse. That day they will be forcibly thrust into the fire of Hell.

"This is the fire you denied. Is it really fake, or do you not understand? Burn therein. Bear it patiently or not patiently; it's all the same for you. Truly, you receive the recompense of your deeds."

They will argue with each other in the fire. The feeble-minded will say to the arrogant, "Indeed, we followed you [as our role models]. Can't you relieve us of some of our fire?"

The arrogant will say, "Indeed, we are all in this together! Truly, Allah has judged among the servants."

—QUR'AN 52: 1-16 AND QUR'AN 40: 47-48

Daily living tip: Choose your role models carefully. Most people don't share our values and ethics. You can't blame your role models for leading you down the wrong path. You are responsible for your own deeds. Be a weirdo and be happy about it.

Today's prayer: O my Lord, bless me with role models I can look up to you and depend on not to lead me the wrong way.

Unforgiven Sinners Will Be Held Accountable.

Every soul will be held accountable for its misdeeds. The exception is the companions on the right. From gardens they will ask one another about the sinners. "What led you into Hell?"

They will say, "We were not among those who prayed. We did not feed the poor. We talked [in vain] with gossipers. We denied the Day of Judgment, until the certainty [of death] came upon us."

Then, mediation of intercessors will not profit them. What is wrong with them that they refuse warning as if they were frightened donkeys fleeing a lion? It seems that each one of them wants to be given unrolled scrolls [detailing their misdeeds]. Undoubtedly, they do not fear the hereafter.

No doubt, this surely is an admonition! Anyone who will keep it in remembrance should do so. None, however, will keep it in remembrance except as Allah wills. He is the Source of Reverence and the Source of Forgiveness.

—QUR'AN 74: 38-56

Daily living tip: The religion is easy: pray without ceasing, give charitably to help the poor, be kind and loving, and live righteously. Don't let people try to make it hard by adding manmade rules. People are always making up stuff and trying to say it came from Allah. Leave those people to their own struggle. Don't make it yours.

Today's prayer: O my Lord, make my religion easy to follow and keep me from following people who would make it hard.

Beware the Deafening Noise.

Humanity should consider his/her food. [He/she should consider] how We pour water in abundance. We fragment the earth in cracks. From it are produced grain, grapes, nutritious herbs, olives, date palms. [Also produced are] luxurious, enclosed gardens, and fruits and fodder as provision for you and your cattle.

Someday the deafening noise will come. That day a person will flee from his/her own brother and from his/her mother and father and from his/her spouse and children. Every person, that day, will have enough worries of his/her own.

Some faces that day will be beaming, laughing, rejoicing. Some faces that day will be dingy. Darkness will cover them. Such will be the disbelievers, the sinners.

Truly, from their Lord, that day, they will be banned. Truly, they will enter the fire of Hell. Also, it will be said [to them], "This is that which you rejected as false."

—QUR'AN 80: 24-42 AND QUR'AN 83: 15-17

Daily living tip: People often see things they don't understand and think it's the end of the world. Examples of those things are volcanic eruptions, the aurora borealis, and fiery comets. When the day actually comes, however, there will be no doubt. It will be a day of terror for the wicked. Do your best to be on the right side of things so that you don't have to fear that day.

Today's prayer: O my Lord, help me to live my life in such a way that I do not have to fear the day that is beyond human imagination.

What is the Calamity?

The calamity! What is the calamity? What will explain to you the calamity?

A day when people are like scattered moths! The mountains will be like fluffs of wool. Whoever has a heavy balance is heavy [of good deeds] will have a joyful life.

Whoever has a light balance will have the pit [of Hell] as his/her mother. What will make you know what that is? A fiercely blazing fire!

(The disbelievers) refute the hour, but We have prepared a blazing fire for those who deny the hour. When it sees them from a distant place, they will hear its fury and its raging squall. When they are cast, bound together, into a constricted place therein, they will plead for ultimate destruction.

On this day, do not plead for a single destruction; plead for a continuous destruction.

Say, "Does that sound better or the eternal garden promised to the righteous? For them are a reward and a goal. For them will be all they ever wanted. They will live forever. That is a promise for which should be petitioned from your Lord."

—Qur'an 101 and Qur'an 25: 11-16

Daily living tip: The descriptions of Hell are metaphors for an existence we cannot comprehend. Being burned alive is the closest thing in human language that describes the terror. This should be enough for you to realize you really don't want to be in that hot mess.

Today's prayer: O my Lord, save me and all my loved ones from the torment of Hell.

Earth Will Shake into Convulsions.

When the earth is shaken into convulsions! And the earth spews its burdens! And humanity cries, "What is wrong with it?" On that day (Earth) will declare its account. Your Lord will have given it inspiration.

On that day, people will proceed in various groups to be shown their deeds. Anyone who has done an atom's weight of good will see it. Anyone who has done an atom's weight of evil will see it.

Who will advance to Allah a beautiful loan? Allah will multiply it to his/her credit, and he/she will be rewarded liberally.

One day you will see the believing men and the believing women, how their light goes forth before them and from their right hands. "Good news for you this day: gardens beneath which rivers flow for your eternal dwelling." That is indeed the biggest success story!

Truly, the righteous will be in bliss. [They will be] looking from thrones. You will know them from their faces, beaming with wonderful delight. Their thirst will be slaked with pure nectar, sealed with musk. For this, may those with aspirations aspire.

—QUR'AN 99 AND QUR'AN 57: 11-12 AND QUR'AN 83: 22-26

Daily living tip: A wonderful day will come when you can stand with the believing men and believing women. Don't blow it. Don't be a loser. Strive for this greatest success you could ever have.

Today's prayer: O my Lord, may my living and my dying be embraced by your grace and mercy.

Angels Will Stand in Ranks.

Consider the panting steeds. They strike sparks of fire. They charge at dawn. They raise the dust. Together, they penetrate the midst.

Truly, humanity is ungrateful to his/her Lord. Truly, to that he/she bears witness. He/she is truly intense in the love of wealth.

Is he/she not aware of when the graves will be cast forth? [Does he/she not know] that what is in the hearts will be known? Truly, their Lord will be fully aware of them on that day?

The day that the Spirit and the angels will stand in ranks, none shall speak except any permitted by the Most Gracious, and each one will speak what is true.

That day will be the sure reality; therefore, anyone willing [to come to God] may return to his/her Lord.

Truly, We have warned you of an advancing penalty. [That will be] the day when humanity will see what his/her hands have incurred.

The disbelievers will say, "Oh, if only I were dust!"

—Qur'an 100 and Qur'an 78: 38-40

Daily living tip: Imagine the day when you will see the angels standing in ranks. This will be your personal Day of Judgment. Take it seriously. Prepare today for that awesome day of reckoning. It will be the most serious moment you ever experience.

Today's prayer: O my Lord, may everything I do pave a successful path for me to arrive on the Day of Judgment well prepared to face the angels.

Beware the Day the Sky Splits.

Consider the hurled (gusts), one after another. Consider the winds blowing violently and scattering far and wide and then making distinction. Consider those who relay the reminder [of God's Word], whether explanation or warning.

Honestly, what you are promised will come to pass. When the stars are smothered! When the sky splits apart! When the mountains convulse and crumble. When the messengers are each appointed a time. For what day are these postponed? It is the Day of Judgment. What will explain to you what the Day of Judgment is?

Beware that day, rejecters of truth.

Depart to that which you rejected as false. Depart to shadows of three columns. No cool shade is there and no shelter from the fierce blaze. It becomes a tower of shooting sparks. It looks like [a race of] yellow camels.

Beware that day, rejecters of truth.

That will be the Day of Judgment. We shall assemble you and your predecessors. If you have a scheme, go ahead and use it against Me [your Lord].

Beware that day, rejecters of truth.

—QUR'AN 77: 1-15, 29-33, 37-40

Daily living tip: Do you like to watch movies about natural disasters? Watch movies about earthquakes, firestorms, volcanoes, and meteor strikes. Multiply that terror many times, and you may get an idea of what the end of the world will be like. Make sure you get your ticket out of here and into Paradise.

Today's prayer: O my Lord, may the rejecters of truth wise up before it is too late for them.

Mountains Will Vanish, and Oceans Will Swell.

When the sun folds! When the stars fade away! When the mountains vanish! When the full-term, pregnant camels are abandoned! When the wild beasts herd together! When the oceans are swollen! When the souls are paired [with their bodies]! When the baby girl, buried alive, is questioned for what crime she was killed! When the scrolls are laid open! When the sky is stripped! When Hell is ignited! When Paradise is presented! Each soul will then know what it has forwarded.

Truly, I [the Lord] attest by the planets that recede, orbit, and set. [I attest by] the night as it dissipates; and the dawn as it breathes.

Truly, this is the statement of a most honorable messenger [the angel Gabriel]. [He is] empowered and honored before the Lord of the Throne. [He is] respectful and faithful.

Also, your companion [the Prophet] is not possessed [of an evil spirit]. Without a doubt, he saw (Gabriel) on the horizon, clearly. (The Prophet) does not withhold knowledge of the unseen. It is not the word of Satan, the condemned.

—QUR'AN 81: 1-25

Daily living tip: When Prophet Muhammed (peace upon him) recited the Qur'an, people thought he was whack. The powerful and terrifying verses about the end of the world present a story like a horror movie. Some people do not want to believe these things will really happen. Don't deny the realities of the future events for our world. Your survival guide is the Qur'an.

Today's prayer: O my Lord, help me be prepared for spiritual survival by packing all the truths and guidance of the Qur'an.

Stars Will Scatter, and Graves Will Erupt.

When the sky splits! When the stars scatter! When the oceans burst! When the graves are overturned! Each soul will then know what it has forwarded and withheld.

O Humanity, what has deceived you from your Lord the Most Generous? The One who created you fashioned you in appropriate stage. He arranges in whatever He wants. Shame! You, however, deny the judgment.

Truly, over you are guardian angels. [They are] honorable in recording [your deeds]. They know all that you do.

As for the righteous, they will be in bliss.

The wicked will be in Hell. They will enter it on the Day of Judgment. They will not be able to avoid it.

What can explain to you what the Day of Judgment is? Again, what can explain to you what the Day of Judgment is?

It is the day when no soul can help another. The command that day will be with Allah.

—Qur'an 82

Daily living tip: How will graves be overturned? According to one scientific theory (the Omega Point theory) the continually expanding universe will suddenly stop expanding. Time will move in reverse. Everything that has ever lived will be resurrected. The more you learn about science, the more the Qur'an makes sense.

Today's prayer: O my Lord, may my Day of Resurrection be one of glory and not of shame.

You Will Meet Your Lord.

O Humanity, truly, you are toiling onward towards your Lord, with effort, but you will meet Him. One who is given his/her record in the right hand will receive an easy reckoning for his/her account. He/she will turn to his/her people, rejoicing.

The one who is given his/her record behind his/her back will soon cry for destruction. He/she will enter a blazing fire. He/she certainly went among his/her people, gleefully. He/she really thought that there was no return [to Allah]. How senseless! Truly, the Lord was always watching him/her.

Oh, I attest by the glow of sunset, the night and all it gathers, and the moon in its fullness. You will certainly journey from one point to another.

What is wrong with (the disbelievers) that they won't believe? When the Qur'an is read to them, they do not prostrate. On the contrary, they reject it. Allah has full knowledge of what [ill thoughts] they harbor. So proclaim to them a harsh penalty. The exception is for those who believe and work righteous deeds. For them is an infallible reward.

—QUR'AN 84: 6-25

Daily living tip: "You will certainly journey from one point to another." In Islam, we believe a passage called barzakh is like a worm hole that connects this world to the next. When a person dies, the soul travels through this tunnel. How you live your life today determines if your journey will be beautiful and peaceful or terrifying.

Today's prayer: O my Lord, may my journey to the next life be one of beauty and peace, and I pray the same for my family and friends and all believers.

The Vengeance of the Lord is Strong.

Consider the sky with its constellations. Consider the promised day. Consider the witness and the subject of the witness.

Cursed are the makers of the pit. [It is] the fire fed by fuel [for torturing and murdering the believers]. They took seats [near the fire]. [As spectators,] they watched what they were doing to the believers. They tortured them for no other reason than that they believed in Allah, the Victorious, the Praised One. He owns the dominion of Heaven and Earth. Allah witnesses everything.

As for those who persecute the believers –men and women— and do not repent, they will incur the penalty of Hell. They will incur the penalty of the burning fire.

As for those who believe and perform righteous deeds, they will live in gardens beneath which rivers flow. That is the great salvation!

The vengeance of your Lord is truly strong. He creates from the very beginning, and He can recreate. He is the Most Forgiving, Full of Loving Kindness. [He is] Owner of the Throne of Glory. [He is] Performer of All His Intentions.

—QUR'AN 85: 1-16

Daily living tip: Whenever you are bullied for your faith, remember that whatever you have to endure was endured much worse by the first believers in the Qur'an. You are in good company. It's like a club membership. You are in a club of the divine.

Today's prayer: O my Lord, bless and protect all believers from those who would harm us.

Seek Salvation.

O Believers, save yourselves and your families from a fire with fuel of humans and brimstone. It is a fire over which are stern, severe angels. They do not flinch at the commands they receive from Allah, but do exactly what they are told.

[The angels will say:] "O Disbelievers, make no excuses this day. You are only being rewarded for all that you did."

O Believers, turn to Allah with sincere repentance in the hope that your Lord will cover your sins and admit you to gardens beneath which rivers flow. On that day, Allah will not permit the humiliation of the Prophet and those who believe with him. Their light will radiate before them and from their right hands as they pray, "Our Lord, perfect our light and grant us forgiveness, for You have power over all things."

We know how it breaks the heart of (the Prophet) because of what people say [against him]. But celebrate the praises of your Lord and be among those who prostrate [in adoration]. Serve your Lord until that certain hour [of death] arrives.

—QUR'AN 66: 6-8 AND QUR'AN 15: 97-99

Daily living tip: When you get your feelings hurt, remember that Prophet Muhammed (peace upon him) got his feelings hurt even worse. Allah will make it right on the Day of Judgment. You will be able to raise your fists and say, "Whoop! Whoop!" You got this!

Today's prayer: O my Lord, peace and blessings upon Prophet Muhammed and all the prophets who suffered bullying and abuse. Help me to endure as they did.

Consider from What You Are Made.

Consider the sky and the night visitor. What will explain to you what the night visitor is. The star of piercing brightness!

There is no soul without a protector over it.

May humanity consider from what he/she was created! He/she was created from an ejected fluid. [This fluidity began] from between the backbone and the ribs. Surely, He is able to resurrect him/her.

[Consider] the day when secrets will be made known. Humanity will have no power and no helper.

Consider the sky and its cycle. Consider the earth that cracks [with the sprouting of seeds]. Truly, this is the Word that distinguishes. It is not a thing for fun.

Indeed, they are plotting a scheme. I too am plotting a scheme. Therefore, grant a delay to the disbelievers. Give a small respite to them.

If We had already inflicted punishment upon them, they would have complained, "Our Lord, if only You had sent us a messenger, We surely would have followed Your signs before we were humiliated and shamed."

Say, "Each of us is waiting, so just wait. Soon you will know who among us is on the Straight Way and has received guidance."

—QUR'AN 86 AND —QUR'AN 20: 134-135

Daily living tip: The jerks will claim that the Bible, the Qur'an, and other holy books are all fairy tales. They make fun of believers. Be assured the Qur'an is not a comic book. The superheroes in the Qur'an are real!

Today's prayer: O my Lord, give me superhero powers to be able to walk bravely upon this earth in defiance of all those who mock believers.

What is the Reality?

The Ultimate Truth! What is the Ultimate Truth? What will cause you to realize what the Ultimate Truth is?

When one blast peals from the trumpet! [When] the earth and mountains are lifted and then crushed to powder in one event! That day the episode will come to pass. The sky will rip apart, for on that day, it will be dilapidated. The angels will be on its sides. On that day, eight will bear the throne of your Lord above them.

On that day, you will be exposed. Not one of your secrets will remain hidden.

The one who receives his/her record in his/her right hand will say, "Now read my record. I really did understand that I would be held accountable." He/she will be in a life of bliss in a garden on high, where fruits hang near.

The believers and their believing family members will be reunited. We will not deprive them any of their earnings. Each individual is pledged for his/her deeds.

We will bestow upon them fruit and meats as they desire. They will exchange, one with another, a cup free of foolishness, free of sin.

—QUR'AN 69: 1-3, 13-23 AND QUR'AN 52: 21-23

Daily living tip: When the world as we know it comes to an end, we will experience a different type of reality. Life as we know it is like looking through fog. In the hereafter, we will see things clearly and have greater understanding. When the life of this world seems like a mess, remember that Allah has a plan to make everything right.

Today's prayer: O my Lord, prepare my soul for the inevitable reality fully known only to You.

The Time-Space Continuum is Allah's Reality.

A petitioner asks about a penalty to befall the disbelievers. [It is a penalty] which no one can avert. [It is a penalty] from Allah, the Owner of the Staircase.

The angels and the Spirit ascend unto Him in a [cosmic] day, the measure of which is fifty thousand [Earth] years. So be patient with a content patience. (People) see (the last day) as far away, but We see it as near.

That day the sky will look like molten metal. The mountains will become like [fluffs of] wool. [Out of dread] no friend will ask about another friend. [That is] even if they are put in sight of one another.

The [unforgiven] sinner will wish that he/she could redeem him-/herself from the penalty of that day with his/her children. [He/she will wish for redemption by using] his/her spouse, his/her sibling, his/her relatives who sheltered him/her, and all else on the earth that might deliver him/her. But no! There is only fire plucking to the skull. [The fire will be] inviting those who turned their backs and rejected [the truth] and who amassed and hoarded.

—QUR'AN 70: 1-18

Daily living tip: Learn as much as you can about quantum physics and other sciences so that you can understand more about how the Qur'an addresses the subject of time and the end of time.

Today's prayer: O my Lord, make me one who never tires of gaining knowledge.

When is the Day of Resurrection?

I call to witness the Day of Resurrection. I call to witness the self-reproaching spirit.

Does humanity think that We cannot assemble his/her bones? Certainly, We are able to put together in perfect order even the very tips of his/her fingers.

But humanity prefers to debase whatever is in front of him/her.

The question is asked, "When is the Day of Resurrection?" When the sight is dazed! And the moon is eclipsed! And the sun and moon merge! That day people will ask, "Where do we go for refuge?" By no means will there be a place of safety. To your Lord, that day, will be destiny. That day humanity will be confronted with every positive and every negative deed. Every person will be his/her own witness, even if he/she makes excuses.

Do not move your tongue in haste while reciting the Qur'an [without taking time to understand it]. It is up to Us to render it and to recite it. Once We have recited it, follow its narration. Then it is up to Us to explain it.

—QUR'AN 75: 1-19

Daily living tip: Do not be disrespectful or unkind. Don't be a jerk to anybody. Don't creep on people. You don't know when it's your time to rise on the Day of Resurrection and face up to whatever you have done.

Today's prayer: O my Lord, may my Day of Resurrection be one of gladness and not shame.

A Single Blast Will Portend the Judgment.

The trumpet shall be sounded when, behold, from the graves they will rush forth to their Lord. They will say, "Oh, woe to us! Who has raised us from our beds of repose?"

[In answer:] "This is what the Most Gracious promised, and the messengers told the truth."

No more than a single blast will there be when, behold, they will all be brought before Us. On that day, not a single soul will be wronged in the least, and you shall be repaid only for your past deeds.

Truly, the Companions of the Garden will have joy that day in everything they do. They and their spouses will be in shady groves, reclining on couches. Fruits will be there for them. They will have whatever they request.

"Peace!" That's the word from the Most Merciful Lord.

—QUR'AN 36: 51-58

Daily living tip: If you knew what terrific things were waiting for you on the other side of this life, you wouldn't even think of messing up. Do what's right. It's worth the effort!

Today's prayer: O my Lord, may I enter the next life, hearing words of peace and comfort.

Past Deeds Will Be Presented.

Present them the simile of the life of this world: It is like the rain which We send down from the skies. The earth's vegetation absorbs it, but soon the plants become dry stubble, which the winds scatter. Allah prevails over all things.

Wealth and children are fascinations of the life of this world, but the things that endure, good deeds, are best in the sight of your Lord in terms of reward and hope.

One day, We shall remove the mountains, and you will see the earth barren, and We will assemble them, and We will not leave out a single person. They will be marshaled before your Lord in ranks. "Now you have come before Us as We first created you. You thought We would never fulfill this appointment made for you."

The Book will be placed, and you will see the sinful in great terror because of what is therein. They will say, "Woe to us! What manner of book this is! It leaves out nothing, small or great, but takes account thereof." They will find all their deeds presented, and your Lord will not cause injustice to anyone.

—QUR'AN 18: 45-49

Daily living tip: Time is a book recording all your deeds, both good and bad. Make time your friend by doing your best to have a longer list of good deeds than bad. Repent of your bad deeds, and, insh'Allah, they will be erased from time.

Today's prayer: O my Lord, I repent of all my wrongdoings, so please erase them. Empower me to do better and to create a long list of good deeds.

Our Own Skins Will Testify.

On the day that the enemies of Allah will be assembled for the fire, they will be assembled in rows. Finally, when they reach it, their hearing, their sight, and their skins will testify against them for their deeds.

They will say to their skins, "Why do you testify against us?"

They will answer, "Allah has made us able to communicate. He is the One who gives speech to everything. He created you for the first time, and unto Him you were to return. You did not seek to hide yourselves, lest your hearing, your sight, and your skins should testify against you. Instead, you thought that Allah did not know many of the things that you used to do. Your assumptions that you entertained, concerning your Lord, has ruined you, and now you are among the lost."

If they endure, the fire will be their residence. If they beg for favor, they will not be among those who receive favor.

Further, we have destined for them companions who made their past and present [deeds] seem justifiable, but the sentence has already been passed against them, along with previous generations of spirit-beings and people. Indeed, they were losers.

—Qur'an 41: 19-25

Daily living tip: We now know that things such as fingerprints and DNA can testify against criminals. On the Day of Judgment, your whole body will testify for or against you. If you use drugs or alcohol or any other bad substance, your body will blab about it. If you watch porn videos, your eyes will testify. Make your body your friend –not your plaintiff.

Today's prayer: O my Lord, may my body have only good things to say about me.

No Living Thing Has Been Omitted
from the Book of Life.

Lost indeed are those who disregard the fact that they must meet Allah. Suddenly the hour [of judgment] is upon them. They will say, "Oh, disaster is upon us because we did not give serious thought." The weights of their sins are borne on their backs. What a miserable burden!

The life of this world is merely entertainment and amusement. Better yet is the home of the hereafter for those who live righteously. Don't you understand?

There is not a creature on the earth, not even a being that flies on wings, that is not part of a community, just like you [humanity]. We have omitted nothing from the Book [of Life]. They all shall be assembled before their Lord.

Those who reject Our signs cannot hear or speak and are in the dark. Allah leaves whom He will to wander. He places whom He will on the Straight Way.

Say, "Do you think that, if the wrath of Allah or the hour [of judgment] suddenly came upon you, you would call on anybody other than Allah, if you are honest?"

—QUR'AN 6: 31-32, 38-40

Daily living tip: All creatures are Muslims because they do whatever they were created to do. If you have a pet or love all animals, you can be happy that they are written in the Book of Life. Paradise will have plenty of animals for you to hug. Be kind to all animals because they are Muslims like you.

Today's prayer: O my Lord, bless all the animals so that their struggles are easier for them.

Day
344

Consider the Parable of a Man and His Donkey.

Consider this parable:

A man passed through a ghost town all in ruins; even the roofs had fallen.

He said, "Oh, how could Allah ever bring life back to this town?"

Allah caused him to be dead for a hundred years, and then revived him.

(Allah) asked [him], "How long have you been here?"

He answered, "About a day or so."

Then (Allah) informed [him], "No, you've been here for a hundred years. Your food and drink show no signs of decay but look at your donkey [which is decayed]; of it We will make a sign for you which will benefit all people. Watch how we bring the bones together and clothe them with flesh."

When this was shown to him, he said, "I now realize that Allah is in complete control!"

—QUR'AN 2: 259

Daily living tip: This parable, which is also in Jewish tradition, shows that Allah has a plan to resurrect all living creatures. Don't be so arrogant that you think the Day of Resurrection is only for people. All creation is within the heart of Allah and destined for Paradise.

Today's prayer: O my Lord, may Your help come to relieve creation from the burdens humanity has placed on it by his/her reckless exploitation of natural resources.

Consider Your Original Creation.

O Humanity, if you have doubts about the resurrection, [consider that] We indeed created you from dust, and then from sperm, and then from a mass clinging [to the uterine wall]. [We continued with] an embryonic lump, partly formed and partly unformed, so that We may clarify to you [the wonder of creation]. We cause whom We will to remain in the wombs for an appointed term, and then We bring you forth as babies so you may attain maturity. Among you is one who dies [before old age] and one who is returned to a feeble age until he/she knows nothing after having known.

Further, you see the earth barren, but when We pour rain upon it, it is stirred, it swells, and it puts forth every kind of lovely plant. This so because Allah is the Ultimate Truth. He gives life to the dead, and He has power over all things.

The hour [of resurrection] will come. No doubt about it! Allah will raise all who are in the graves. Yet, among humanity is such a person who argues about Allah, without knowledge, without guidance, and without a Book of enlightenment.

—Qur'an 22: 5-8

Daily living tip: Whether you have a wonderful mother or a rotten mother, be grateful to her for the time she carried you and gave birth to you. Your mother was the vessel from which you traveled from the spirit world to the physical world. Don't talk smack to her.

Today's prayer: O my Lord, may every person know the love of a good mother whether or not she is his or her biological mother. Bless all mothers who fulfill their role with love and grace.

Allah Can Restore Life.

The disbelievers say, "What! When we and our ancestors become dust, shall we really be resurrected? Sure, we and our forefathers were promised this before, but that was nothing but ancient folktales."

Say, "Travel about the earth and see what became of the guilty."

Do not grieve over them, however, or be upset over their plots.

Don't they see that Allah –who created the skies and Earth, never tiring from their creation— is able to restore life to the dead? Yes, truly, He has power over everything.

[Said] on the day that the disbelievers are placed before the fire: "Is this not the truth?"

They will say, "Yes, by our Lord!"

He will say, "Then taste the penalty that you denied."

Have patience, therefore, as did the patient messengers of strong will. Do not be in haste about the (disbelievers). On that day, they will see what has been promised them, as if they had lingered [in death] no more than an hour of a single day.

Only give notification. Shall any be destroyed besides the sinners?
—QUR'AN 27: 67- 70 AND QUR'AN 46: 33-35

Daily living tip: People must be whack if they think the creation will not be restored. Allah made it the first time. Why would anybody think He can't do it again? Don't be like the disbelievers and poo-poo everything about faith.

Today's prayer: O my Lord, bless all creation to endure the struggle until Your awesome plan of resurrection unfolds.

Three Classes of People Will Be Resurrected

When the inevitable event comes to pass, no one will be able to deny its reality. It will debase; it will exalt. The earth will shake violently. The mountains will crumble and collapse.

You [humanity] will belong to three classes: [1] The companions of the right: what will be the companions of the right? [2] The companions of the left: what will be the companions of the left? [3] The foremost will be foremost. These will be those nearest [to Allah]. [They will be] in gardens of bliss. [They will be] a number [of people] from ancient times and a few from later times. [They will be] on ornate thrones, reclining on them, facing one another. Around them immortal youths will serve goblets, pitchers, and a flask filled from pure, flowing fountains. (The companions) will not get a hangover or suffer intoxication. They will have any fruits they may select and any poultry they want.

Companions with attractive eyes, wide [with delight], will be like safely guarded pearls. A reward for the deeds of their past will be no frivolous talk heard therein and no taint of hostility. [They will hear] only the saying, "Peace! Peace!"

—Qur'an 56: 1-26

Daily living tip: Live so that you will be among the most favored on the Day of Judgment. Don't let your buddies try to convince you that wrong deeds are okay. If Allah says it's wrong, it stays wrong even if everybody is doing it. You are responsible for your actions. It doesn't matter how weird you seem to other people. Being weird is cool.

Today's prayer: O my Lord, let me not be persuaded to do things that You have already said are wrong.

Day
348

The Good Finale is for the Righteous.

We shall give the House of the Hereafter to those who seek no supremacy or evil on Earth, and the good finale is for the righteous. Whoever performs goodness will receive a reward far better than his/her deed. Those who do evil, however, are punished only in relation to their deeds. Truly, He who ordained the Qur'an for you will bring you back to the place of return.

Say, "My Lord knows best who conveys true guidance and who is in evident error."

You never expected that the Book would come to you except as a mercy from your Lord; therefore, do not lend support in any way to the dissenters. Let nothing keep you away from the Scriptures of Allah after they have been revealed to you. Invite people to your Lord, and do not be among the polytheists. Do not call on any god other than Allah. No god is there except Him! [Eventually] everything will perish except His face! To Him belongs the command! To Him you will return!

—Qur'an 28: 83-88

Daily living tip: Don't bully anybody no matter what his or her condition is. Bullying is not cool. Don't make fun of people. Look for opportunities to be kind to people and animals. Stick up for people even if they act stupid. Everybody has poopy-head moments.

Today's prayer: O my Lord, give me the courage to do the right thing even if I'm the only one doing it.

Hell is for the Unforgiven Sinners.

[To the unforgiven:] "O Sinners, depart on this day! Did I not enjoin on you, O Children of Adam, that you should not revere Satan because he was your avowed enemy? [Did I not say] that you should worship Me? That was the Straight Way. He led astray many multitudes of you. Did you not then understand?

"This is Hell, about which you were warned. Embrace it this day because you would not believe."

On that day, We shall seal their lips, but their hands will speak to Us, and their feet will bear witness for all their deeds.

If it had been Our will, We could certainly have poked out their [spiritual] eyes and left them groping for the path, but then how could they have seen [even if they had wanted]? If it had been Our will, We could have transformed them into immovable objects wherever they settled [in spiritual matters], and then they could not have returned [even if they had wanted]. [But God continued allowing free will.]

—QUR'AN 36: 59-67

Daily living tip: Everybody goofs up sometimes. Everybody does stupid things. You don't need to carry around guilt. Repent with a sincere repentance. When Allah forgives, your goof-ups get erased.

Today's prayer: O my Lord, forgive me for my mistakes and sins and save me from the Hell fire.

What is Hell?

O enveloped one, arise and warn! Glorify your Lord and purify your garments. Abandon all sin. Do not expect anything in return for your giving, but be patient for the sake of your Lord.

When the trumpet is sounded, that day will be the day of distress. [It will be] far from easy, for the disbelievers.

Leave Me alone with the one I created barren. I granted him/her abundant resources and the presence of children. I made his/her life comfortable, but he/she wanted Me to give more. Ridiculous! He/she has been oblivious to Our signs. I will soon burden him/her with hardship!

I will cause him/her to suffer in Hell. What will explain to you what Hell is? It permits nothing to endure but allows nothing to be consumed. It scorches human skin.

Consider the moon and the night as it retreats, and the dawn as it shines forth. This is only one of the awesome warnings to humanity. [It is] to any, whether you choose to press forward or lag behind.

—QUR'AN 74: 1-17, 26-29, 32-37

Daily living tip: The metaphors of Hell are to explain to us the horror of an existence that we cannot comprehend. Nobody fully understands what Hell is like. All we know is it's not a place cool dudes and gals want to go to.

Today's prayer: O my Lord, save me, my family members, and friends from the terror of the flames of a dreaded existence.

Hell is an Ambush.

Truly, Hell is an ambush. For the transgressors [it is] a destiny. They will dwell therein for ages. They won't taste anything cool. There will be no drink except scalding water and paralyzing cold [like freezer burn]. That is a fitting recompense because they never expected accountability. They treated Our signs as false.

One day Earth will be changed to a different Earth, and the skies will also change. (People) will emerge before Allah, the Only One, the Prevailing Force. You will see the [unforgiven] sinners that day bound together in shackles. Their garments will be of liquid tar, and their faces will be covered with fire.

Allah will repay each soul according to what it deserves. Truly, Allah is swift in calling to account.

Here is a message for humanity. May they take warning from it, and may they know that He is One God. May people of understanding take heed.

—QUR'AN 78: 21-28 AND QUR'AN 14: 48-52

Daily living tip: Be kind to everyone. By your kindness, Allah may become known to those who do not know Him. Your kindness may be the cause of saving someone from Hell. Don't be someone's hell on earth by being a snob.

Today's prayer: O my Lord, make me to be a kind and respectful person.

Hell Will Never Be Too Full for One More.

One day, We will ask Hell, "Are you full?"

It will say, "Are there any more?"

Paradise will be brought near to the righteous –no more a distant thing. "This is what was promised for you –for everyone who repented, who was protecting [of the faith]. [It is for the one] who feared the Most Gracious in the unseen, and approached with a repentant heart. Enter there in peace and security. This is a day of eternal life!"

For them will be whatever they want, plus more with Us.

How many generations before them did We destroy, stronger in power than they? They wandered through the land; was there any place of escape?

Truly, in this is a message for any who has a mind, or who listens and earnestly witnesses.

We created the skies and Earth and all among them in six days, and no exhaustion ever touched Us.

Endure with patience all that (the disbelievers) say. Glorify your Lord before the rising of the sun and before the setting. During part of the night, glorify Him, and at the ends of prostrations.

—Qur'an 50: 30-40

Daily living tip: You may feel like you're missing out on a lot: beer busts, wild parties, unchaperoned dates, bar hopping, etc. The best thing you can miss out on, however, is Hell. Avoid activities that may lead you into a mess of trouble. Always have someone to call on for help if you do get in a mess and need to leave.

Today's prayer: O my Lord, help me avoid situations where the wrong things can happen. Grant me opportunities for good, clean fun.

Relief Will Be Forbidden.

Between (the faithful servants and the unforgiven sinners) will be a partition. On the heights will be people who recognize others by their marks. They will call to the companions of Paradise, "Peace to you!" They [the forgiven servants] will not have yet entered the garden, but they will already have the assurance.

When (the forgiven servants') eyes turn toward the companions of the fire, they will say, "Our Lord, do not send us into the company of sinners."

The companions on the heights will call to certain people whom they will recognize from their marks. [They will say,] "No profit to you were your hoarding and whatever caused your arrogance. Are these [forgiven servants] not the same people of whom you said Allah would never bless with His mercy?"

"Enter Paradise. No fear or grief will be upon you."

The companions of the fire will call to the companions of Paradise, "Pour upon us water or anything that Allah has provided you."

They will say, "Allah has certainly forbidden these things to those who would not believe. [They are] those who acknowledged religion to be mere amusement and play and were deceived by the life of this world."

That day We will forget them as they forgot the meeting of this day of theirs, as they tended to reject Our signs.

—QUR'AN 7: 46-51

Daily living tip: If you are invited to a party or other event, ask questions. Who will be there? Who will chaperone it? Will there be alcoholic drinks or illegal drugs? Find out as much as you can to ensure that you will not be with those who love to do what is wrong. Some people live like they want to be hotdogs roasting in Hell. Be kind to everyone but don't accept everyone as your buddy.

Today's prayer: O my Lord, make me wise enough to know how to stay out of trouble.

What Did Your Lord Reveal?

[On the Day of Judgment], it will be said to the righteous, "What did your Lord reveal?"

They will say, "All that is good."

For those who do good, there is goodness in this world, and the home of the hereafter is even better. Excellent indeed is the home of the righteous. It is Gardens of Eden, which they will enter. Beneath them, rivers will flow. They will have therein all that they wish. Thus does Allah reward the righteous! [The righteous are] those whose lives are in a state of purity when the angels take them. [The angels] say, "Peace to you; enter Paradise because of what you did."

Do (the disbelievers) wait until the angels come to them or some command from their Lord comes to them? So did those who went before them, but Allah did not cheat them. They cheated their own souls. The evil results of their deeds overwhelmed them, and that which they had scoffed surrounded them.

—QUR'AN 16: 30-34

Daily living tip: You may feel left out sometimes when you have to turn down invitations to haram activities. Remember that when you get to Paradise, you'll really be in with the in-crowd. Look forward to that.

Today's prayer: O my Lord, bless me with friends who know how to have fun without doing stupid stuff.

The Righteous Will Be Rewarded.

For the disbelievers, We have prepared chains, yokes, and a blazing fire.

As for the righteous, they shall drink from a cup, a mix of [a soothing tonic of] camphor. [It will be] from a fountain where the worshipers of Allah drink. I will flow in unhindered abundance.

(The righteous) perform vows [of spiritual service]. They fear the day from which dread flies far and wide. They provide food, in spite of their own want for it. [They provide it] to the indigent, the orphan, and the captive. "Truly, We feed you for the sake of Allah alone. We expect no reward or thanks from you. We fear from our Lord a day of severe difficulty [if we do not follow His will]."

But Allah will deliver them from the harm of that day and will shed over them radiance and joy.

Because they were patient, He will reward them with a garden and silk. Reclining in (the garden) on raised thrones, they will experience neither the sun [ie, unbearable heat] nor excessive cold. The shades [of the garden] will hang near them. Bunches of fruit will hang low and accessible.

—QUR'AN 76: 4-14

Daily living tip: Be generous to others, and Allah will be generous to you. You will find joy in this life and rewards in the next life. Don't be greedy and stingy.

Today's prayer: O my Lord, grant me opportunities to share what I can with others. May Your help come to all those who are suffering and struggling.

The Righteous Will Be Pampered.

Among them will be passed vessels of silver and goblets of crystal. [They will be] crystal clear and with silver. They will determine however much they want. They will be given to drink a cup, mixed with ginger. [It will be] from a fountain called Seek the Way.

Around them will be immortal youths. If you saw them, you would think of them as scattered pearls [so unblemished are they].

When you look around, you will see a blissful and magnificent realm.

Upon (the believers) will be green garments of fine silk and heavy brocade. They will be adorned with bracelets of silver. Their Lord will give them a pure and holy [non-intoxicating] drink.

Truly, this is a reward for you, and your endeavor is recognized.

The righteous shall be amid shades, fountains, and fruits –all that they desire. Eat and drink to your heart's content because of your works.

Thus do We certainly reward those who live righteously.

—Qur'an 76: 15-22 and Qur'an 77: 41-44

Daily living tip: We cannot imagine how splendid Paradise is. We are given metaphors to let us know that it will be wondrous, peaceful, and sublime. When life gets tough, stay tough yourself as you remember the rewards that await you because you struggled and won against temptations.

Today's prayer: O my Lord, make me tough enough to endure with joy in the pursuit of pleasing You.

For the Righteous Are Gardens of Eden.

Truly, as for those who believe and perform righteousness, We certainly shall not allow the perishing of the reward of any soul who does a good deed. For them will be the Gardens of Eden, beneath which rivers flow. Therein, they will be adorned with bracelets of gold, and they will wear emerald garments of fine silk and elaborate brocade. They will recline therein on fancy couches. How wonderful the reward! How comfortable a bed on which to recline!

Truly, for those who believe and perform righteous deeds, there are Gardens of Paradise for their leisure. They shall dwell there forever and will not desire anything different.

Say, "If the ocean were ink for the words of my Lord, the ocean would be exhausted before the words of my Lord would end, even if We added another [such ocean] like it to supplement it."

Say, "I [your Prophet] am merely a man like you. Inspiration has come to me, saying that your God is One God. Whoever expects to meet his/her Lord should live righteously, and, in worshiping his/her Lord, allow no partner.

—Qur'an 18: 30-31, 107-110

Daily living tip: You likely see opportunities every day to do a good deed, but you may overlook some of them. Picking up a piece of trash is a good deed. Giving food to a stray dog is a good deed. Leaving a bucket of water for wild animals is a good deed. Putting up a bird feeder is a good deed. Make a list of simple things you can do that count as good deeds.

Today's prayer: O my Lord, help me to not overlook any opportunities to do good deeds for people, animals, and the environment.

Excellence Awaits in Heaven.

The righteous will be in the midst of gardens and springs. [They will] enjoy the things that the Lord gives them because of the good lives they had lived. They had a habit of sleeping only a little at night. The hours of early dawn would find them praying for forgiveness. From their wealth and resources was provided the right of those who asked [for help] and those who were deprived.

On the earth are signs for those of assurance [in faith]. [There are] also [signs] within your own selves. Will you not understand? In Heaven is Your sustenance, as you are promised. Consider then the Lord of Heaven and Earth. This is the very truth –just as real as the fact that you are able to converse.

We constructed the sky with skill, and We are expanding it.

We unfurled the earth. How excellently We prepared it!

We created everything as a pair. Perhaps you will reflect.

Hurry then to Allah! I am merely an advisor from Him, bluntly calling you [to accept His message]. Do not make another into an object of worship with Allah. I am an advisor from Him, bluntly calling you.

—QUR'AN 51: 15- 23, 47-51

Daily living tip: Excellence awaits in Paradise for those who strive for excellence in this life. You will make mistakes. Everybody does. Ask for forgiveness and carry on trying to live in the most admirable ways.

Today's prayer: O my Lord, help me to live an excellent life so that I may be rewarded with the excellence of Paradise.

Behold Paradise!

As for those who believe and live righteously, no burden do We place on any soul except what it can bear. They will be companions of Paradise, where they will dwell forever.

We will remove from their hearts any lurking malice. Beneath them will be flowing rivers. They will say, "Praise Allah who has guided us to this. Never could we have found guidance had it not been for the guidance of Allah. The messengers of our Lord really did bring us the truth."

They will hear the proclamation, "Behold Paradise! You have been made its inheritors for your deeds."

The companions of Paradise will call out to the companions of the fire, "We have indeed found the promises of our Lord to us true. Have you also found your Lord's promises true?"

They shall call, "Yes," but a crier shall proclaim among them, "The blame of Allah is on the sinners. [They are] those who hinder from the path of Allah and seek in it something crooked. They denied the hereafter!"

—Qur'an 7: 42-45

Daily living tip: It is natural to grieve the death of a loved one. When a good person dies, however, it is a time for joy as well as grief. You are sad because you will miss the person. After your grieving, be happy because that person will be rejoicing in Paradise.

Today's prayer: O my Lord, may all those who achieve a life of good deeds be rewarded with the glories of Paradise.

Security Will Be There.

The sincere servants of Allah will have a determined provision. [That includes] fruits. They will have honor in comfortable gardens. [They will] face one another on thrones. Passed around will be a cup from a crystal clear fountain –sterling crystal, of a taste delicious to those who drink. It will be free from causing dizziness, and they will not suffer intoxication. With them will be companions who are not flirtatious, having beautiful eyes. [They will be] as if they were eggs carefully protected.

The righteous will be in a position of security. [They will be] among gardens and springs. [They will be] dressed in fine silk and rich brocade. They will face each other. Thus shall it be. We shall join them to companions with beautiful, wide, lustrous eyes.

There they can ask for every kind of fruit, in security. They will never taste death, except the initial death. He will save them from the penalty of Hell. [That will be] a grace from your Lord. That will be the ultimate achievement!

—Qur'an 37: 40-49 and Qur'an 44: 51-57

Daily living tip: We must earn a record of good deeds, but salvation is only by Allah's grace. His grace and mercy grant us peace and security in Paradise. We won't have to worry about being hungry or paying bills. Make life easier on your parents or guardians by being mindful of not wasting things like food, electricity, and supplies.

Today's prayer: O my Lord, help me to find ways to make life easier for my parents (or guardians.

Glory to the God of the Miraculous Night Journey!

Glory to the One who took His servant [for a journey] by night from the Haram Mosque [in Mecca] to the farthest mosque. We blessed those precincts in order that We might show him some of Our signs. He is the All-hearing, the All-seeing.

We gave Moses the Book [of Torah] and made it a guide to the Children of Israel: Do not take other than Me as disposer of affairs.

Descendants of those We delivered along with Noah, truly he was a most grateful servant.

We gave warning to the Children of Israel in the (Bible) that twice they would cause corruption upon the earth and be elated with mighty arrogance.

When the first of the two predictions came to pass, We sent against you Our servants given to terrible warfare. They entered the very inmost parts of your homes, and it was a prophecy fulfilled.

We then granted you victory against them. We gave you increase in resources and sons and made you more numerous.

—Qur'an 17: 1-6

Daily living tip: Some people will try to tell you that this story is just a myth. They think it is impossible. When you study quantum physics, try to figure out how it is possible. Don't let your mind be confined to the reality of this world. Allah's reality is greater.

Today's prayer: O my Lord, help me in my schoolwork so that I may understand more about Your awesome realities.

Day
362

Consider the Book Filled with Wisdom.

Ya Seen! Consider the Qur'an filled with wisdom. You [Muhammed] are indeed among the messengers. [You are] on a Straight Way. It is a revelation bestowed by the Almighty, the Most Merciful. [It is] so you may warn a people whose forefathers had received no warning and who therefore remained heedless.

Certainly, the Word is proven true against the majority of them for they do not believe. Indeed, We have put yokes around their necks up to their chins so that their heads are forced up. We have put a barrier in front of them and a barrier behind them, and We have covered them, so that they cannot see. It is the same to them whether you warn them or not; they will never believe.

You can only warn one who follows the reminder and fears the Most Gracious in the unseen. Therefore, give such a one good news of forgiveness and a generous reward. Truly, We will give life to the dead. We record what [deeds] they sent before and their footprints [ie, their legacy]. We have taken account of all things in a concise register.

—QUR'AN 36: 1-12

Daily living tip: Seek the wisdom of the Qur'an. Try to find how you can apply it to your daily life. Also, seek the wisdom of older people who have already learned how to live by the Qur'an. Don't think the old people are out of touch with your world. Their experiences are different, but they have learned how to cope with life's challenges. Don't be such a brat that you can't learn from those who already know better.

Today's prayer: O my Lord, make me wise through the Qur'an's messages and through the experiences of others who have already learned.

Consider What Allah Has Given You.

To Allah belongs the mystery of Heaven and Earth. The advent of the hour [of judgment] is as the twinkling of an eye or even quicker. Indeed, Allah, over everything, is All Powerful.

Allah brought you from the wombs of your mothers when you knew nothing. He gave you hearing and sight and affection so you may give thanks.

Do they not look at the birds held poised in the midst of the sky? Nothing holds them up but Allah. Truly, in this are signs for those who believe.

Allah made your homes to be places of rest. He made for you, from skins of animals, tents that you find convenient when you travel and when you camp. Out of their wool, fur, and hair [He made] rich furnishings and provisions for a time.

Allah made for you, out of the things He created, shade. He made for you, from the mountains, shelter [ie, caves in which to dwell]. He made for you garments to protect you from heat, and heavy coats [of armor] to protect you from your violence. Thus does He complete His favors on you so you may submit [to His will].

—QUR'AN 16: 77-81

Daily living tip: Don't be a sassy brat that doesn't appreciate things. We live in a beautiful world. Don't take it for granted and don't mess it up. Be grateful for every little thing that makes this life beautiful, comfortable, and amazing.

Today's prayer: O my Lord, thank you for Your grace and mercy in making a world full of wonder.

Consider the Signs of Science.

Truly, in cattle you will find a lesson. We give you drink from what is in their bellies; from between bowels and blood. There is milk, pure and appetizing for those who drink it.

From the fruit of the date palm and the grapevine, you receive wholesome drink and food. Indeed, in this also is a sign for those who use reasoning skills.

Your Lord inspired the bee to build its nests in hillsides, in trees, and in buildings. He inspired it to eat of all fruiting plants and follow the spacious paths of your Lord. From within their bodies comes a drink [honey] of varying colors, wherein is healing for people. Truly, in this is a sign for those who ponder.

Allah creates you and takes your souls at death. Of you there are some who are sent back to a feeble age so that they know nothing after having known. Indeed, Allah is the All-knowing, the Most Capable.

—QUR'AN 16: 66-70

Daily living tip: When you look at the world around you, take time to think about all the miracles of the sciences involved. Allah is the Master Scientist. Humanity has done nothing that was not already done in some form in Allah's creation.

Today's prayer: O my Lord, thank you for the wonders of Your amazing creation.

Consider the Signs of Nature.

Certainly, Allah causes the seed grain and the date stone to split [and sprout]. He brings life from the dead, and He brings death from the living. Such is Allah! How then are you deluded?

He cuts the break of day. He makes the night for rest, and the sun and moon for calculating [time]. Such is the order of the Exalted in Power, the Omniscient.

He is the One who made the stars for you so you may navigate, with their help, through the dark spaces of land and sea. We certainly clarify Our signs for people who know.

He is the One who produced you from a single soul. Here [on Earth] is a place to live and rest. We certainly clarify Our signs for people who understand.

He is the One who bestows rain from the skies. With it We produce vegetation of all kinds. From some We produce foliage out of which We produce heaps of grain; out of the date palm and its sheaths, clusters of dates hanging low and near; and gardens of grapes, olives, and pomegranates, each [garden] similar yet unique. Look at the fruit when it emerges and ripens. Indeed, in that are signs for people who believe.

—QUR'AN 6: 95-99

Daily living tip: Some people are blockheads. They walk around without noticing the messages nature has for us. Don't be a blockhead. Teach yourself to be observant of every little thing Allah has created. Nothing was created without a lesson for you.

Today's prayer: O my Lord, help me to hear the quiet voice of creation telling me of Your wondrous deeds.

Allah's Command is Coming!

The command of Allah is on the way! Do not seek to hasten it. Glory to Him! He is exalted above having the partners (the idolaters) ascribe to Him.

He sends His angels with inspiration of His command to any of His servants as He pleases: "Warn that no god is there except Me, so fear Me."

He has created the skies and Earth for just means. He is exalted above having the partners they ascribe to Him.

He has created humanity from a single cell; look how the same becomes a public disputant.

He has created herds for you. From them, you get warmth [from skins] and numerous other benefits, including what you eat. You admire their beauty as you drive them home [in the evening] and as you lead them forth [to pasture in the morning]. They carry your heavy loads to lands that you could not otherwise reach except with great difficulty. Your Lord is indeed the Kindest, Most Merciful.

He has created horses, mules, and donkeys for you to ride and use for shows. He has created things about which you have no knowledge.

Unto Allah leads straight the way, but there are ways that divert. If Allah had willed, He could have guided all of you.

—QUR'AN 16: 1-9

Daily living tip: If you are a Muslim, you are a weirdo in this world. That's okay. Enjoy being weird. That kind of weird is what is going to secure you on the Day of Judgment. On that day, the real freaks are going to be wishing they were weird like you.

Today's prayer: O my Lord, help me to stand secure in the knowledge of You and Your awesome plans for this world and the hereafter.